BENEATH THE FAULT LINE

The Popular and Legal Culture of Divorce
in Twentieth-Century America

BENEATH THE FAULT LINE

The Popular and Legal Culture of Divorce
in Twentieth-Century America

J. Herbie DiFonzo

HQ
834
.D49
1997
West

University Press of Virginia
Charlottesville and London

THE UNIVERSITY PRESS OF VIRGINIA
© 1997 by the Rector and Visitors of the University of Virginia

First published 1997

∞ The paper used in this publication meets the minimum requirements
of the American National Standard for Information Sciences—Permanence
of Paper for Printed Library Materials, ANSI Z39.48-1984.

Library of Congress Cataloging-in-Publication Data
DiFonzo, J. Herbie.   ·
   Beneath the fault line : the popular and legal culture of divorce
in twentieth-century America / J. Herbie DiFonzo.
      p.   cm.
   Includes bibliographical references (p.   ) and index.
   ISBN 0-8139-1707-7 (cloth : alk. paper)
   1. Divorce—United States—History—20th century.   2. Divorce—Law
and legislation—United States—History—20th century.
HQ834.D49   1997
306.89'0973—dc20   96-41268
                                                                        CIP

Printed in the United States of America

*To Pat and Drew,
who have supported and
suffered me through it all.*

CONTENTS

ILLUSTRATIONS

TABLES

ACKNOWLEDGMENTS

When I attend a movie, I stay and watch until the end of the credits. I also read the acknowledgments pages in other people's books. I realize this behavior may be odd, but I believe in the importance of thank you's.

My obligations to several members of the faculty at the University of Virginia come first. Brian Balogh helped me obtain a more panoramic view of recent American history. Joseph F. Kett encouraged me at all times to ask probing question and then play with the answers. Walter Wadlington helped me to see the context in legal reforms, both English and American. Most significantly, Charles W. McCurdy prodded me to set the framework, then persevered with me through the details, even— or especially—when the facts radically altered the frame. Chuck and I have been friends for many years, and his support has always spurred me to reach beyond my initial grasp.

Other colleagues have facilitated this project in different ways: I thank Dean Stuart Rabinowitz of Hofstra University Law School for his generous support; Michael Grossberg for his knowledgeable reading of the text; Mary F. Hayes, S.N.D., for personal encouragement and for providing me with opportunities to teach and thus to learn; Robert Tuttle for his hospitality and conviviality; and Lindsey Robertson for his friendship and contagious enthusiasm. Many thanks to my editor, Richard Holway, who nursed this book through repeated ups and downs. Donna Posillico, Lenore Glanz, Nita Kane, and Heather Golin also helped keep the text together whenever it threatened to come apart.

The illustrations from *Vanity Fair* have been published courtesy of *Vanity Fair.* Copyright © 1927 (renewed 1955) by the Condé Nast Publications, Inc. Portions of chapter 1 have appeared as "The Feminization of Divorce after World War I," *Journal of Unconventional History* 5 (Winter 1994): 39–67. Portions of chapters 2 and 3 have appeared as "Alternatives to Marital Fault: Legislative and Judicial Experiments in Cultural Change," *Idaho Law Review* 33 (1997). Portions of chapters 4 and 5 have appeared as "Coercive Conciliation: Judge Paul W. Alexander and the Movement for Therapeutic Divorce," *University of Toledo Law Review* 25 (1994): 535–75. Portions of chapter 6 have appeared as "No-Fault Marital Dissolution: The Bitter Triumph of Naked Divorce," *San Diego Law Review* 31 (1994): 519–54.

I express the final and most heartfelt appreciation for my family: to my parents, Charles and Aida DiFonzo, for their love and steadfastness; to my spouse, Patricia N. Marks, for helping me see our own family in many different ways; and to my son, Drew, whose mischievous delight inspires me daily, and whose witticisms on the law include his remark that an alibi "is what lawyers sing to their children at night."

BENEATH THE FAULT LINE

The Popular and Legal Culture of Divorce
in Twentieth-Century America

THE RIVAL ARENAS OF DIVORCE

> The perfect marriage is perhaps more worth fighting for
> than the imperfect marriage is worth protecting.
>
> *Katherine Fullerton Gerould, "Divorce"*

In the middle of the twentieth century, the American way of divorcing presented a gaggle of radically competing norms and operations. Divorce statutes everywhere held marriage to a high standard which limited dissolution to cases demonstrating proof of a serious assault on the marital vows by either wife or husband. But half of all American legislatures also nominally broadened the divorce apparatus to encompass breakdowns caused merely by separation over long periods of time, or even by temperamental incompatibility. Appellate courts often restricted these fault-free alternatives, pronouncing instead a vision of divorce law limited to coping with the occasional seismic shudders that tore apart many families and paradoxically serving to emphasize the overall stability of family life in American society.

A look at the working world of divorce courts revealed quite different practices, more attuned to the fissures in American domesticity. Trial judges mediated between the formal requirements of their appellate masters and the surging mass of insistent and divorce-minded litigants. Finally, the scripted courtroom behavior of most divorcing wives and husbands played scenes from an adversary theater of the absurd. Wives breathlessly testified to their husbands' beastliness toward them, while their spouses almost always passed up their right to respond, many waiting outside the courtroom door for their freshly divorced ex-wives to bring them the good news of the successful verdict both had conspired to obtain.

At bottom, this disjointed portrait of American divorce presents the paradox of different arenas for processing marital dissolution. These cultural and legal spheres sometimes intersected and at other times remained parallel as if oblivious to the rivals' existence. I believe that each of these arenas produced law. Each one carved out a cultural territory with distinct rules, patterns of behavior, and constituency. Each arena, moreover, worked toward a different goal than the others. And each changed over time, at its own rate. The two generations that lived between the end of World War I and the spread of California-style no-fault in the 1970s were both creators and victims of this geometric madness, in which the Euclidean universe of divorce law and culture imploded.

Most historical accounts contend that twentieth-century divorce reforms were attempts to liberalize family law to conform with the ever-increasing demand for divorce.[1] But I believe that formal changes in the rules for divorce, from the "living apart" statutes, which spread to almost half the states by midcentury, to California no-fault itself, were conservative sallies aimed at reversing or at least slowing the overflowing divorce rate. As the popular culture ignored or circumvented each revision of the formal rules, worried legislators became convinced that the fault requirement for divorce had become more a sieve than a screen. The attempts to dam the flow grew more desperate, culminating with the fervent if ultimately unsuccessful campaign to channel all divorce-minded couples into a therapeutic family court. This pastiche of divorce reform, retrenchment, and ultimate failure was also staged in Great Britain. Anglo-American cultural and legal ties made the British adventure at times a model of family law reform and at other times an admonitory tale of disaster. British divorce reforms were particularly influential in the origins of California no-fault, and so this study of American popular and legal culture occasionally makes a transatlantic crossing.

The Historiographical Context

Despite its popular and controversial appeal, only three full-range histories of divorce in America have been published in the twentieth century, and only two since 1904.[2] The most recent, Glenda Riley's *Divorce: An American Tradition*, treats divorce legislation as epiphenomenal, merely responsive to variable social pressures exerted on busy legislators. Divorce reforms were, in her view, "often hasty, ill-conceived, and adopted under pressure from whichever faction had momentary influence with a particular group of legislators."[3] A generation earlier Nelson Manfred Blake had explored the "Land of Make-Believe," his term for the fraudulent practices of divorce. Writing in 1962, Blake described the therapeutic divorce court as the "Path of Reason," whose spread he both anticipated and welcomed. This cross between psychiatric couch and courtroom chair was intended to defang the adversary system as it enhanced the integrity of the divorcing process by removing the need for character assault or concocted evidence.[4]

All accounts of modern divorce emphasize the wide divergence between the formal rules for divorcing and the actual behavior of litigants. But the crux of historical explanation requires a showing of when and why the split occurred and how this resulting legal hydra could maintain itself for at least two generations. Some explanations, like Riley's, suggest that legal reforms track social changes at a distance, and thus the uneven rate and direction in the latter have resulted in the odd shape of the formal rules. Lynne Carol Halem offered a more sophisticated version of this argument in her 1980 study, *Divorce Reform*, which focused on the interplay of shifting theories of divorce and their adaption in legal policies. Halem contended that all discussion of divorce in the past presumed pathology, and that the central transitions in the perceptions of divorce shifted from moral to social to psychopathological. As with Blake's earlier history, Halem was concerned with both the therapeutic uses of law and the failure to uproot the damaging pathology of the adversary system.[5]

The various efforts to alter the law of divorce in this century have been denominated "reforms," although the aim of the reformulation has not always been clear. Most historians claim to have seen the banner of divorce reform flying above a liberalizing impulse, that is, a conscious effort to lower the barriers to divorce. Writing in the 1970s, Max Rheinstein claimed that no-fault statutes had been passed because "conservatism has weakened to the point of allowing the liberalism of the law in action to be recognized and find expression in the law of the books."[6] The reformers were motivated, in this view, not by any urge to increase the rate of divorce, but by a desire to have the divorce rate ascend to match the rate of marital breakdown.

In his extensive and multifaceted survey of divorce and marriage breakdown in Western culture, Roderick Phillips concluded that traditional societies generally featured stable marriages, and that the last century has seen a dramatic rise not only in the divorce rate but also in the rate of underlying marriage breakdown. Phillips identified the several surges of divorce law changes since World War I as part of a "general trend of liberalization" in American culture. Although he recognized that no-fault reforms were a compromise between liberal and conservative forces, he clearly located no-fault within the "more liberal attitudes toward authority and institutions" of the 1960s.[7]

Herbert Jacob provided a different reading of the evidence in *Silent Revolution: The Transformation of Divorce Law in the United States*. Jacob examined why the radical legal changes in divorce procedures in the no-fault era were enacted with virtually no interest group pressure and with relatively little publicity. He found that the no-fault reformers successfully cast their ventures as routine legislation, aimed only at streamlining the legal process. On moral issues these leaders adopted a "pro-family vocabulary" and "as conservative a guise as possible" so as to secure passage with little fanfare. Because the creators of modern no-fault "did not speak the language of the political conflict," their reforms slipped smoothly through the legislative process.[8]

Some writers have contended that the 1960s changes in divorce laws that resulted in no-fault in California, as well as in England and in several other nations, originally were conceived as conservative campaigns to retard the divorce rate. The reformers demolished fault because it had failed in its historic mission of separating the many unnecessary divorces from the few essential ones. Replacing fault with therapy under a no-fault rubric represented, in this view, an attempt to reverse history. Therapeutically oriented courts, backed by specialized social workers and psychiatrists, would refuse to grant divorces merely because a chimerical "fault" ground could have been asserted in an uncontested hearing. The courts were to evaluate the whole marriage to determine its viability under the best psychological criteria of the day.[9]

But no study has taken these insights on the California and English campaigns and used them to evaluate the evidence on earlier divorce "reforms." Such a perspective might fragment the current interpretive whole in the course of emphasizing the multitude of voices that constituted rival systems of divorce law during the twentieth century. In contending that divorce reforms always have responded to social pressure, Glenda Riley echoed the functionalism of Lawrence M. Friedman's observation that "divorce law was a compromise between the instrumental demand for divorce and the opposing moral postulate." The dean of the drift and default school of legal history, Friedman viewed divorce laws as weaving a zigzag course between the push of moral reformers and the pull of unhappy spouses. "Law is a mirror," Friedman asserted, of society's "ragged multiplicity." He answered the question of the lack of congruity between formal rule and social behavior by positing the latter as too complex, variable, and uncontrollable to project any neat reflection onto the legal code. Friedman insisted, as well, on the limitations of his mirror metaphor by denying that the law has any original outputs. All law is an image, however distorted, of society.[10]

This book examines the interrelationship of popular culture and legal rules in order to explore the causes and effects of American divorcing patterns throughout the century. Divorce reforms are shown as campaigns by actors in some of the divorce arenas (sometimes the legislatures, sometimes the appellate courts) to change the operating standards of their rivals (often the trial judges, always the popular litigants). Complicating the analysis is the public's attitude, which grew progressively more liberal toward divorce while remaining largely conservative toward divorce law.[11]

In the course of my research, I came to believe what functionalist historians deny, that "the law is more than just an arena for struggle: the law itself is an actor in the contest."[12] But this book equally fails to uphold the extreme claims of some segments of the critical legal studies movement. Radical indeterminacy, political legitimation, and the ideological essence of law are, of course, part of the story. Indeed, the colossal failure of the California no-fault divorce reform may best be explained as a tale of law's outputs dramatically changing social behavior, rather than the other way around. But the historical artifacts of divorce do not easily conform to a single mold. In certain contexts and time periods, social changes resulted in alteration of the formal legal norms; elsewhere, a recombination of the formal mix fueled the engine of widespread cultural conversion. This double proposition will be rejected by both doctrinaire functionalists and radical "crits," but it fits the evidence of American family development better than either theory-driven extreme.

I have, in other words, tried to bridge the gap between the current twin paradigms of historical scholarship about legal institutions: "For advocates of critical legal studies, law is a central cultural and social institution; their paradigm suggests too strong an influence of law on social behavior and too large a role for law in the construction of the social world. In contrast, the law and society tradition often provides too small a role for law in constituting social life."[13] I have tried to strike a more sensitive balance, mindful of the lyrical wisdom of E. P. Thompson about the ubiquity of law in culture:

> I found that the law did not keep politely to a "level" but was at *every* bloody level; it was imbricated within the mode of production and production relations themselves (as property-rights, definitions of agrarian practices) and it was simultaneously present in the philosophy of Locke; it intruded brusquely within alien categories, reappearing bewigged and gowned in the guise of ideology; it danced a cotillion with religion, moralizing over the theatre of Tyburn; it was an arm of politics and politics was one of its arms; it was an academic discipline, subjected to the rigour of its own autonomous logic; it contributed to the definition of the self-identity both of rulers and of ruled; above all, it afforded an arena for class struggle, within which alternative notions of law were fought out.[14]

Scholars as different as Lawrence Friedman and Robert W. Gordon have warned of the danger in allowing appellate cases to stand in for the entire legal process.[15] The same caveat should accompany any narrow-gauged approach to a broad cultural question. In that light, this study examines law texts, scholarly journals, and statutes, as well as the yield of both trial and appellate courts. But its main concern is cultural shift, and its primary source is the popular press. Accordingly, I have surveyed virtually every article on divorce published in popular magazines from the end of World War I to the 1950s, as well as many from the preceding and following eras. Mass circulation magazines examined formal law and social consequences earlier and far more frequently than their counterparts in the legal press. For example, the call for a sociological view of divorce arose in legal journals in the 1940s, but the popular press had already been scouring the subject for two decades. As prominent divorce reformer and judge Paul W. Alexander admitted in 1952, "Whatever attention has been paid to the cause, cure and effect of divorce, as distinguished from the law of divorce, has been left almost entirely to the tender mercies of the lay writers in popular periodicals."[16]

J. Willard Hurst declared that the law tracks the "main currents of American thought." This insight is, however, occasionally misleading. At times the law does not mirror social policy, however belatedly, but both reflects and helps construct cultural contingency. Many voices have created the law of divorce, and their story lines deserve a respectful audience. Much of this study is an effort to allow the many actors on the divorce stage in the twentieth century to tell their story. In a sense I am responding to Robert Gordon's complaint that a society "whose history is so full of mass reform movements should have produced such a Tory legal literature, narrowly focused on official agencies, especially the courts, and almost completely indifferent to extra-institutional law-making."[17]

The Parallel yet Intersecting Arenas of Divorce

The central paradox of twentieth-century family law is that legislatures, appellate tribunals, trial courts, and unhappy wives and husbands formed and maintained separate domains of divorce law. This puzzle is best approached within the larger realm of popular legal culture. Noted anthropologist Clifford Geertz suggested that culture patterns provide a "template or blueprint for the organization of social and psychological processes." The cultural "tone" derived from a "system of shared meanings and values" tends to color the perspective and heavily influence the actions of participants in the society. Indeed, some critics believe that popular culture is a powerful mechanism through which a society "most firmly and decisively implants values and maintains the norms it considers desirable."[18]

Legal culture has been appropriately defined as a "network of values and attitudes . . . which determine when and why and where people turn to law or government or turn away."[19] Popular legal culture, for the purposes of this study, refers to the orientation of the vast majority of divorce-minded wives and husbands, untrained (and usually uninterested) in the minutiae of legal scholarship. How their experience was attuned to action is the central theme of this story, bearing in mind Stewart Macaulay's dictum that Americans "freely improvise on the law."[20]

How did the separate divorce arenas develop? Legislators generally tried to articulate policy norms and translate them into statutory commands. They were most influenced by organized public opinion, such as the media, interest group lobbies, and, especially early in the century, formal religion. By contrast, appellate courts aimed at guiding the evolution of the stately common law, relying on the judicial tradition of formal legal reasoning to adapt statutory language to the perceived needs of the day. The lawmaking goals of both the legislative branch and the appellate bench were to reduce the divorce rate.

Both systems acted as if divorces threatened marriages, oblivious to the truth of Mary Ann Glendon's dictum that Americans "like marriage so much that they do it over and over again."[21] These two legal arenas also viewed morality as their exclusive province. Both legislative hall and appellate tribunal crafted their work product in order to induce individual behavior into meeting the standard of lifelong marital commitment, deviation from which was sanctioned only under extremely limited circumstances. Neither would understand the streetwise probity articulated in 1924 by William Seagle in the *American Mercury*: "It is immoral to compel a husband and a wife to live together when they hate each other."[22]

Moreover, legislative and appellate chambers at times shot their operational arrows at cross-purposes. Statutory attempts to reduce the realm of fault in an effort to slow divorce were obstructed by some courts of appeals that were reluctant to let go of a fault conceptually, even while they shriveled the prerequisites for a fault divorce to a bare formulaic ritual. Trial judges who handled the hurly-burly of the daily divorce dockets followed quite a different agenda from that of their statutory or case law masters. Divorce judges needed to process their overloaded court calendars with fairness to the litigants and, especially in urban jurisdictions, with a maximum of speed. Although their formal role required them to apply positive law and judicial precedent to the case at hand, the pressures of the divorcing population often swayed trial judges to reverse the process. Divorce courts ended up making the law fit the facts.

Neither state legislators nor appellate judges were in attendance in divorce courtrooms. Although the statutory code and the case reports were often close by behind the bench, divorce judges faced in the other direction, seeing wives and husbands, every day, thousands upon thousands, each with their own story, and yet each with the same story. What was the narrative told by divorcing husbands and wives? The overwhelming evidence is that they told one story to each other and a different one in court. Among themselves, the parties usually negotiated a bittersweet end to their unhappy marriage.[23] At times, one party just gave up and let the other have her or his way. The courtroom yarn could be anything but the truth, however, or the judge would be obliged to enforce the door-closing devices of condonation, collusion, connivance, or recrimination. Rather, the parties (or usually the wife alone, in her culturally conditioned role as the designated driver of divorce) related a fable of marital fault. Usually the parable involved cruelty; sometimes, in a state such as New York which did not grant divorces for cruelty, the fiction portrayed adultery.

In their close dealings with the parties, the trial courts adopted a ministerial role, and the lawmaking tendencies of wives, husbands, and judges merged. Since contested divorces were quite rare (approximately 15 percent throughout the century), the most likely outcome was the ratification of party agreements, under appropriate disguises that would insulate them from further scrutiny. The desire of trial judges not to be reversed blended with the determined couples' demands for prompt and final divorce and produced, for the most part, a record which spoke in equal parts of law and of fantasy but—most importantly—could not be appealed.

The failure of the formal law arenas to regulate divorce effectively is best understood in the context of contrasting goals. Legislatures articulated divorce policy norms but made only intermittent efforts to implement their policy priorities in the light of appellate decisions. The occasional statutory reforms were often misunderstood by the courts and usually ignored by the divorcing population. Statutory provisions, as a result, had very little relationship to the regulation of divorces. Similarly, appellate tribunals succeeded in their traditional role of designing and navigating formal legal rules. But by truncating the legislature's few efforts to undo the fault system and insisting upon the false veneer of fault to grant divorces, courts of appeals insulated themselves from the reality of divorce. Trial courts early on gave up any role they might have had as regulators. Presiding over charades of fault, trial judges usually acted as registrars ratifying divorce plans worked out by the parties.

By contrast, the law system erected by a million litigants who cleverly and doggedly pursued their autonomy succeeded in regulating divorce behavior, because its principal goal was divorce by mutual consent. The regularization and falsification of the fault grounds well served this law arena in its attainment of the only working divorce law in midcentury America. Perhaps what is most significant about the lay system of law is that it alone reflected the belief that divorce was a bulwark for marriage. Katherine Fullerton Gerould aptly summarized the prevailing ethos: "The perfect marriage is perhaps more worth fighting for than the imperfect marriage is worth protecting."[24] Only the popular arena understood that marriages were driving divorces, and that the prospect of conjugal happiness fueled the divorce rate most of all. As a writer in the *New Republic* recognized in 1925: "The printed laws are powerless before the Juggernaut car of American custom. The divorces are going to keep on being good because those who get them will fight for them, and those who have the right to fight against them will lie down and be rolled over."[25]

This book describes the dramatic shift in the moral boundaries of divorce in the twentieth century. This expansion of the cultural perimeter was staged in the several arenas of divorce struggle, primarily during the fifty years from the end of World War I through the California and English divorce reforms that began the 1970s. As William O'Neill established in his excellent study *Divorce in the Progressive Era*, the debate over the viability of divorce raged in the four decades that bracketed the turn of the twentieth century. By the end of World War I, however, the religious and ethical view that refused to sanction any divorce had decisively lost. From then on, the debate centered over the contours of the new right to divorce.[26]

Chapter 1 examines this new divorce freedom, showing how the writings of popular journals in the 1920s and 1930s defended and expanded this right, claiming for their own a legal arena which sometimes engaged but often outflanked the formal legal rules. With the lessening of the traditional stigma against divorce, the popular mood sounded a largely utilitarian theme as it identified liberalized divorce as women's particular cultural contribution. The second chapter examines this popular system of divorce in depth, exploring the concept of incompatibility as it resounded through popular psychology and jurisprudence beginning in the 1920s. The expansion of the divorce ground of cruelty to include mental anguish was not an attempt to broaden divorce grounds but rather to define the range of the existing cruelty principle in terms of the new psychological understanding. Divorces had infiltrated the consumer culture, and the voices of the trial judges sliced through the thick web of formal divorce grounds and defenses.

Chapter 3 considers legislative responses in the 1930s to the new divorce freedom: a veritable boom in state statutes presenting nonfault divorce alternatives. While a surface reading of these "living apart" and "incompatibility" laws suggests a legislative design to ease the burdens of divorcing couples, a look underneath reveals other motives. These early nonfault reforms may well have been attempts to slow down the rate of divorce, reflecting legislative awareness that the sandbags of fault had seriously eroded. The popular reaction to these nonfault progenitors was not, however, what the legislatures had hoped. The number of intended consumers who purchased their marital freedom in this fashion remained negligible. Nor did the statutory reforms find universal favor among appellate courts, which often had difficulty interpreting these novel laws except within the fault-oriented matrix of traditional divorce procedures. Chapter 4 presents the often farcical interactions between the formal and the popular divorce arenas at midcentury. Sometimes the farce turned ugly. Complaints about the demoralization of modern marriage cast woman as the scapegoat. After World War II the portrayal of women in the popular press shifted. Attacks on woman's "emotional cannibalism" and greed for alimony marked her as the responsible party in the now unseemly rush to the divorce court.

The world of therapeutic divorce in the decades between the 1940s and 1960s is presented in chapter 5. As the structure of American family life intensified its transition from the institutional to the companionship mode, divorce reformers focused on efforts to recast the divorce court as a psychoanalytic institution, modeled after the juvenile court. In an effort to win acceptance for their radical move to stem the rising divorce rate, Judge Paul W. Alexander and his allies proposed to substitute therapeutic for fault divorce. But the true agenda of social control revealed itself in the new institution's coercive conciliation procedures. Therapeutic divorce represented compelled nondivorce, holding families together through directive psychiatry. Chapter 6 describes the last hurrah of therapeutic divorce. Realizing that fault no longer served as a barrier to divorce by mutual consent, conservative reformers in both England and California staged a dramatic gambit. In this last and sometimes comic scenario, reformers gambled that eliminating all fault grounds would be a sufficient enticement for divorce-minded couples to submit to a reconciliation-minded social welfare establishment. This clash of minds was supposed to yield a lower divorce rate. The reformers nearly succeeded. But the resulting fiasco not only facilitated a divorce boom, it enshrined in divorce law a predilection for ersatz gender egalitarianism. What was once bargained for in the shadow of the fault regime is now litigated for in the brave new day of no-fault. The process of deciding the critical issues of custody, child support, and spousal maintenance by all accounts has become more acrimonious rather than less, and many women are up in arms over the loss of bargaining power resulting from the formal legal changes.

Given the continuing extent of sexual discrimination, as manifested primarily in the labor force and in the cultural assumptions about the primacy of women's maternal and custodial role, a divorce regime mandating strict equality in support and property distribution serves to perpetuate the disadvantaged situation in which most women find themselves after divorce. The reification of no-fault ideology has yielded divorce on demand, with little heed to the inequities of property division and child and spousal support. As if to display the awesome contingency of history, the rival law arenas have been made one, but order has not brought sanity.

ONE

THE FEMINIZATION OF DIVORCE
AFTER WORLD WAR I

In America, divorce is a growing female institution.

Henry R. Carey, "This Two-Headed Monster—The Family"

The much-ballyhooed "New Woman" of the 1920s had older sisters who were similarly inclined, whose voices were clearly heard through the popular press.[1] In 1910, for instance, Margaret Deland noted a distinct change in the "feminine ideal," which she elucidated for readers of the *Atlantic* as a move from selflessness to individualism. Divorce was a necessary solvent for the flawed bond caused by overhasty marrying. Deland was quite explicit about the danger posed by bad marriages: "To imprison hatred within the little circle of a wedding-ring does not often make a family, it generally destroys a home. Divorce is sometimes the only way to safeguard the family idea."[2]

Similarly, journalist and feminist Rheta Childe Dorr advised readers of *Forum* magazine in 1911 to consider divorces as "mere legal ratifications" of marital dissolutions arranged by the parties themselves. Dorr, who had been separated—but not divorced—from her husband since 1898, believed that most divorces were obtained by mutual consent, arrived at after years of sincere efforts to make the marriage succeed. As for the argument that divorce breaks up the family, Dorr countered that any home where the wife has been abandoned or physically or mentally abused already has been destroyed by the husband's action. Dorr attributed America's higher divorce rate than Europe's to the greater gender equity enshrined in our laws. Women now could take charge of their own lives and again seek marital bliss despite earlier failure. "Americans," she concluded, "will not accept any marriage but a happy one."[3]

Even before World War I the "divorce movement" was seen as an expression of women's growing independence from men. Women's hope for emancipation was founded on the mirage of female economic breakthrough, an illusion which provided many women with the courage to call for liberation from cruel and unhappy marriages. An abused woman no longer felt compelled to remain with an unfit husband "whose touch is pollution." Buoyed by the examples of women in the labor force, a wife who sought her exit from a dying marriage at least could contemplate financial autonomy without enduring the pangs of guilt Victorian spouses would have felt about destroying the family, described by Henry James as "the original germ-cell which lies at the base of all that we call society . . . [and] the sole nursery of the social sentiment in the human bosom."[4] The social sentiment altered as the economic basis for families changed. During the Progressive Era the state began to take over an increasing number of traditional family functions, at least for the lower and lower-middle classes. As historian David M. Kennedy noted, "Social critics from John Spargo to Theodore Roosevelt endorsed the Socialist idea of the state as an 'over-parent' which should provide schools, housing, sanitation, and recreation in the crowded cities." In 1909 critic Edward Alsworth Ross observed that the "old economic framework of the family has largely fallen away, leaving more of the strain on the personal tie."[5]

This greater emotional content of family relations elevated the stakes in marriage, making domestic life delightful when it succeeded and devastating when it failed, as was now more likely to happen. This alteration of family dynamics may be seen as a wave in the sea change in American culture. As Warren I. Susman has argued, the nineteenth-century ideals of self-restraint, a bounded universe, and personal character gave way to the new age's more audacious tropes of self-presentation. Even the early years of the twentieth century were characterized by new cultural patterns of consumption, the cult of personality, and worship of the "brazen calf of Self." And this rampant individualism crossed gender lines. Although one writer believed that women were the weaker sex and thus lost "infinitely" more than they gained in any loosening of the marriage tie, she acknowledged that hers was "not a popular view."[6]

The popular view of divorce may be seen in the explosion of debate that appeared in the pages of *Good Housekeeping, Harper's*, the *Ladies' Home Journal, Atlantic, Literary Digest, American Mercury, Saturday Evening Post*, and many other widely read journals during the period between the two world wars. These sources detail how the popular culture viewed both the concept of divorce and its practitioners through the Jazz Age and the Depression. In volley after volley of informal essays and in responsive letters—popular commentaries—to the editor, we find American voices not always heard in the legislative halls that produced the statutes under whose terms divorces were prosecuted, in the courtrooms in which the decrees were granted, or in the appellate chambers whose robed authority reviewed trial court judgments and crafted guidance for new cases.[7]

In these popular journals we find the voices of well-known literary and legal figures, as well as those of anonymous writers chronicling the passing cultural parade. Letters to the editor expressed the vox populi even more directly. Social theorist Jurgen Habermas suggested that the letter exchanges in newspapers and magazines replaced personal letter writing, and thus "the sphere generated by the mass media has taken on the traits of a secondary realm of intimacy." That periodicals, through their letters columns, were serving an increasingly confessional purpose was noted by advertising executive and inspirational writer Bruce Barton in a 1926 *Good Housekeeping* article: "In the old days people confided their problems to their pastors or their parents or each other; now the editor of a national magazine is the recipient of confidences more intimate than his readers would ever think of making to anybody else."[8]

The functional history argument generally holds that voices such as these affected the lawmakers, who in time changed the laws. Popular culture is supposed to stimulate legal change by a process of accretion: as the impetus for social reform mounts, legislators and judges finally respond by altering the legal forms to comply with the popular will. I maintain, however, that these popular writers spoke to and helped create a cultural outflanking of statutory reality, effectively deploying an alternative system of divorce in the 1920s and 1930s.

But how could law be made independent of the authorized legal structure? My research into divorce culture led me to conclude that disaffected spouses neither agitated for formal change nor chafed under an unresponsive legal structure. Rather, they created their own operational law of divorce, a legal structure which became far more vigorous and entrenched than the official legal apparatus. How the mass of divorce-minded spouses were able to establish this alternative arena for processing divorces is the focus of the first two chapters of this book. In short, I contend that divorcers co-opted the trial bench, by and large, ignoring the fault threshold to divorce encoded in statute and case precedent and substituting a formulaic ritual which masked the underlying reality of mutual consent. Divorce courts agreed to this subversion of the litigative process in part because they came to acquiesce in this sub-rosa revolution. Equally significant, however, the fact that the substituted rationale was based on mutual consent rendered trial courts immune from appellate reversal, since neither party would appeal a result demanded by both. Thus, the vanguard of dissolution-minded spouses indeed made law outside the normal registers of legislative or appellate mandate.

The change in the status of divorce also reflected a significant transformation in women's station in life. Women's customary work had largely been displaced after World War I. Homemakers evolved from producers to consumers, from baking and making to trying and buying. Middle-class white women compensated for this functional displacement by enlarging women's roles to encompass increasingly more public stages.[9] Between 1897 and 1921 the net national product increased from $15.8 billion to $70.3 billion, and the per capita national product rose from $231 to $793.[10] While the Victorian home had fancied itself a moral haven, the emerging modern home of the 1920s served as a consumption center. With materialism, ironically, came romance. The rigidity of the former generation's moral rules was undone, not by any desperate desire for licentiousness, but rather by the shifting social patterns brought on by a rising tide of disposable income. Romance is, after all, a leisure-time activity.[11]

But there was another side to this modulation of woman's role. In the context of family mores, women in the 1920s increasingly believed themselves liberated from the financial fiefdom which had constrained their mothers' marriages. The statistical improvement in women's economic condition did not appear to warrant the change in attitude. But the tone of popular culture in the 1920s was unmistakable: women's new earning freedom rendered it unnecessary for her to remain in a beastly marriage. Victorian unions, as historian Elaine Tyler May noted, had been based on "duties and sacrifices, not personal satisfaction."[12] But self-sacrifice, whether in politics or in manners, was in retreat as a clarion call in the years after World War I.

The popular press provided various estimations of the weakening of the divorce taboo. Some writers warned of divine retribution or social Armageddon if marriages continued to be dissolved. Others proposed specific solutions for the divorce "problem" or "evil." Still others prized divorce as an outright benefit to society. Many drew upon the tools of religion, law, eugenics, or psychology to craft both issue and resolution. The cumbersome choir of popular periodicals did not, however, produce cacophony. One tone may usually be heard above the others. This voice emphasized the evils of the particular marriage in question and sympathized with the need to escape domestic hell. While admitting that some people obtained divorces "frivolously," the popular concern focused on those wretched individuals "who run out of their marriage as one runs out of a burning house because one is not safe there." Many writers would have winced at her bluntness, but they would have agreed with critic Ruth Hale that "we must have divorce . . . preferably cheap, easy, collusive divorce and nobody's business why."[13]

Here

Woman the Culture Changer

But divorce appeared to be everybody's business why. It touched a nerve in the body politic, exposing the raw point of friction between the old morality and the new. A 1921 article in *Current History* magazine reminisced on the earlier reluctance "to label oneself as a divorced person; the idea was personally and socially repugnant." But far from fearing the stigma of divorce, many spouses in the 1920s considered marriage a simple contract whose fate was entirely up to them, as Clarence Darrow informed readers of *Vanity Fair*.[14] Popular columnist Dorothy Dix noted that while a divorced woman was once a "disgraced woman," society after World War I found it useless to keep "two people together who have come to hate each other." Only six months after Armistice Day, Boston probate judge Robert Grant told the readers of *Scribner's* that the law was verging close to divorce on demand. But not quite. Even this judge was astonished when a woman asked him if she could divorce her husband for smoking in bed.[15]

Clearly, the culture had shifted. As a popular doggerel of the 1920s put it: "Still the Census taker tarried / With a poised and ready pen; / 'One more question, Are you married?' / Came the answer, 'Now and then.'"[16] But what was driving the shift? And why? The answer given in the popular press of the 1920s was unequivocal: women had changed. World War I had "taught thousands of women that they could work, that work was agreeable, and that it brought an exhilarating sense of independence. They have not forgotten. Wives who would once have been afraid to attempt self-support, feel no such timidity now; when marriage becomes detestable, they revolt."[17] The president of the National Women's Trade Union League exclaimed that the First World War represented "the first hour in history for the women of the world." Women's war work was seen as the key to their immediate social evolution; *Good Housekeeping* noted that "one can not exaggerate the effect upon women of their massive effort on munitions, in government offices, in every trade." By earning war wages, women not only saw the workaday world in a different light, but they also "discovered men as comrades and as rivals[;] they discovered themselves as equally able in many trades; [and] they learned to question male commands." Benjamin P. Chass insisted in the pages of *Current History* that World War I ended the myth of women's "supposed weakness" and demonstrated that "the hand that rocked the cradle could rock the world."[18]

Women's perceived economic and moral independence allowed them to seek the "overthrow of old customs and sex ideals." Indeed, the new woman looked upon her Victorian predecessors with distaste, believing that no "real morality" could be achieved so long as women were dependent upon men for economic necessities. Under the old conjugal arrangements, New York psychiatrist Beatrice M. Hinkle pointed out, the "higher love impulse was largely undifferentiated from the impulse of self-preservation," so that the free blossoming of moral actors could not take place. The attainment of suffrage and the increasing opportunity for self-support fostered women's new moral sway. But women also simultaneously "commenced to find themselves interesting."[19]

Marital upheavals were inevitable, as W. L. George advised the readers of *Good Housekeeping*. "The modern woman," he wrote, "seeks in marriage what her grandmother sought—love, children, security—but she also demands that she shall be allowed to remain a human being, with views, power to make a career—power to contradict."[20] The Pittsburgh *Gazette Times* agreed, foreseeing failure in the efforts from the pulpit to stem divorce. The newspaper saw the hand of woman in the rising divorce rate, which it attributed to the mammoth changes in American social structure, including "the reorganization of household economy, the independence that has come to woman, the non-necessity for enduring an unhappy relationship, and popular sanction of divorce as an appropriate and not disgraceful way of escape."[21] Pointing to one small sign of this new autonomy, Charlotte Perkins Gilman praised those women who kept their last names after marriage. In earlier days, she asserted, this gesture would have been meaningless, as the appropriate question then was not "Who is she?" but "Whose is she?"[22]

A Muncie divorce lawyer told Robert and Helen Lynd that "if a woman has ever worked at all she is much more likely to seek a divorce." Elaine Tyler May's research into samples of 1920 divorce records from New Jersey and California demonstrated that women suing for divorce were considerably more likely to be employed than married women generally. The same refrain was heard from a chorus of divorce judges interviewed by New York writer Mabel Potter Daggett, who recorded her observation that divorce in the 1920s "looks like a walk-out. The woman with the wage envelope has broken the lock from wedlock." With his characteristic light touch, Cole Porter poked fun at the female-driven push to the courthouse in his 1929 Broadway success, *Fifty Million Frenchmen*, telling "modern wives" that if they "led more domestic lives" the results would be dramatic: "There'd be no more divorce in Paris and / Of course there'd be no more annulments in Rome." In one stroke, Porter touched on both the fashionable French divorce of the 1920s and the alternative for Roman Catholic couples, the annulment.[23]

Breadwinning Wives but No Homemaking Husbands

That women had magically achieved economic freedom was the gospel of the 1920s. This claim was repeated so often that it reflected a universal perception. Charlotte Perkins Gilman, Ben B. Lindsey, and many others weighed in on the announcement of the economic roots of social change.[24] A wife's new economic status allowed her, these writers said, to refuse to be subordinated to, or exploited by, her husband. The New York *World* agreed that women's growing economic power led to a higher rate of divorce but insisted that it represented fundamental fairness: "The abused and mistreated wife need no longer submit to a cruel spouse in order to get her bread and butter." As Judge Grant parsed the same point, financial autonomy meant that wives need no longer "endure brutes or utter sensualists."[25]

This striking image of women's new diversity and freedom was not borne out by the hard numbers of economic transformation. Historian William H. Chafe has called the notion that wartime labor force participation transformed women's economic status one of the "popular misconceptions" about the 1920s. Chafe pointed out that the experience of women workers during the war "generated widespread enthusiasm among women leaders and led many observers to declare that women had reached a new plateau of economic equality." But the statistics do not support this confidence.[26] Only 5 percent of female wartime workers were new to the labor force. The overwhelming majority of wage-earning women merely had moved up temporarily from lower-paid jobs. The armistice brought large-scale regression. As New York's Central Federated Union proclaimed in 1919, "The same patriotism which induced women to enter industry during the war should induce them to vacate their positions after the war."[27] In some cases, it undoubtedly did. On many other occasions, however, the patriotic fervor to resign their posts had to be enforced by government and private employers. As Chafe concluded, "Although the continued growth in clerical positions [in the 1920s] offered middle-class women a greater opportunity to work, there was little basis, on balance, for concluding that women had substantially expanded their economic role or risen to a new level of equality with men."[28]

The Women's Bureau of the Department of Labor took heart in what it viewed as long-term trends. Its director, Mary Anderson, proudly announced in 1923 that while men's employment over the period 1880–1920 had increased 124.2 percent, women's gainful employment was up 223 percent. Anderson did acknowledge that the primary shift during the war decade had been from one occupation to another, with increases in business and professional jobs more than offsetting losses in domestic service and farmwork. Calling women workers the "real pioneers in the feminist movement," Anderson concluded that the income of women who worked outside the home was generally necessary for the support of their families.[29]

Women's industrial penetration was, at best, only half of the equation. As noted feminist Crystal Eastman remarked, many married women have worked for pay, but "these bread-winning wives have not yet developed homemaking husbands." Marriages were unequal partnerships. An employed wife "simply adds running the home to her regular outside job."[30] A 1931 Department of Labor pamphlet confirmed that working women continued to labor at home as well:

> There are some people who believe that women go into stores, factories, and mills because they prefer that kind of labor to housework. If those theorists could take a peep into the homes of most wage-earning women, they would discover these same women after 8 or 10 hours of industrial work toiling in the home, at the stove, or over the dish pan, washtub, or sewing machine. Housework must be done before and after factory work each day, even though women get up at 4 in the morning and go to bed at midnight.[31]

Whose job was it to run the home? The almost unanimous response was that the new woman must continue to perform her old tasks. Jazz Age hedonism even condemned women for the ultimate flapper sin: boredom. F. Scott Fitzgerald leveled this charge in a 1923 article for the *Ladies'*

Home Journal: "The average home is a horribly dull place." According to Dr. Abraham Myerson, housework was not only banal but nerve-racking. In *The Nervous Housewife* and in several magazine articles, Dr. Myerson articulated the thesis that the isolation, routine, and mentally unfulfilling nature of the housewife's career led women to an emotional dead end. In portraying Carol Kennicott as "a woman with a working brain and no work," Sinclair Lewis provided in *Main Street* a fictional insight into the ossifying monotony of some housewives' lives.[32] W. L. George ventured to speculate that homemaking was not indelibly part of female nature, and that for some women the home could be a prison. George even predicted the eventual extinction of unpaid housewifery. In the coming future of sexual equality, he predicted, women would compete with men in the professions, with paid workers performing housework. *Good Housekeeping* published George's essay, but it could not resist an editorial wink at its largely female readership on the front page of George's "No Housewives, No Homes" article: "We Don't Believe It; Do You?"[33]

The overwhelming chorus sounded the note of women's continued sole stewardship of the home. Challenges to the perceived natural division of labor were viewed as threats to the underlying social and family structure. As Henry Carey wrote in *Harper's*, a woman "cannot be a man and hold a man." Carey laid the rise in the divorce rate after World War I at the feet of those unnatural wives who "have been exceedingly aggressive in legally disrupting the family. They are becoming more so with every succeeding year. In America, divorce is a growing female institution. . . . Any step which tends to make [the sexes] alike in function, manners, or appearance is a step away from nature and towards sexual chaos."[34]

Social conservatives like Carey blamed the sexual chaos on one man: Sigmund Freud. Although Freudian psychology had reached America before World War I, it became a national fad in the 1920s. In the understated words of Havelock Ellis, Freud "taught the world that the sexual impulse . . . has even wider and deeper implications than has usually been suspected."[35] While Freud had attributed a sexual origin to most neurotic symptoms and conduct, his popularizers turned an explanation of causes into an apologia for behavior. Thus, Freud became as much a symbol of the Jazz Age as the speakeasy.[36] Unlike environmental explanations of human behavior, locating libidinous drives within the self promoted individualistic responses to the crises of life. Young women after World War I engaged in what psychiatrist Beatrice Hinkle described as a "mighty struggle towards differentiation and an individual direction." These women demanded "recognition as individuals first, and as wives and mothers second." The flowering of the sexual instinct may also be seen in the results of a 1938 survey of 777 married women. Twenty-six percent of those born between 1890 and 1900 reported having experienced sexual intercourse before marriage. Of women born after 1910, however, two-thirds had lost their virginity before taking nuptial vows.[37]

In a remarkable article in *Harper's*, a woman defended her affair with a married man on the grounds that his marriage was loveless. While acknowledging the "common assumption" that the First World War had altered moral standards, she begged to differ: Sigmund Freud and Havelock Ellis were the true catalysts. The new psychological literature, she claimed, "made me see for the first time that the miracle of sex can exist quite independently of the institution of matrimony, and be none the less beautiful."[38] Freud's emphasis on irrational impulses and on the role of the unconscious also provided a plausible scenario for many who could not otherwise understand the horrors of the First World War. Revulsion at the war's atrocities combined with the theological liberalism that swept the Protestant churches after 1910 to eviscerate popular belief in authoritarian religion and its God. The loosened grip of formal religious morality allowed divorce to ease away from public opprobrium. In arguing for divorce as a moral and divinely sanctioned act, one wag reversed the biblical dictum to read, "What God hath put asunder, let no man hold together."[39]

As always, changes in marriage drove divorce patterns. Young women interviewed by researchers Phyllis Blanchard and Carlyn Manasses in the late 1920s affirmed that they "ask of life . . . a new kind of marriage, one in which a man will have to do more than provide a living for his wife and children, or else fail." The interviewers concluded that the "modern union of man and woman is visioned as a perfect consummation of both personalities that will involve every phase of mutual living." Over 90 percent of the women who responded to Blanchard and Manasses agreed that divorce was the solution to dissatisfied marriages. What else could be expected in an age when commentators in *Vanity Fair* mocked "the species commonly known as 'first husbands'" and professed that a "reckless gusto becomes marriage," which "to be any good must not be allowed to become a symbol of duty." As historian Paula S. Fass noted, the sexual revolt of the twenties did not target marriage for extinction but consisted of a "revolution within marriage, and as such it recharged the momentum toward marriage as the consummation of love." Dorothy Dunbar Bromley made the same observation more bluntly in a 1927 article in *Harper's*: the new woman expected to be satisfied "as a lover and as a companion."[40]

In terms of the division of function within a home, both sexes believed that biology determined who should handle childbearing, child rearing, and home management. Higher education was an "irritant" to the normal woman raising children and cleaning house, and most observers assented to Worth Tuttle's conclusion in the *Atlantic* that women "cannot utilize the mechanism they have for bearing children and live the lives of men." Novelist Pearl S. Buck agreed, but she blamed American culture for subsisting "in a medieval state of mind about the place of women." By the same token Anne Shannon Monroe argued that the decision whether to divorce should be the woman's, because she stakes the most on the marriage venture. In this new age a woman's biological and socially conditioned subservience to men was transformed into her right to an exit visa from an unhappy union.[41] Charlotte Muret had experience as a nurse before working as a bacteriologist for the Rockefeller Foundation. She studied at Columbia University, then traveled to France to gather materials for her Ph.D. dissertation. A prolific writer and lecturer, she insisted that women's true career was marriage. A woman's psychological differences render it fitting that she subordinate herself to a man. "Men should be catered to," she wrote, "because the truth is that a man wants to be the center of his wife's universe. He wishes her emotional interest to be focused on him, and in so far as a career diverts it, he feels forlorn and cheated." Although more women were saying they were not satisfied with marriage as a career, Muret insisted that women still have "an almost voluptuous pleasure in yielding."[42]

Support abounded for Muret's conclusion that marriage and career made an unstable mix for women. Former newspaper reporter Judith Lambert wrote of her failure during the mid-1930s at juggling home, child, and job. Even when she worked full-time as a reporter, the home responsibilities were entirely hers. Lambert did not suggest that she made any effort to have her husband accommodate to a revision of sex roles. Critical of the myth of women's emancipation, she quit her job, concluding that the "50–50 arrangement [was] a romantic delusion that has since gone the way of World Peace and the Versailles Treaty."[43] A totally egalitarian marriage was still a cultural impossibility. The debate raged over the viability of women's careers outside the home. But no disputation troubled the issue of women's career inside the family residence. While her church obligations encompassed by the traditions of *Kinder, Kirche, und Küche* had weakened, the remaining two corners of women's domestic responsibilities remained strong. Children and kitchen were a wife's unquestioned bailiwick.[44]

Despite the image of the 1920s as the roaring decade of speakeasies and flappers, major cultural developments reinforced women's exclusive responsibility for child rearing and child spacing. In an age in which respect for the sagacity of experts fueled the bounding engine of consumerism, women received mountains of advice on child care and housework from professionals and advertisers. From birth control to microbes, the "100% Mother"[45] became an amateur child psychologist, dietitian, and perpetual laundry machine.[46] The initial venture of the federal government into social welfare legislation, the Sheppard-Towner Maternity and Infancy Protection Act of 1921, bolstered this view of woman's role as custodian of motherhood and of the next generation.[47] The sharp disparity in marital expectations about each sex was illustrated by Leonard McGee's 1924 *American Magazine* lists of "Don'ts for Wives" and "Don'ts for Husbands." McGee was attorney-in-chief of the New York Legal Aid Society, which handled four thousand divorces a year. His twin decalogues of advice included the admonition that a wife should not let her home get dirty because a "clean house re-freshes a man." A husband was warned not to interfere with his wife's management of the home, for she "is a better housekeeper than you." The married men were advised about good grooming; women received the same advice, with the asterisk that a "slovenly wife makes a truant husband." McGee reminded wives that men "like to be coaxed, but resent being driven." He counseled husbands not to "hurt your wife's feelings. A woman is a bundle of nerves, and she is far more easily hurt than you are." Women were often seen as fragile and consequently edgy. As a male Middletowner told the Lynds, "There's something about the female mind that always short-circuits a general statement into a personal criticism."[48]

"Super-Wife" and the Double Standard

The battle over the readjustment of the sexes was never ending. In 1929 *Harper's* published an article by Floyd H. Allport, professor of social and political psychology at Syracuse University, which questioned the prevailing assumptions about gender. Allport challenged the belief in inborn differences between the sexes on the ground that most such thinking assumed that women were different from men, who were presumed to represent the norm. He asserted that a woman should have the same right to full employment as a man, suggesting that the "sweeping claims of the unfitness of women for industrial work" were based in part on "our habits of chivalry" and in part on "a rationalization of masculine economic motives." *Harper's* reported that Allport's essay drew "unanimous applause" from its readers, including one who praised any man who regarded women first as human and then as female.[49]

But the next year found George Jean Nathan harrumphing in the *American Mercury* about the "masculinization of women." The female invasion of "men's sanctums" had proceeded so far that "the purple allure of distance has vamoosed." Writing in *Harper's*, literary critic and novelist Ludwig Lewisohn had no doubt that a "fair" division of the care of infants was in fact "monstrously unfair, since it destroyed the inherent functional differentiation" of the sexes. Marle Beynon Ray suggested in the pages of the *Saturday Evening Post* that gender divergence was hegemonic as well as functional. A veteran magazine editor who had spent five years at *Harper's Bazaar* after ten years at *Vogue*, Ray asserted that the need for a man to feel superior to a woman "is a secondary sex characteristic, as essential to a man's self-esteem as the ability to grow a beard."[50] Even though men aspired to feel superior, a wife was advised to be her husband's "intellectual equal" and "delightful chum," running the home, managing the children, and talking shop with her spouse. She was reminded of her duty to build the emotional home for the family, because men were too "clumsy" for this "delicate" undertaking. In sum, a woman was obliged to become the "modern super-wife."[51]

The challenge of super-wifery was also portrayed as the only refuge for a woman in the 1930s. Harvey Zorbaugh, director of New York's Clinic for Social Adjustment, wrote that marriage was "the only human relationship left that is stable and intimate enough to give an opportunity for self-fulfillment." Zorbaugh's article, condensed by the *Reader's Digest*, told women that they had not yet completed the transition from inferiority to independence because they had been unable to free themselves from traditional attitudes. Women remained torn between self-images as women and as persons. Some readers may have second-guessed Zorbaugh's sanguine view of marriage as a refuge for women, however, for he also wrote that the average husband was "emotionally unable to accept woman's changing role" and exhibits "bewilderment" at it.[52]

The difficult interpersonal dimensions of the task awaiting the "super-wife" may also be seen in some anonymous reflections on a man's view of marriage published by *Harper's* in 1935:

> I have long since come to the conclusion that practically always men marry because they reach a time when their glands impel them to fall in love and at that very moment accident propels some woman into propinquity. Then, after the heat and the fury subside, habit usually takes hold of the married man and binds him tight as any Egyptian undertaker ever wrapped a mummy—habit and the pattern of life each man visions for himself. He thinks "Thank God, now I don't need to worry about women any more. I can proceed with the main business of life, the carving out of a career." More and more, his wife slides into the back of his consciousness. When she moves forward, as like as not, he becomes irritable and peevish, and he says to his friends, "What does she want anyhow? I give her a good home, I provide for the children, I turn over every cent I make." Of course, he doesn't mention his club dues, his tailor bills, his tab at Tony's, or the money he dropped in the poker game. . . . [He] usually assigns her in his not-too-secret thoughts a place in the scheme of things little more than that of mistress and minister to his well-being.[53]

Masculine nature was less frequently an overt topic of discussion in the periodicals, since men were presumed to be the norm from which women differed. Although men were thought to be as locked into their roles as women were to theirs, conflict arose because the culture perceived women as dissatisfied with their portion. Reflections on men's traits may be gleaned from how men wrote about women, as in the preceding excerpt. Occasionally, however, a woman turned the popular microscope on a man. In "I Believe in the Double Standard," a piece which stretched even the *American Mercury's* penchant for notoriety, "A Wife" presented her defense of men's "proneness to philander." Downplaying the impact of adultery, the author insisted that "the average man is not chemically conditioned to be a one-woman commodity." Since monogamy for her husband constituted "emotional mayhem," she was content to be the "chief concubine" in his circle. More than tolerant, she relished the challenge: "That 'there's nothing that keeps a woman young like a fresh love affair' is even more axiomatic if the love affair happens to be her husband's."[54]

Reader response to "I Believe in the Double Standard" was immense and focused almost exclusively on the wife's role in the relationship. The editors published forty-one letters over the next fourteen months either dealing with the original article or attacking other letters that responded to it. The majority of the readers condemned the piece, agreeing with the Bismarck, North Dakota, woman who called it a "putrid article" which belonged "in the waste paper basket or perhaps in *True Story* magazine." Other readers found the article "rotten," chock-full of "erotic rationalizations" and "moronic mouthings," and predicted that the author's children would grow up to be criminals. But one Connecticut wife wondered if the author might be "just ahead of her times, for now that sex is disassociated from religious morality in many minds, we may expect an increasingly casual attitude toward many of its manifestations." While that reader believed the piece looked to the future, a Sedalia, Missouri, correspondent expressed her opinion that the author was merely reiterating the Victorian code by which women were commanded to bear patiently their husband's sexual proclivities.[55]

Other responses revealed how genuinely multifaceted the issue of sexual relationships was in the two decades after the First World War. While a Chicago "Bachelor" said he had been looking for a "Double Standard" woman for twenty-five years, a Philadelphia man gave more thought to the issue and hoped that the article would encourage wives to be more sexually interested in their husbands. He remarked that "the seeds for most divorces are planted in the bedroom, but that is never brought out in the evidence." From Oak Park, Illinois, came the plaint of a woman frustrated because her lover was already married. Maintaining that her love for him was just as natural as that of his wife, she remonstrated, "Why should children of mine be illegitimate just because another woman met the man I love before I did and exchanged vows with him?" Finally, a New York City woman commented that while ultimately monogamy led to the "greatest happiness," the trek to that goal should include "the time-honored roll in the hay . . . [for] both sexes." She expressed a confident hope that "neither my sons nor my daughters marry virgins or *as* virgins, and that hand in hand with experience they will bring to the marriage bed a knowledge that both sexes being human, the standard should be single but tolerant." [56] In mid-twentieth-century America, the sexual standard was growing more tolerant but was still far from being single. [57]

Women's Work in the Depression

The ultimate—if somewhat wishful—praise for the "super-wife" came in the suggestion that women adapt their natural talents to areas of political concerns in which men had proved to be failures. In the 1930s articles in the popular press intimated that women had a greater capacity for organization than men, and that the task of getting the nation out of the Depression could be handled appropriately by women. Katherine Burton, assistant editor of *Redbook* magazine, suggested in *Commonweal* that woman, "the home's housekeeper, is getting dizzy at the doings of man, the world's housekeeper." The Depression had caused women to do what they always did, budget and innovate, only more carefully. Men, however, seemed traumatized by the economic crisis and failed to cope. Burton illustrated her point with a Betty Crocker analogy: "When a woman has made enough cookies for her family she stops making them until they are eaten up and cooks something else. Men don't—they just think up new ways to persuade the children to eat the cookies." [58]

The rumblings of another European conflict in the 1930s led some writers to consider a further field for women's involvement. They argued that woman's natural domesticity need only be extended to the larger world stage of peace, war, and global economic issues. An article in *Good Housekeeping* asking "Should Women Take over the World?" was illustrated by a drawing of a female figure with a broom sweeping an outline map of the world. Clearly, domesticity was being stretched, not discarded.[59]

But most Americans in the nineteen thirties worried far more about the Depression than about *Anschluss*. Some commentators heralded the newfound family togetherness resulting from the economy's meltdown. A Muncie, Indiana, newspaper editorialized: "Many a family that has lost its car has found its soul." A more common sentiment, however, recognized that the Depression had savaged America's families. The divorce rate slowed its increase, but desertions skyrocketed. By 1940 over one and a half million married women lived apart from their husbands. Custodial placements for children rose 50 percent during the first two years of the Depression, and hundreds of thousands of vagrant children wandered the country after their families disintegrated.[60] The preoccupation with material survival yielded, not the expansion of women's sphere to the wider world, but rather a paradoxical shift regarding women's employment outside the home. Women entered the labor force in large numbers in the 1930s. They did so, however, not for reasons of gendered emancipation or psychic satisfaction, but to assist in the struggle for survival of their families in the Depression. At the same time women's increased labor force participation generated a reaction aimed at excluding them.[61]

Married women often were fired and replaced by men, thus reflecting society's assumption that providing work for men was the best way to safeguard the family's well-being. *Independent Woman*, the journal of the Association of Business and Professional Women, vigorously protested the discrimination against women workers, many of whom were their family's breadwinner. But more was at stake than national economic planning, as may be seen in *Commonweal*'s support for the firing of women. Allowing married women to work, according to the Catholic periodical, "weakens the family." The editors proposed instead that a "family wage" be paid a man so he could support his family.[62] "Are Married Women People?" told the story of a woman's firing by a school district because she was married at a time when her husband was unemployed and she was the family's only source of support. Complaints to a school superintendent only brought the reproach, "Divorce your husband if you want a job."[63] Although this incident showed extreme bureaucratic myopia, hostility was displayed toward married women workers across the nation.

Section 213 of the 1932 National Economy Act prohibited any family from having more than one member on the civil service payroll, thus forcing wives (who routinely earned less than their husbands) out of their government jobs. Reinforcing the gendered nature of the statute, the comptroller general ruled in 1933 that female government workers had to assume and report their husbands' last names or face disciplinary action. No matter what the analysis, men still hated women who competed with them in the workplace. American society reverted to old understandings under pressure. As New York's Senator Robert Wagner concluded, the woman wage earner was "the first orphan in the storm."[64]

The Churches: "Militant but Legislatively Powerless"

Although the generation after World War I quickly adopted a more favorable view of divorce, dissenting views were still heard. The storm within the churches on the issue of divorce died a hard death. Implacable opponents of divorce, usually religiously oriented, dramatically declined in number during the interwar period. But those remaining in the fold could still shout. Divorce was a "national calamity," reported the *Literary Digest*, due to the "free-and-easy public mind" of the 1920s, the "jazzing wife," and restless ex-soldiers.[65]

The *Catholic World* denounced in sexually barbed terms the permissive legal system that yielded the growing number of divorces: "In the lawlessness of such a moral tumult the State provided a livelihood for a corps of lawyers by legally interpreting the mad delirium of lechery as the exalted sentiment of love. The Court then became the fertile mother and polite patroness of a tragic horror." Even the normally equable Judge Grant could be moved to proclaim that in an age of limitless divorce, "we are in grave danger of losing our national moral sense." But Grant admitted that "the great public seems unperturbed" and the churches "militant but leg-islatively powerless," and so his "Call to a New Crusade" had the ring of a merely formal protest.[66]

Other voices expressed concern that the cultural norm bespoke moral slippage. *Collier's* reflected the shift in the Weltanschauung from charac-ter to personality in worrying that "we have grown used to the thought that the remedy for marital tiffs is not self-control but a change." The di-vorce laws were to blame, asserted Gustavus Myers, for encouraging di-vorce on trivial grounds. The *Literary Digest* referred to the "national spiritual deterioration" brought on by the rapidly increasing divorce rate. Episcopal bishop Charles Fiske decried divorce as a "ready release from the difficulties of readjustment" and blamed it on the "amazing aimless-ness and emptiness of modern life."[67]

The Roman Catholic Church provided much of the artillery in the battle against divorce, reaching its audience through the pulpit and the periodicals *Catholic World, Commonweal,* and *Catholic Mind.* In 1930 Pope Pius XI promulgated his encyclical letter "On Christian Marriage," which had been written, he remarked, because errors regarding the sanctity of Christian wedlock were "gradually gaining ground." The pontiff observed that the "divine institution" of marriage was under attack; "openly, with all sense of shame put aside, now by word, again by writings, by theatri-cal productions of every kind, by romantic fiction, by amorous and fri-volous novels, by cinematographs portraying in vivid scene, addresses broadcast by radio-telephony, in short, by all the inventions of modern science, the sanctity of marriage is trampled upon and derided."[68] By the "sanctity of marriage," the pope meant, not only the preservation of monogamy and the eradication of divorce, but a specific gender stratifi-cation. The pontiff stressed the "primacy of the husband with regard to the wife and children, and the ready subjection of the wife and her willing obedience." Indeed, the papal letter recognized the connection between divorce and the "social, economic, and physiological emancipation of women," which it condemned as debasing the character and dignity of both women and the family. Divorce was itself roundly denounced at length, with the pontiff contending that amity and benevolence in the daily life of marriage were "miserably weakened by the presence of a facility for divorce."[69]

The *Literary Digest* remarked in 1931 that "all the world buzzes" with discussion of Pius XI's encyclical, which made "not the slightest concession to modernism." But the Catholic Church had almost no power to influence American divorce culture. Novelist Theodore Dreiser hewed much closer to the national norm when he identified marriage as "an unstable equation" and found divorce justified on the grounds of "inharmony, schism, and in consequence bitter contention."[70] Playwright and novelist Rupert Hughes summarized the growing rift between old church doctrine and modern life when he condemned the traditional view as a belief that "pain, suffering, sacrifice and sorrow are the ideal conditions for this earthly life as a preparation either for eternal bliss or eternal blisters." Clearly, the "jazzing wife" and her male counterparts felt otherwise. The *New Republic* argued that the guidance of the Christian Church over youth in matters of relations between the sexes "has either been negative or negligible" and claimed that the relationship between church and society was antipodal: "Possibly Christianity's most grievous failure in teaching the good life may be associated with its impotence to create a domestic atmosphere in which sexual and religious experience were not either hostile or irrelevant to one another." Many Americans were beginning to agree with liberal Episcopalian minister Percy Stickney Grant that "you cannot make the Bible a handbook for modern law-makers."[71] Even more pointed were the words of a letter writer to *Collier's*, who embraced the cultural change with religious zeal: "I say God bless the laws which grant divorce!" *Collier's* received 1,328 letters in response to an article about divorce. While many readers called for more reverence for marriage, only a few opposed an escape hatch for truly miserable couples. The majority agreed with the letter writer who stressed that abolishing divorce would be "a crime against love, happiness and Christianity."[72]

"Romantic Divorce" in Fiction

The social conflict over divorce was also played out in fictionalized treatments of struggling marriages. Early criticism condemned contemporary novels and short stories as "tainted with an insidious form of free love presented in literary form" and as "swing[ing] entirely upon the pivot of sex as set forth by Freud."[73] One critic lambasted Edith Wharton's *Glimpses of the Moon* for attributing "precocious cynicism" to a child when she wrote: "The little girl wound her arms about Susy's neck and leaned against her carelessly. 'Are you going to be, soon, then? I'll promise not to tell if you don't want me to.' 'Going to be divorced? Of course not! What in the world make you think so?' 'Because you look so awfully happy,' said Clarissa Vanderlyn simply."[74]

But the fact that dissolution resolved the difficult marriages of at least six individuals in Charles Norris's 1921 novel, *Brass*, reflected the prevalence of divorce as an accepted form of ending marital stress; Norris's story is exceptional only in the number of compressed instances, not the novelistic treatment of each. In *Support* (1922), M. E. Ashmun wrote of a divorce premised on no more than the parties' conclusion that life would be more pleasant for each without the other. Divorce as a matter-of-fact solution to long-standing conjugal maladjustment is portrayed in Robert Herrick's 1923 novel, *Homely Lilla*.[75]

Fictional versions of divorce in the interwar period reflect the same themes as the periodical literature, including the strength of feminism, the adverse impact of alimony on the husband's second marriage, the emotional wounds suffered by children of divorce (particularly wealthy children), the use of psychological constructs to interpret marital relationships, and the frequency of the marriage versus career dilemma for modern women.[76] The problem with marriages, wrote Gina Kaus in *Good Housekeeping*, was that young people "regard marriage as far less important than love." Kaus decried novels, motion pictures, songs, and the theater for focusing on romantic love "as the only real goal of life." In the 1920s the Lynds found that the residents of Muncie, Indiana, considered "the demand for romantic love as the only valid basis for marriage." Indeed, in *Happiness in Marriage*, Margaret Sanger insisted that the "nuptial relation must be kept romantic. . . . Do not be afraid to take the brakes off your heart, to surrender yourself to love."[77]

With such emphasis on romance as life's central attraction, it was not long until American culture manifested "romantic divorce." Katherine Fullerton Gerould defined this cultural term as ending one's marriage in the hopes of preserving the passionate quest by finding a new love object. In envisioning this idealized conception of love, "we have demanded a white-hot emotional perfection," remarked Gerould. "Needless to say, we have very seldom got it." This theme of romantic divorce is portrayed in Ursula Parrott's novel *Ex-Wife* and in Katherine Mansfield's short story "Marriage à la Mode." That romanticism did not remove the bitterness underneath "the etiquette of divorce" is portrayed in Maude Parker's aptly titled short story "Till the Courts Do Us Part."[78]

By far the most influential divorce novel, both in England and the United States, was A. P. Herbert's *Holy Deadlock*. Herbert's tale of the ready manufacture of "hotel evidence" and the pervasive fraud in the procurement of English divorces played a leading role in changing public opinion and pressuring Parliament to expand the grounds of divorce in 1937. The *Literary Digest* noted that *Holy Deadlock* made a sensation on both sides of the Atlantic and quoted Herbert's assessment of divorce as a "release from misfortune and not a crime."[79]

The gaudy divorce behavior of the Hollywood "smart set" received its share of censure. The merry-go-round marriages of stars such Gloria Swanson, William Powell, Jean Harlow, Carole Lombard, and Cary Grant were carefully scrutinized and then criticized for setting the tone of loosened morality for the general public. After a time, of course, the marital carousel seemed almost natural. Mary Pickford and Douglas Fairbanks were two of the most adulated film actors of the era. In 1920 each obtained a divorce in order to marry the other. Seven years later their marriage was described as "amazing" for having endured while those of other celebrities failed. But the Pickford-Fairbanks love match ended in divorce court, and each tried again with a third spouse.[80] *Good Housekeeping* tracked the celebrity wedding ring-toss, sagely observing that those who "marry for a season are few in number, but impressive in influence. They belong to the group which sets our fashions in clothes, resorts, amusements; in time their morality tends to become our own."[81]

Finally, poetry too served as a vehicle for describing the changed mores of divorce. Humorist Ogden Nash quipped that "women are dictators all," and that "a little incompatibility is the spice of life, particularly if he has income and she is pattable." In one Nash poem, a wife poisoned her long-suffering and empathic mate because "she could no longer stand being perpetually understood." In another, a husband divorced his wife for adultery, which was not his real objection to her, "but he didn't want to blast her reputation." In "Advice outside a Church," published in 1935 in the *Saturday Evening Post*, Nash addressed a man who believed that marriage would allow him permanently to shelve his bachelorhood. Nowadays, Nash noted, "lawyers make bachelors of us all." He remarked on the transitory state of modern marriage, in which "no one belongs to anybody." With the traditional marital warranties no longer in effect, conjugal bliss required constant wooing: "Strong are the couple who resort / More to courtship and less to court."[82]

In the words of one of the era's most incisive critics, Katherine Fullerton Gerould, "As long as personal happiness is made the only desideratum in marriage, the divorce courts will be full. . . . You cannot have the right to expect perfection, without the right to discard imperfection."[83] This introduction to the popular culture of the early twentieth century has stressed the changing dynamic of gender roles. In the broader society women made gains toward self-determination, including suffrage, some improvement in employment prospects, and an expanded resort to divorce. Within the home, however, women continued to be not only prisoners but wardens. The next chapter explores how the popular culture created its own legal system of divorce and forced trial courts to defy both their appellate and legislative masters in transmuting the effective law to allow divorce by mutual consent.

1. Nineteenth-century poster: the father is awarded custody.
(Drawn by P. Krafft; The Bettmann Archive)

TARZAN TAMED
Are women *really* the weaker **sex**?
Obviously not, thinks our artist, who
shows us here, how Hugo, a hulking he-
man, is instantaneously transformed by
marriage into a tea-time cake-carrier

DEGRADATION
Even mother-love is surpassed by
Woman's passion for Authority,
as witness his mother's very public way of slapping Cecil, right
before a brace of his schoolmates

2. Parodies of the emerging cultural dominance of women.
(Illustrated by FISH for *Vanity Fair*, November 1927)

THE DANCING BEAR

Portly Adolph is another shining example of how women shape the destinies of mere men. Loathing dancing extremely, Adolph is forced nightly to trip the light fantastic—with the accent on the trip

DISILLUSIONMENT

Cast your eye on Reggie who discovers his sweetie in the arms of another. This picture shows how quickly a lover may be reduced to the sighing furnace state

MISS NANCY

How an inferiority complex may be fastened on a male is shown by the plight of little Peter whose sissified garb fills his manly boy friends with glee

3. More illustrations of women's "diabolical power" over men.
(Illustrated by FISH for *Vanity Fair*, November 1927)

THE BOLD BRITON

Behold the English ménage. Egbert would a-golfing go, and his wife accompanies him . . as caddy. Note the concealed reporter recording legal evidence, should she dare to think of disobeying her liege-lord

IN ARCTIC CIRCLES

When the Eskimo husband falls for a fascinating, fur-bearing flapper, his pleasant custom is to put his regular wife in cold storage until her jealousy is thoroughly cooled

4. Women of other lands portrayed as subservient.
(Illustrated by FISH for *Vanity Fair*, May 1927)

THE LAND OF THE FREE

And here we see the glorious American wife. No second-fiddling here. Nay! at her husband's suggestion that they spend one evening at home, she cries, "Stay home forever, if you like. I'm going into the movies!" And off she hops to Hollywood, that haven for independent women

5. American women, by contrast, have declared independence from their husbands.
(Illustrated by FISH for *Vanity Fair*, May 1927)

THE INNOCENT ON-LOOKER

Gertrude is the newest of new parents in every sense of the word. Her marriage to Freddy is no bar to a light petting party with Herbert whom she has known for years and years. Fortunately, Freddy Junior, who is seen supine in the foreground, is at that convenient age where children see but do not tell. He will some day be taught to call Herbert "Uncle", which is the generic title of all detached males whom it is pleasant to have around the house

6. The changing mores of Jazz Age parents. (Illustrated by FISH for *Vanity Fair*, February 1927)

THE CHILD-CHAPERONE

Many a poor little rich girl is toted about merely to preserve appearances—such as they are. This is the fate of Dottie, who spends tedious hours at the Ritz while Mama dances with a gentleman of whom Dottie only knows that he isn't Papa. Some day she may tell this to the judge, and oh, won't that be fun?

A FLOP

Henry Higbie, the poor deluded old father, still believes in parental authority, guidance, firmness and all that sort of tosh. He is shown trying to give a piece of his mind to his hopeless hopefuls. The going is rough. Henry, Jr. says, "Dad, you're better than Burton Holmes," but his daughter is less encouraging. She only cries, "Funnier, but not so loud." Verily, the old fashioned Pop is a flop

7. Cultural change in the parent-child relationship in the 1920s.
(Illustrated by FISH for *Vanity Fair*, February 1927)

TWO

THE POPULAR ARENA OF DIVORCE

Public sentiment is stronger than any courts.

Judge Robert Grant, "A Call to a New Crusade"

Arthur Garfield Hays described divorce in the 1920s as a "beating of wings against a cage—an endeavor to obtain a legal paper with a red seal which will avoid a situation which two people find intolerable." Hays was a prominent civil rights lawyer who served as counselor for the American Civil Liberties Union and participated in the *Scopes* evolution trial in the 1920s and the race-baiting Scottsboro trial a decade later. His personal experience of divorce in 1924 triggered a flurry of publications on the subject. Hays took an aggressive stance, condemning the immorality of any couple who stayed married after they no longer loved each other. In "Modern Marriage and Ancient Laws," Hays contrasted the cultural hare with the statutory tortoise. Anyone who supported divorce on demand, he remarked, was castigated as "a wrecker of our institutions." But society was edging closer and closer to pure individualism. Hays saw nothing beneficial in holding on to the cultural husk while morality evolved into another form. "Revolutionary changes occur unnoticed," he announced, "while our delusions persist and our sense of conservatism is gratified."[1]

In Sync: The New Psychology, the New Jurisprudence, and Marital Incompatibility

Judge Grant, frequent contributor to the popular press, noted in three post–World War I articles for *Scribner's* and one for *Good Housekeeping* that women's economic emancipation had made compatibility the test of marital survival. But the problem with an incompatibility standard for divorce, he argued, was that it made the formal dissolution process "hinge on caprice instead of some tangible grievance." More than economics was at issue. Grant viewed women as cultural captains in the campaign to capture divorce: "If sundering the marriage tie for mere incompatibility is to involve no social reproach, it will be because the women of the United States are in favor of it."[2] Women were perceived as the prime agitators for greater divorce, not—said the *World's Work*—because they were immoral, but because they were self-respecting and would no longer submit to "indignities."[3]

Women were indeed the captains of divorce not only culturally but especially in the courtrooms. Henry R. Carey complained that women's economic freedom allowed an unhappy wife to replace the court as the judge of what was "unbearable." Carey pointed with exasperation to the fact that over two-thirds of divorce decrees were awarded to women.[4] Since men had access to roughly the same number of divorce grounds as women, the enormous disparity reflected a strong cultural preference for women as the champions of new divorce values.

At first glance the formal requirements of the fault system might seem to explain why wives were usually the plaintiffs. Only an innocent spouse could receive alimony, and although the presumption that custody should go to the wife while the child was in its "tender years" was in full sway, the courts still favored "innocent" over "guilty" spouses whenever possible. However, alimony turns out to have been a surprisingly insignificant factor in the cases, and most divorces were legal ratifications of brokered endings negotiated by the parties themselves. The predominance of women

Table 1. Percentage of absolute divorces and annulments, by party

| Year | Granted to: | |
	Husband	Wife
1867–70	36.0	64.0
/////		
1916–20	32.6	67.4
1921–25	31.8	68.2
1926–30	28.7	71.3
1935	26.9	73.1
1940	26.0	74.0
1945	28.6	71.4
1950	27.5	72.5

Source: Paul H. Jacobson, *American Marriage and Divorce* (New York, 1959), table 58, at 121.

Note: Not only were women granted decrees twice or thrice as often as men, as the table shows, but wives were also more successful as divorce plaintiffs than husbands. In 1939, for example, of the 65,740 decrees issued in suits brought by husbands, the men were awarded the decree 95 percent of the time (with their wives awarded 5 percent of the decrees, presumably on cross-motion). Of the 185,260 decrees issued in actions taken by wives that year, women were successful 99.5 percent of the time. Jacobson, *American Marriage and Divorce*, table 56, at 120.

divorce plaintiffs probably owes more to the rise of cruelty as the most popular divorce ground and the sense of most couples that it would be easier for a woman to admit that she had been slapped by her mate than vice versa. An anonymous female contributor to *Harper's* declared that male gallantry was the cause: "It is in the divorce courts of to-day that chivalry at its most absurdly romantic is to be found. What were the courtly sweeps of Elizabethan plumed hats compared to the American husband automatically permitting an adulterous wife to sue him for 'cruel and barbarous treatment' in order that she may marry her lover? It is a supreme gesture, daily accepted as a matter of course."[5] Table 1 confirms the predominant role that women achieved as formal initiators of divorce.

Despite widespread exposure in fiction and the periodicals, incompatibility did not exist as a statutory divorce ground in the 1920s.[6] Spouses in dissolving unions may have perceived irreconcilability as the underlying ground for the divorce, but this truth was not cognizable in court, where "divorces are obtained for alleged causes, wholly different from the real causes." Nancy M. Schoonmaker called for an end to this dissonance between law and life: "If we insist upon divorce, no matter how our preachers and teachers rail at us, then certainly the more decently the divorce can be obtained the better for the individuals directly concerned and for the body social as well."[7] The concept of incompatibility also rang true to a generation bursting with psychological explanations for all behaviors.

Incompatibility turned the legal rationale for divorce on its head. The tradition of ecclesiastical and statutory law had deemed divorce a consequence of certain proscribed behaviors. The nineteenth-century view of divorce had been consonant with orthodox formalism, an ethos insisting on rigid boundaries for classifying all human behavior and its legal consequences. In this categorical universe law served as the impartial and apolitical police officer. Indeed, nineteenth-century divorce doctrine provided a classic example of legal formalism. A marriage was deemed indissoluble, save when the complainant established a fault ground. At that point formal dismemberment of the union was mandatory. The underlying reality of the marriage was never the focus of the judicial inquiry. Technical grounds served as the unrebuttable barometer of the health of the marriage, and their presence meant its absence, with no occasion provided for the court to inquire behind the mask of the formal law.[8]

In a similar vein the arena of formal divorce was a haven for logical puzzle making. As one illustration of the legal acrostics, courts under the fault requirement occasionally faced the prospect of determining whether a single instance of marital intercourse betokened condonation by the complainant of a single instance of prior extramarital sex by the defendant, resulting in the latter's immunity from an adultery action. Further along the looking-glass path of formal divorce law appeared this example: did a postcondonation violation of the marital vows by the original guilty party constitute a revival of the earlier fault ground that the condonation had previously rendered unavailable? These conundrums may fairly be characterized as the acrobatics of logic over experience, particularly as courts sought their resolution in the realm of syllogistic reasoning rather than in a consideration of the well-being of the flesh-and-blood marriage at stake.

But the rising tide of psychology flooded over legal designs that evaluated an act without examining the motivation of the actor. Where the formal divorce system stressed logic, the new understanding of divorce evidenced a utilitarian basis. In place of the traditional cause-and-effect scheme in which one act of adultery or desertion warranted the penalty of divorce, the emerging psychological insight opened the door to innumerable causes and thus questioned the necessity of any punishment at all.

This elevation of the psychological elements in American life was evident in the strength of scientific naturalism after World War I. This experimentally based ideology undermined the absolutist moral foundation of society in the 1920s and 1930s. At the same time the rise in popularity of cultural anthropology led many Americans to question their assumptions about fundamental values. As Edward Purcell has written, by "rejecting the possibility of demonstrating the truth of ethical propositions by either induction or deduction," scientific naturalists "left moral ideals without a rational, theoretical basis."[9] The psychological, naturalist, and anthropological strains are all reflected in the era's changing jurisprudential thought. Nineteenth-century formalism genuflected to the axiological god of logic and abstraction. But the instrumentalist revolt, led by Oliver Wendell Holmes, Jr., prayed for facts. Law is no more than "what the courts will do in fact," Holmes asserted in his seminal essay on "The Path of the Law."[10] In valuing substantive concerns at the cost of logical cohesion, the instrumentalists dealt a significant blow to all legal systems that had been maintained as comprehensive orderings of their societies.

While the instrumentalists were primarily utilitarians who believed, with Holmes, that judges made law only at the margins, a younger breed of legal theorists went much further. John Chipman Gray asserted that only judges made law. Legislation, in his view, was merely a source of law, fuel for the law-producing engine of the courts. Roscoe Pound hailed judges as "social engineers," and Karl N. Llewellyn criticized judges for not admitting that the adherence to precedents and legal rules was a pretense.[11] These legal realists insisted that the categories of orthodox formalism were social constructs, not natural boundaries. The pragmatic temper of the early twentieth century had dismissed the claims of philosophical idealism. In a similar fashion legal realism's "cognitive relativism" fostered a "hermeneutic understanding of reality," highly skeptical of classical boundaries.[12] Some of this new skepticism about the certainty of legal postulates was due to the vast expansion of the National Reporter System since the West Publishing Company had begun its compilation in 1870. By the 1920s the growing formless and limitless mass of state and federal decisions had destroyed the pretense of categorical organization. The syllogistic precision of formalism was exposed as a fraud, and the whole question of determining law was reopened. In this process of discovery, the rules of law were much more likely to be Roscoe Pound's flexible "general clauses"[13] than any specific formula deduced from an antiquated hierarchy of values or an impossible ocean of case volumes.

One significant manifestation of the sloughing off of rule-based jurisprudence was the invention of the juvenile court. Beginning at the turn of the century and spreading rapidly across the nation, juvenile courts embodied the reigning psychological and jurisprudential drift in elevating rehabilitation over punishment and preferring easy confession to painstaking proof. Juvenile judges disdained lawyers, precedents, the adversary process, and rules of any kind: what mattered in this quintessential revolt against formalism was the judge's perception of the child's welfare.[14] In sidestepping the presumption of innocence, juvenile courts signaled their belief that the fate of the child was too important to be sacrificed to the dominant legal conventions.

That same impatience to get at the underlying reality—with identical hazards to the truth-seeking process—propelled divorce courts effectively to jettison fault grounds in favor of a generalized incompatibility standard. The real force of the incompatibility concept was made manifest in the mistaken belief of some writers that incompatibility had actually been generally enacted as a valid legal ground for divorce. Historian George L. Koehn, for example, showed his ignorance of formal legal standards in the 1920s by affirming that the "ambiguous term incompatibility is elastic enough to stretch to any lengths the plaintiff desires, and to cover likewise those innumerable cases wherein both agree to disagree and then amicably decide to employ 'incompatibility' as convenient grounds."[15] In sum, the popular culture acknowledged a non-Euclidean procedure whose coordinates did not fit within the classical geometry of the legal system. To borrow the words of Thurman Arnold, such a conflict was a struggle between "an ideal and a social need not accepted as legitimate or moral." This informal "law" of incompatibility, as developed and ratified by assertive litigants and agreeable trial judges, proved to be the stronger determinant of the fate of unhappy marriages in the divorce courts, no matter what the legislatures and appellate courts said.[16]

Divorce Courts and Their Consumers

While much of the literature on domestic relations focused on divorce, relatively little described marriage. American laws regulated marriage quite lightly, and the average citizen could only "visualize state regulation of the marriage relationship" through the rules on divorce.[17] Despite its overarching purpose to preserve marriages, family law was generally visible to the public only when it regulated their demise. The three principal statutory divorce grounds, cruelty, adultery, and desertion, illustrated the murder-of-marriage theory posited by Protestant theology and adhered to by legislatures and appellate courts attuned to classical legal thought. The canons of divorce aimed at rewarding the faithful and punishing the offender. Fault both heated and illuminated formal divorce policy, and divorce grounds and defenses orbited around the concept of guilt. Rather than attempt to evaluate the marriage as a whole, divorce law considered only the statutorily specified grounds. This narrowness of gaze displayed a systemic bias in favor of an adversary process oriented toward particular incidents of conduct capable of courtroom proof.[18]

Demonstration of a divorce ground led to legal recognition of marital breakdown. Empirically, this analysis was at best eccentric, as the advocates of "therapeutic divorce" would convincingly demonstrate in the following decades. Many marriages were shipwrecked despite the absence of a legislatively proscribed ground, and proof of a single occasion of statutory sin did not necessarily mean that the marriage was doomed. When the conjugal falling out could not be attributed to a statutory ground, the prevailing theory left the hapless couple legally stranded because the truthful form of action had not been officially approved. On the other hand, the commission of a specified act by one spouse gave the other substantial leverage as to the fate of the relationship. These power vacuums and struggles were often the unintended consequences of relying on a grounds-based divorce system.

Litigation over grounds represented the fundamental view of legislatures and appellate courts that divorce was a club with which to wallop transgressors of social and religious mores. Statutory adultery, desertion, and cruelty furnished specific standards against which to measure the quality of a marriage. This categorical thinking indulged the legal proclivity for substituting verifiable pieces for an interpretive whole.[19] Writing about the state of American divorce in the generation before the 1920s, historian William O'Neill described matrimonial litigation as a morality play:

> Divorce was comfortingly well-regulated at a time of growing moral confusion. . . . While slackness and moral relativity seemed everywhere on the increase, the divorce court was one of the few places where the old beliefs still obtained. There was a guilty party and an innocent party. The innocent party was rewarded, the guilty punished, right prevailed over wrong, and the American verities were reaffirmed. Society at large might wink at adultery and assorted other breaches of law, custom, and good taste, but the divorce court did not. In this sense, divorce, though offensive to traditional values reinforced them all the same.[20]

Before World War I the issue of whether divorce would permanently scar or enhance American culture was an open question. As Herbert Croly phrased the quandary in 1909 in his celebrated *The Promise of American Life*, "public opinion does not appear to have decided" whether the prevalence of divorce represented "an abuse or . . . a fulfillment of the existing institution of marriage."[21]

In the 1920s public opinion decided. Beginning in that decade divorce courts faced an avalanche of wives and husbands who demanded nothing less than that the court "wink"—to use O'Neill's word—at the wholesale breach of the fault-driven system of divorce law. Trial judges largely accommodated these commands from below, keeping the blindfold on formal justice as they opened their eyes to the demands of what Llewellyn called the "law-*consumer*."[22] This shift away from enduring connubial woe and toward freer divorce as a positive cultural and psychological good was consistent with what historian T. J. Jackson Lears described as "a shift from the Protestant ethos of salvation through self-denial to a therapeutic ideal stressing self-realization in this world—a paradigm characterized by an almost obsessive concern with psychic and physical health defined in sweeping terms."[23]

Even had legislators and appellate judges the inclination to make dramatic pronouncements in favor of broadening access to divorce decrees—and there is no evidence that they did—their work product appeared in much too public a forum to have avoided tremendous controversy. While many voices in the interwar period praised the pioneers of expanded divorce, a good number of cultural and religious leaders continued to condemn the rise in the rate of divorce. As the popular literature reflected, the public proved increasingly sympathetic to multitudinous cases of individual relief through the divorce courts. But it became difficult to disagree with society's elders that there was nothing beneficial about the booming divorce rate increase itself.

This cultural standoff was matched by a legal draw, in which appropriate divorces were granted but the statutory dam still blocked the flood of open divorce. Nor did public opinion force the issue of broad legal reform. The growing ease of divorcing, particularly for the well-off and middle classes, militated against any movement for reform. Katherine Fullerton Gerould remarked on the "tendency among civilized people, who live 'above the law,' to underrate the sensitiveness of the average man, whose weaknesses laws are designed to control. Did you ever know anyone who admitted that laws existed to control him?"[24] The Roman Catholic bishop of Boston would make the same point a generation later: "There are many citizens of highest calibre who profess to be shocked and horrified by the statistical reports of divorce throughout the nation, but yet have upheld and defended individual cases among their personal acquaintances. . . . The theoretical condemnation of divorce in general has not persuaded these citizens to any judgment against divorce in individual cases."[25] This "moral snobbishness," as Gerould phrased it, helps explain why no League of Wrechedly Unhappy Spouses ever launched a lobbying campaign. Moreover, divorce statutes were "precise enough to satisfy the moral predilections of the clergy," while divorce practice was "lax enough to satisfy the most fickle spouse."[26]

When it became clear that divorces were flowing at the will of the parties, the legislative response produced reforms seeking to block the avalanche of divorce. Appellate courts, by contrast, broadened the range of cruelty and developed the doctrine of mental cruelty as a viable divorce ground. The courts' expansion of cruelty was effectively penned by Sigmund Freud. In an age which featured ubiquitous psychological determinants of behavior, the acknowledgment of cruelty's mental component is not surprising and did not stem from any ostensible intention on the part of appellate judges to widen the aperture of divorce. The Louisiana Supreme Court typified the movement to extend cruelty's domain, holding that "any unjustifiable conduct of the part of either husband or wife which so grievously wounds the mental feelings of the other, or such as in any other manner utterly destroys the legitimate ends and objects of matrimony, constitutes cruelty, although no physical or personal violence may be inflicted or threatened."[27] Minnesota's highest court succinctly embraced the current psychological discourse: "Mental anguish may more perniciously affect health and life than bodily bruises."[28]

Unlike their appellate superiors, trial judges actually dwelled in the lower emotional latitudes of the law. They daily confronted, not the rarified doctrines of collusion and recrimination, but the human agony of matrimonial disruption. While this division of labor between lower and higher courts had always existed, never before had the assertive individualism and consumerism of a vastly increased number of divorce litigants descended upon the courts. Several factors allowed trial judges to join divorce litigants in creating a rival—and nearly untouchable—divorce system. If, as Joseph Walter Bingham claimed, law's substance was found in the "cases in all their concreteness of causes and effects,"[29] then divorce judges could be legal realists par excellence. Trial court rulings announced

Table 2. Appeals from Philadelphia divorce proceedings

Year granted	Divorces	Appeals to superior court	Appeals to supreme court
1938	1,713	9	0
1944	2,933	8	0
1948	3,866	7	0

Source: Note, "The Administration of Divorce: A Philadelphia Study," *University of Pennsylvania Law Review* 101 (1953): 1222 n.87.

no public policy findings or deviations. They simply pigeonholed facts into legal boxes to resolve one case at a time. Since nearly all divorces were uncontested, and the decrees unappealed, it was virtually impossible for appellate courts to review the judgments granting divorce. A Philadelphia study (summarized in table 2) illustrated the irrelevance of appellate courts to the vast majority of divorcing couples.

In the world of American divorce, "only the exceptionally abnormal case" ever needed appellate resolution.[30] In terms the Advertising Age would have understood, trial courts adopted a policy of responsiveness to their clients, and the satisfied customers joined the trial judges in evading review by their off-floor managers, the appellate courts.

The "Unholy Trinity" of Divorce Grounds

Adultery, which H. L. Mencken quipped was "the application of democracy to love," derived from the English ecclesiastical practice of allowing divorce *a mensa et thoro* (from table and bed). This limited divorce separated the parties but left them in spousal limbo by forbidding them to remarry during the lifetime of the other. Adultery was the earliest and most widespread divorce ground in America. It also constituted a capital offense in several New England colonies, but for innocent spouses it at least represented an improvement by allowing remarriage. Although very few philanderers were executed in colonial America, the law served both as a deterrent and as an unmistakable expression of society's devotion to the principle of sexual exclusivity within marriage.[31] Second in the "unholy trinity" of major fault grounds was desertion, which was seen as an abdication of one spouse's lifelong responsibility to the other. All the states imposed minimum time periods, at least one year but usually longer, to ensure that the spousal abandonment was complete.[32] The final divorce ground, cruelty, also branded one spouse as a legal offender, for proof of cruelty was the domestic relations analogue to a criminal conviction for assault and battery.[33]

Of the three grounds, only cruelty became the "dazzling success story of family law" because its plasticity allowed it rapidly to outpace adultery and desertion as the favored ground for divorce.[34] In the 1860s cruelty

Table 3. Percentage of absolute divorces and annulments
in the United States, by divorce ground

Year	Adultery	Desertion	Cruelty
1867–70	26.4	35.4	12.4
/////			
1916–20	12.1	36.9	27.8
1921–25	10.7	33.3	35.2
1926–30	8.4	29.9	39.9
1935	6.9	26.1	44.4
1940	6.2	25.1	47.8
1945	5.6	20.0	54.6
1950	2.7	17.6	58.7

Source: Jacobson, *American Marriage and Divorce*, table 58, at 121.

accounted for only one-eighth of all decrees. By 1922 it was the most popular ground, and reliance on cruelty continued to increase, as table 3 indicates. Cruelty's share as a ground for all divorces rose from one-eighth in 1870 to two-thirds in 1949. The utter malleability of this ground was noted by *World's Work* magazine in 1919, when it editorialized that cruelty "embraces almost anything from violent and constant attacks upon the person, endangering life, to 'severity' of manners or deportment, or treatment involving the 'dignity' of husband or wife." The periodical concluded that cruelty had come to mean that the "husband and wife do not like each other and would be much happier if they could dissolve an unfortunate partnership."[35]

Support for a broad reading of the cruelty ground came from many sources. Almon Hensley, president of the New York Mothers' Club, argued that "constant nagging is [a] better justification for divorce . . . than misconduct." Doris Stevens believed that cruelty grew out of incompatibility and included mental anguish. An anonymous writer in *Harper's* noted that her husband did not physically mistreat her but merely forbade her to smoke and attempted to censor her reading matter. She had no doubt that she could obtain a divorce on grounds of cruelty. *Time* noted in 1937 that the ground was so easy to prove that plaintiffs who normally would have pleaded adultery instead were alleging "excessive cruelty" out of squeamishness. As University of Minnesota law professor William L. Prosser acknowledged to readers of the *Forum* magazine, mental cruelty "is an inevitable accompaniment of any marriage which has been a failure."[36]

Double-Barreled Fault: The Role of Defenses

Divorce defenses also revealed the legal system's emphasis on critical moral distinctions proved by specific acts. In fact, the legal defenses focused attention on the formal system's requirement of double-barreled fault: not only must the defendant be guilty, the complainant must be innocent. In the looking-glass morality of divorce law, forgiveness was taboo. The resumption of sexual relations after learning of the existence of a fault ground was deemed to be conclusive proof that the innocent spouse had condoned the guilty spouse's misconduct. An act of forgiveness was not evaluated in the context of the whole of the marriage. Mercy constituted a devastating error, for a single act of intercourse would bar the innocent spouse's access to the divorce court.[37]

Collusion and connivance reinforced the law's preoccupation with adversarial divorce. Husbands and wives were forbidden to agree upon a divorce ground. Collusion, a defense presumably raised *sua sponte* by the court, would defeat a divorce action upon discovery that the couple had cooperated in seeking to obtain it. In fact, such a mutual desire was regarded officially as "morally reprehensible"[38] and "several degrees worse than murder."[39] A few states went so far as to create the office of divorce proctor or *defensor vinculi* (literally, "defender of the [marital] bond"), charged with rooting out collusion in divorce cases. Connivance, a variant of collusion, would deny a divorce to a spouse who had "corruptly" agreed that his or her spouse could commit a marital offense.[40]

Anne Shannon Monroe argued in the pages of *Good Housekeeping* that the single-act theory of divorce law was psychologically warped. She insisted that the "very thing that will positively defeat an attempt to obtain a divorce—the agreement of the two that it is the wisest course—is the one absolute reason why a decree should be granted." Katherine Fullerton Gerould summarized the argument against the bar of collusion: "Why do your best to prevent people's divorcing when both of them want to? The cry against divorce on the score that in most divorces one person is sacrificed becomes absurd enough when you realize that only on the basis of one person's wanting it and the other person's not wanting it is a divorce obtainable at all." As Robert Grant concluded, collusion converted every divorce ground into the catchall moral ground of incompatibility.[41]

Unrelentingly opposed to all marital dissolutions, *Commonweal* argued that collusion flowed from the existence of divorce, and that proscribing collusion was as pointless as forbidding bootlegging during Prohibition. It was in the nature of divorce law "irresistibly" to broaden all exceptions: "If unfaithfulness or physical cruelty are causes, why not incompatibility? If incompatibility, why not boredom? What court can say which causes less subjective suffering, or which should be denied relief?"[42] Paradoxically, the iron logic deployed by this Catholic periodical would become the operating wisdom of the popular law of divorce in America, with unmitigated individualism destroying—as *Commonweal* predicted—all barriers to "free" divorce. The blurring of specific grounds with their psychological components lifted the lid on the Pandora's box of divorce. Wives and husbands became convinced that no court had the right to evaluate how much conjugal suffering merited the redemption of divorce. No rules could govern subjectivity. And trial courts began to agree.

Recrimination was the divorce defense that most peculiarly—but most convincingly—demonstrated the formal system's priority on penalizing malefactors. Recrimination represented legal theory's determination to deny divorce to wives and husbands who had violated their marital vows. It provided the means by which a defending spouse could "admit even the most repellent charges made in the complaint and still prevent the plaintiff from securing a divorce." In such a case of mutual fault, the court was bound to withhold its decree, thus visiting the parties with "the Sartresque punishment of remaining together and hating it."[43]

Like collusion, connivance, and condonation, recrimination had its distant genesis in Roman property law. The legal charter of antiquity had been recast by twelfth-century canonists so that "the Church might intervene in a divorce suit which, if successful, would have turned a wife loose on a society in which unattached women had no place." These origins suggested that recrimination focused more on property issues than on divorce itself.[44] The modern twist given this doctrine served only to block the decree and appeared to ignore any financial consequences of divorce. Ironically, however, recrimination generally was raised as an issue only when one party was dissatisfied with the property arrangements. Litigated recrimination cases generally involved a spouse "forced to resort to the defense of recrimination because he [or she] has failed to bargain successfully outside of court." In those cases the parties wielded the cudgels of moral fault in a combat over finances.[45]

Recrimination fared no better than collusion in the popular journals. As Ruth Hale phrased the conventional wisdom, "That spiritual perceptiveness which holds that a divorce must on no account be granted if both persons . . . have been unfaithful to the marriage, instead of merely one, can hardly be respected as a source of law or precept." Although mocked by many, the formal legal system insisted on the letter of its peculiar anti-windfall logic: since divorce could only be awarded to an innocent husband or wife, a guilty spouse could not benefit from the other's marriage-destroying misconduct. Recrimination thus banned divorce unless both barrels of the fault system were loaded.[46]

What the Divorce Judges Said

A trial judge handling divorce cases in the 1920s and 1930s faced the dilemma of resolving the conflict between, on the one hand, the instructions laid down by legislatures and appellate courts and, on the other, the pervasive, unending, quotidian pull of divorce litigants. The formal system began with the proposition that, subject to certain narrow exceptions, marriage was a permanent commitment. But this premise was regularly and stoutly denied by the consumer culture, which acted on the opposite assumption that "unhappy unions" were disgraceful and should be dissolved in divorce. Ludwig Lewisohn declared in the *Nation* that marriage should be held to a basic standard of contentment: "To fall below that minimum is to cheat both the self and society, both the present and posterity, to sacrifice honor to a fetish and vitality to decay." Thus, the popular view reversed the formal postulate and its exceptions, holding that the pursuit of happiness mandated ready divorce, subject to prohibitions upon particular circumstances. As English preacher and feminist A. Maude Royden declared in the *Atlantic*, the "real immorality" consisted of pretending that a marriage was working when it had broken.[47]

Popular voices complained that the necessity of proving fault in order to obtain freedom was indecent. Katherine Fullerton Gerould believed incompatibility was "certainly as reasonable a ground as any" and far better than the requirement of "mud-slinging." In response to the moral calumny that religious conservatives launched at those disdainful of the immutability of the conjugal commitment, Gerould argued that a spouse who refused divorce to a partner desiring it was "beneath contempt." Since society permitted easy marriage, it should guarantee divorce on demand, for the two were linked. The *Nation* agreed, calling for "decency in divorce."[48] These cultural heralds also challenged the logic of the fault grounds themselves. Royden highlighted the inconsistency of defining marriage as indissoluble by its nature yet permitting dispensations for specific reasons. Adultery, for instance, offended the "carnal side" of marriage. But to grant divorce only for adultery was to elevate the physical bond over the whole relationship. The legal system's pretense that grounds subsumed "causes" was fake, Royden insisted, and led to the "legal fictions" of perjury and collusion.[49]

What happened to these "legal fictions" in court? The evidence shows that trial judges treated them as page-turning, case-disposing best-sellers. In three substantial articles in *Good Housekeeping*, Mabel Potter Daggett reported on her 1925 nationwide survey of divorce judges. Their confessions about their attitudes and rulings, together with other commentary by bench and bar in the popular press, reveal a law system completely at odds with both statute and case law.[50] What the judges said about divorce reflected the changing culture more than the unchanging law. According to Salem, Oregon, judge John McCourt, "Until a few years ago public sentiment deterred many a woman from divorce. Now a changed public sentiment, together with the economic emancipation of woman, accounts in large measure for the heavy increase in the ratio of divorce to marriage." The formal premises of the divorce law were of no consequence to Judge S. S. Sherman of Montrose, California, who maintained that "divorce is not an evil. It's the mending of a marriage mistake." Nor was Baraboo, Wisconsin, judge James H. Hill respectful of the traditional legal policy when he observed that "on the whole, there are not divorces enough."[51]

The judges tended to be older than most divorce litigants, but in this generational clash the senior culture yielded. To Judge Peter Shields of Sacramento, California, the "theoretical ideal" of marriage must give way before the concrete pressure of wives and husbands seeking personal fulfillment: "We of an earlier age may deplore divorce and regret that youth does not have the fortitude to bear the sorrows of a mistaken marriage for duty's sake. But today the world supports the married person who will not endure an existence in which happiness is impossible or sacrifice the realities of life to a theoretical ideal."[52] Trial judges acknowledged divorce as a "fire-escape from a domestic hell" and believed that "the moral atmosphere is better with divorce easy and rapid." They supported women divorcing husbands who refused to grant them equality in marriage, and they also viewed woman's emancipation in economic terms, remarking that "how much a woman will forgive today is almost in inverse ratio to how far is the factory." Judge John S. Dawson of Topeka, Kansas, took pride in his state's elevation of women to a position of gender equality: "The old theory of dominion of the husband over the wife is, in Kansas, as dead as Tut-ankh-amen. And I say Hurrah."[53]

While the judges worried about the effect of divorce upon children, they voiced a cheer even for some parents seeking to break up a family. Judge Grier M. Orr of St. Paul, Minnesota, declared that in a home in which parents clashed openly and often, it was their duty to divorce. Similarly, Judge Hill believed that "no divorce can scar the soul of a child more than that hell, a home devoid of all the bonds of affection that sanctify marriage."[54] Ready divorce converted marriage into trial marriage. Judge Chester F. Miller of Dayton, Washington, focused on the evils of "hurried courtship," which left young couples unprepared for conjugal rigors. When a "little hell on earth begins . . . divorce is the best solution." After the court-sanctioned marital breakup, "the boy and girl who've had their lesson can each select a second partner with greater care." Judge Ben B. Lindsey's once-controversial suggestion that a young couple experiment with marriage before settling down to the institution in a serious manner now appeared more routine than radical. Physician and statistician I. M. Rubinow observed that the popularity of Lindsey's "companionate marriage" proposal "cannot be explained on the ground that he has suggested a new way out. It is only evidence that society will always vociferously approve something it is already practicing."[55]

As the trial judges saw it, the problem was not divorce but marriage. The condition of matrimony had changed; divorce merely followed and obeyed the altered cultural norms. As Daggett summarized their sentiments, "Divorce is going to be worse until marriage is better." The consensus view was expressed by Judge W. A. Reynolds of Chehalis, Washington. Laying to one side the teachings of appellate courts and the pronouncements of the legislatures, he observed that divorce in the 1920s was "an established, accepted exit from an unpleasant or irksome though not necessarily intolerable situation."[56]

The cognitive dissonance between the court's duty to uphold the formal law and its intention nevertheless to accede to the demands of the consumers of justice was never far from the judicial consciousness, as a Muncie, Indiana, judge disclosed to the Lynds: "A judge never knows the inside reasons in divorce cases. A divorce case comes up, and it's just another court case to be disposed of. I never look over the records. The lawyers get all those details. You see, if the judge knew these details, he might not grant the divorce."[57] Accordingly, divorce judges treated cruelty as a blanket legal allegation covering up the truth of simple incompatibility or mutual consent. What other conclusion could there be, after consideration of the types of divorces granted on the ground of cruelty? Stephen Ewing collected several examples of such awards in his 1928 report in *Harper's*:

to a husband because the sound of his wife's voice injured his delicate health;

to another who claimed his spouse was "disagreeable in words";

to a wife on the ground that her mate had been "intolerably cool" to her;

to another whose husband had told her to go to hell once too often; and

to a husband whose wife made him get up five or six times a night to look after her cat.[58]

Helen and Robert Lynd reported in 1929 that "loss of affection [during] marriage was not legally recognized as sufficient reason for dissolving a marriage until recent years." Since no changes in the formal law system occurred in the 1920s, the Lynds' account of the changing law must have reflected a mutual acknowledgment between the court and the spouses that divorce would be granted upon request. Such an interpretation is reinforced by two examples the Lynds provided. In 1924 a divorce was granted to a Muncie couple who reported to the court that they "have no affection for each other and do not want to live together." Another divorce was awarded a husband who pleaded that his wife "says she does not love me and does not want to live with me."[59] Further support for the proposition that cruelty became the cover story for divorces on grounds of incompatibility or mutual consent may be found in the overall divorce data the Lynds provided. The divorce explosion in Muncie may be seen by contrasting its 87 percent increase in population between 1890 and 1920 with the 622 percent increase in divorces, comparing the numbers for the years 1889–92 and 1921–24. During that same generation the percentage of Muncie divorces on the ground of desertion dropped from 29.6 to 14.9. Adultery had provided the divorce ground 23.7 percent of the time in the earlier period, but it decided only 14.5 percent of 1920s divorces. Cruelty, however, increased its percentage from 30.3 to 51.7 of all divorce cases.[60]

That Muncie divorces for cruelty rose from fewer than one-third to more than one-half did not, of course, signify an epidemic of connubial beastliness in Indiana, as the Lynds recognized. They noted that cruelty "may cover almost any variety of marital maladjustment, and the increase in divorces on this charge probably indicates chiefly a growing flexibility which allows divorces on other than specific charges such as 'adultery' and 'abandonment.'"[61] Clearly, though, the pose of cruelty described a dissembling tactic far more than a malicious heart. Roscoe Pound twitted the irrelevancy of statute to conduct when he asked his readers to "consider what any American community would think of a man convicted of extreme physical cruelty to his wife if those words were taken seriously."[62] The contrast between the old and new dispensations on marital dissolution was aptly etched by an article in *Good Housekeeping*, which noted that nineteenth-century marriages were "generally indissoluble, not because divorce laws were more severe than today—the laws have scarcely changed—but because public opinion exercised silent but more implacable pressure."[63] In the interwar period the inexorable force of public opinion remained a constant. But the direction had shifted.

Alimony's Puzzle

One of the thorniest problems confronting a historian of divorce in America is to explain why alimony, along with child custody, child support, and property division, received so little attention in the literature of the 1920s and 1930s, compared with the focus on divorce itself. The principal concerns surrounding family breakup in the last quarter of the twentieth century have revolved around these issues, ones lawyers peculiarly call ancillary matters. It is puzzling to look back from the perspective of the end of the century and discover that sorting out the right to divorce—and seeking to slow the rush toward divorce—occupied such an overwhelming amount of time and effort for our predecessors that they left a meager record of concern for spousal and child maintenance.

Sociologist Lynne Carol Halem argued that the financial and dependency aspects of divorce were separated out by reformers who were trying to replace the fault standard for divorce with one that would legally dissolve a marriage when the partners became incompatible. In order to satisfy a skeptical public that innocent wives and children would not be abandoned, these early proponents of no-fault divorce limited their reform to the action for divorce itself, agreeing to leave custody and property matters under the traditional fault standards. Halem suggested that this "distinction between the legal dissolution of a marriage and the resolution of its by-products . . . has most influenced the course of divorce reform. . . . Perhaps it explains why divorce laws have been the primary focus of reform attempts since the post–World War I epoch while the emotionally charged issues pertaining to children and economics (e.g., alimony, property division) have received only titular consideration."[64] But Halem's suggestion is problematic. There is little evidence that the incompatibility advocates succeeded in attracting much attention for their divorce alternative and its concomitant emphasis on separating out the main from the ancillary jurisdiction.[65] Moreover, even under customary standards of fault, neither the popular nor the formal legal systems of divorce paid much heed to considerations of spousal and child support.

The most striking aspect of alimony was its scarcity. At the turn of the century (1887–1906), 13.4 percent of divorces included requests for alimony, which were granted in 9.3 percent of the cases. In 1916, 20.3 percent of wives demanded alimony, and 15.4 percent received it. Totals for 1922 indicated awards of alimony in 14.7 percent of the cases.[66] Statistician I. M. Rubinow argued that the 80 percent and more of wives who declined to request the courts to order alimony reflected "not only the amicable nature of the divorce but also the moderate financial circumstance of the divorces."[67] But by the same token, in view of the undefended nature of the overwhelming number of divorces, the few that went to trial in a bona fide adversary proceeding must often have litigated alimony.[68] Between 1922 and 1950 the proportion of uncontested divorce cases ranged between 84.3 and 87.9 percent.[69]

The same cultural opening that perceived women's economic progress as generating virtual equality with men closed tightly against most women who received alimony. Spousal support was no longer culturally acceptable for women who were capable of work and who did not have to care for young children. Some authors recklessly presented divorce as an opportunity for women to improve their economic outlook, noting that a divorcée "can earn her bread in any civilized country in the world—and not infrequently a better grade of bread than that provided for her by her former partner."[70] Frances Parkinson Keyes made it perfectly clear how she viewed women who violated this emerging norm of autonomy in her comments to a woman considering divorce: "I will not insult you by assuming that you would be so mercenary and undignified as to accept alimony from a man with whom you are not willing to live, since you are not an invalid, and since your children are no longer so small as to be helpless." But after telling her correspondent that alimony was unthinkable, Keyes informed her that divorce would lower her standard of living dramatically.[71]

Despite the paucity of alimony payments, women who insisted on receiving alimony were often castigated. In 1935 a *Time* report on "Maniacal Wives" discussed the work of Jack Anthony, executive secretary of New York's Alimony Reform League. Anthony, who apparently had spent a term in an "alimony jail," had conducted a three-year investigation into "vindictive" wives who insisted on keeping their husbands imprisoned for failure to pay alimony. Anthony claimed that 69 percent of the ex-wives returning his questionnaire were "maniacs suffering from psychoses bordering on sadism." H. L. Mencken added to the demonizing of women recipients with his gibe that alimony was the "ransom that the happy pay to the devil."[72]

The issue of alimony did not divide purely along gender lines. Anticipating the volley of complaints served up in the 1960s, *Harper's* in 1938 described the plight of women tethered "by the bonds of alimony to other women, whom they frequently despise." The anonymous author of "Wives-in-Law" worked outside the home, and her salary matched the alimony her husband paid to his former spouse. The first wife had been employed before her marriage but now lived on her alimony proceeds, "upon the theory that a few years of marriage entitle a woman to support for life." Calling alimony a "curse" both to the receiving spouse and to the paying husband and his new wife, the author claimed that "it is a rare woman who can achieve emotional emancipation from the man who is still supporting her. Legally she is divorced, but financially and psychologically she is not."[73] Alimony was unaffordable bigamy, rarely available because most Americans realized that "very few men earn enough to support two wives."[74] Even though alimony was "not only rarely awarded but much more rarely collected,"[75] the popular culture continued to perceive alimony as "blackmail"[76] and to insist that divorce proved the wallet's downfall and the pocketbook's windfall. Even though it was a professional journal, *Law and Contemporary Problems* correctly assessed the cultural verdict on this issue: "Alimony perpetuates, in most instances, a relationship passionately undesired and in a way that continues and even increases former antagonisms."[77]

The Uncertain Fate of Divorce's Children

Theodore Dreiser identified the central question for the children of divorce: were they better off in successive marriages or in unions from which love had fled? He suggested that children could cope with the vagaries of divorce better than with their parents' constant fighting. Many agreed, including economist Charlotte Perkins Gilman, psychologist James P. Lichtenberger, and essayist Katherine Fullerton Gerould. So did Judge L. T. Price of Markleville, California, who reversed the argument that divorce breeds delinquency: "The moral atmosphere is better with divorce easy and rapid. If people are compelled to live together with hate in their hearts, the children brought into the world under these conditions will be below par. And in time the state will feel the effects."[78]

But others were convinced that children were victimized by divorce, which rendered them "worse than orphans." William Johnston was so concerned about parents' neglect of their offspring during the heat of divorce that he argued in *Good Housekeeping* for children to receive legal representation in cases where their parents sought a divorce. Sociologist Ernest Mowrer believed that divorce so conditioned children that it increased the likelihood of marital dissolution in the following generation.[79] Many authors believed divorce to be an easy case when the marriage was childless or when the children were grown. But in contested divorce suits, the battleground became child custody, property division, or both. Even when children were not hurled directly into the judicial cauldron, the tug of their care and affection undermined the most amiably intended dissolutions. In the homes of divorce, a child became an "emotional football," carelessly tossed between the parties as each accused the other of destroying the family. The custodial decree could settle parents' legal rights but never children's emotional ties. While the "social ostracism" of marital breakup faded, the dilemma of the children was never resolved.[80]

A divorce with children never really ended. In a widely read article entitled "I Have Four Parents," an eighteen-year-old girl named Joan complained that her parents' "civilized, friendly divorce" had not ended their rivalry. The court's decree merely had altered the field of engagement to one for their daughter's love. Both parents had remarried and campaigned to convince Joan that their new familial arrangements were "ideally happy." From the daughter's perspective, however, Joan's parents made her "bear the brunt of their resentments towards each other," even seven years after their divorce.[81] For every Joan, however, there was a Gretchen. In "I'll Take My Parents Separately," this daughter spoke of the dissolution of her parents' marriage with the air of an optimist: "We were a happy family and that is why we have made good with our divorce." Although Gretchen emphasized the positive results of her parents' divorce, the issue of children's fate in divorce remained clouded.[82]

Far from behaving as a much-maligned ancien régime of oppressive divorce restrictions, the fault system operated as a moral charade. Its trappings served as the divorce emperor's transparent clothes, fooling no one but continuing in use for want of a cultural alternative. With the significant exceptions of spousal support and the uncertainties about the children of divorce, the fault system well served the aims of both dissolution-minded couples and consumer-friendly trial judges. Neither group complained of the mutually beneficial arrangement. Judge Paul W. Alexander understood the paradox: "The trouble with guilt as a criterion is . . . [that it] virtually assures mutual consent as a ground for divorce."[83] The pliant cruelty standard rarely closed the gates on any consensual divorce, and speedy divorce procedures facilitated docket control, increasingly a concern of urban judges.

Because their modus vivendi worked so well, neither trial courts nor divorce seekers were likely candidates to push systemic reform. The call for significant changes to the American way of divorcing came, instead, from the legislatures. The new grounds of incompatibility and living apart were the formal system's attempts to reverse the burgeoning divorce rate. The next chapter describes these alterations by focusing on the route of incompatibility in New Mexico and living apart in North Carolina, two jurisdictions where the reforms had full play. The ultimate failure of these legal gambits illustrates the yawning gap between the formal and popular divorce arenas.

THREE

EARLY NONFAULT EXPERIMENTS

Eight years is a long time in a world where life is short.

William Seagle, "The Right to Consolation"

In the mid-nineteenth century several states had omnibus clauses in their divorce statutes that were broad enough to encompass divorce on the nonfault ground that the parties were incompatible.[1] While few of these omnibus clauses emerged into the twentieth century, the state of Washington's law survived until the close of the Progressive Era. It permitted a divorce for any reason "deemed by the court sufficient," with the proviso that the court "shall be satisfied that the parties can no longer live together."[2] Divorce conservatives criticized such omnibus clauses strongly. In Alvah L. Stinson's words, these laws could "reduce the marriage relation to a mere state of concubinage, at the mercy of the parties and the courts."[3] Although these umbrella clauses disappeared from the legislative arena, they were later resurrected in straitjacketed form as the incompatibility statutes.

Some states realized that the divorce trade brought needed revenue, and that they did not need omnibus measures to attract a divorce clientele. While Nevada served as the primary destination for migratory divorce seekers, South Dakota, Arkansas, Idaho, and several other states competed for the dissolution business. These states did not alter the grounds of divorce but merely shortened the period of residency required for filing a divorce action. In these states, as throughout the nation, it was understood that the actual obtaining of a decree was a formality. But particularly for wealthy would-be divorcees desirous of privacy or a vacation, a trip to Nevada could provide both a diversion and a divorce, particularly after the development of its casinos. Despite the media attention lavished on them, however, migratory divorces never became more than a negligible fraction of all American divorces. Divorce statistician Paul Jacobson estimated that migratory divorces accounted for no more that 3 to 5 percent of the annual divorce tally. Most unhappy spouses lacked either the money or the incentive to leave their home jurisdiction. Their local divorce courts generally were as welcoming as any commerce-driven court.[4]

For want of current domestic models, some Americans in the 1920s looked to Scandinavia for guidance in crafting new divorce laws. The Nordic model offered absolute divorce to a couple when "deep and constant discord" had propelled them to a separation, based on the 1910 recommendation of a joint Norwegian-Danish-Swedish commission. The *Nation* praised these laws for assuring the legal and economic equality of the sexes in divorce proceedings. Arthur Garfield Hays quoted the Danish prime minister's defense of his nation's law on the grounds that it was "morally indefensible" to force two people to stay together when the "real bonds" between them had disintegrated. Nancy M. Schoonmaker in *Current History*, Ruth Hale and Edwin Bjorkman in *Forum*, and Dorothy Dunbar Bromley in *Harper's* advocated modeling domestic divorce statutes on the Scandinavian models.[5]

Stephen Ewing described the Scandinavian divorce process. Couples seeking a dissolution were required to discuss their differences with either their minister or a designated government official. If they did not reconcile, they could receive a legal separation upon agreeing on the custody of any children, as well as on financial arrangements. After a separation of between twelve and eighteen months, the couple could petition for an automatic decree of divorce. If only one party wished to end the marriage, then the length of the requisite separation period extended to between two and two-and-a-half years. Ewing concluded his summary for American readers by observing that in Scandinavia "it never becomes necessary for husbands and wives to attack each other in order to gain their freedom."[6] Half of the American jurisdictions eventually developed a homespun version of Scandinavian living-apart laws, requiring far longer periods of separation. While the stated purpose was to prevent brutalization in the divorce courts, the underlying goal of the American statutes was to induce fractious couples to remain together for five or ten more years.

Incompatibility on Appeal

Between 1920 and 1969 seven American jurisdictions adopted statutes permitting divorce on the ground of incompatibility. The Scandinavian influence can be directly seen in the first such law, passed by the Virgin Islands. For the residents of the former Danish territory, the incompatibility statute merely carried over the substance of prior law, which since 1770 had granted divorces for "irremediable disharmony in common life."[7] In 1933 New Mexico added incompatibility as a divorce ground, followed two years later by the territory of Alaska. Oklahoma joined the list in 1953, followed in the next decade by Nevada, Delaware, and Kansas.[8] Despite their open-faced language, incompatibility statutes failed to trigger a wholesale transformation of pseudo-cruelty jurisprudence. In the absence of evidence of legislative intention beyond the bare addition of this new ground to the divorce statutes, appellate courts often refused to countenance divorces merely upon the couple's demonstration that they could not live together. Rather, they often insisted that a complainant continue to prove blamelessness in the breakdown of the marriage. This grafting of a threshold behavioral requirement demonstrated how difficult it was for the formal legal system to uproot itself from the regime of fault.

Exploring the tortuous path of incompatibility on appeal affords us a window into the ideological dimension of this branch of the formal legal system. Referring to this system, Friedman and Percival have noted that the "study of law in this country is mainly the study of appellate case law." Higher-court opinions, in the words of legal historian Michael Grossberg, "offer the most thorough commentary on the law." Historian Robert L. Griswold agreed, although he conceded that the decisions of appellate tribunals "suggest an elegance and consistency to legal reasoning not evident at the local level."[9] These appellate opinions reveal a legal system remarkably divided about the legitimacy of the popular culture of divorce. Even when the legislative mandate provided an opportunity for bridging the gap between the two cultures, many appellate judges declined the invitation. The nineteenth-century view of divorce, insisting on a bright line between the meritorious and the meretricious, lived on in the ideology of many appellate courts long after the popular culture ceased to pay it even lip service.

New Mexico: Clean Hands versus Trial Marriage

New Mexico adopted the first modern fault-free divorce ground with surprisingly scant notice. Throughout its history New Mexico's divorce jurisprudence had been thoroughly grounded in fault. In 1872 its territorial courts were given authority to grant divorces in cases of adultery, cruelty, and abandonment. In 1887 the legislature provided for divorce in the event of habitual drunkenness or nonsupport by a husband of his wife. Three more grounds made their appearance in 1901: impotency, the wife's undisclosed pregnancy by another man at the time of the marriage, and imprisonment for a felony during the marriage.[10] A generation later, in 1933, the state legislature made a dramatic change in the formal law by adding one word—incompatibility—to the catalog of divorce grounds. There is no legislative history on the passage of the bill; nor do the official governor's messages of the time contain any mention of a proposed change in the divorce law. To trace the winding and rewinding of formal divorcing in New Mexico, we must turn to four decades of appellate decisions.[11]

The first attention paid to the new incompatibility statute by the New Mexico Supreme Court came in an unusual 1935 case, which never formally presented the issue at all. Twenty-four-year-old Margarita Medina de Chavez's marriage to Francisco Chavez, whose age was given as between seventy and eighty, broke up in bitterness and mutual accusation. Margarita sued her husband for desertion and nonsupport. Francisco, whom the trial court described as "decrepit and in his dotage," claimed that Margarita had deserted him and was living with Reuben Garcia. The trial judge answered the question of who deserted whom in favor of Margarita. Further, the divorce judge believed that, since Margarita's adultery with Reuben had occurred after her separation from Francisco, her fault did not count as a valid recriminatory defense for her aged husband. Thus, Margarita was awarded both divorce and alimony.[12]

On appeal, the supreme court held that adulterers can never have clear consciences. Postponing the satisfaction of immoral concupiscence until after separation, noted Justice A. L. Zinn in the majority opinion, does not diminish the absolute sway of the recrimination doctrine. Margarita should not gain a divorce because "whoever appeals to a court for relief must do so with clean hands." The absence of statutory sanction or prior decisional law as to recrimination did not prevent the court from treating it as a concrete pillar of the common law. The justices relied on a variety of cases from around the country, including an 1882 pronouncement of eminent Michigan justice Thomas Benton Cooley: "A proper administration of justice does not require that courts shall occupy their time and the time of people who are so unfortunate as to be witnesses to the misdoings of others in giving equitable relief to parties who have no equities. . . . Divorce laws are made to give relief to the innocent, not to the guilty."[13] Accordingly, the majority reversed the lower court and remanded for a new divorce trial.

The incompatibility statute was examined in two concurring opinions. Justice Andrew H. Hudspeth believed that alimony was at the heart of the Chavezes' dispute, and he strongly disagreed with the majority's revival of the recrimination doctrine. Hudspeth noted the "paradoxical and puzzling" nature of recrimination, as well as the state divorce statute's failure to mention it. He suggested that unless limits were set on recrimination, incompatibility would be a defense in an action brought on incompatibility. He went on to describe the new alternative to fault: "When the legislature wrote this additional ground of divorce into our law, they intended to afford a remedy for a spouse incompatible with his or her mate, and that too without regard to the wishes of the other spouse, or the fact that the other spouse might have a ground for divorce. It is a recognition of the fact that in many cases both spouses are to blame."[14] Similarly opposed to recrimination, Justice Howard L. Bickley argued that divorces should be granted even when irreconcilable spouses are both at fault. Refusing to set such wives and husbands free only led to the commission of more offenses against public morality. Bickley believed that the new incompatibility ground was a legislative "declaration of policy that the district courts have full power and authority to decree divorces from the bonds of matrimony when the court is satisfied that the parties can no longer live together."[15]

Formal affirmation of the ground of incompatibility waited until 1941. Robert C. Poteet and his wife Leera had been separated for twenty years before Robert filed a divorce action based on the new ground. Leera disagreed with his claim of incompatibility, however, characterizing the separation as owing to Robert's desertion. She saw no reason why they could not "live harmoniously as husband and wife" if only Robert would "refrain from associating with other women and be contented with his home life."[16] Robert's plurality of affections was not as central to the litigation, however, as was Leera's ill health. After enduring several operations, she needed Robert's financial support. Either she believed she could expect a steadier income if she remained Robert's wife and could enforce his obligation to provide her necessities, or the estranged spouses had come to an impasse on the amount of alimony to be provided. The trial court found that the spouses were incompatible, thus granting Robert a divorce. In the court's view, "if one party is unwilling to continue the relation there isn't any power on earth—court, or anywhere else—to make it a go."[17]

On appeal, the ailing wife insisted that a divorce should only be awarded to the "injured" party. As Justice Bickley phrased her position for an unanimous supreme court, she "contends for a very strict sociological view, and argues that the attainment of divorce should be very difficult."[18] As the author of the liberal concurrence in *Chavez*, Justice Bickley could not reasonably be expected to espouse the wife's "very strict sociological view," whatever that meant. On the contrary, Bickley declared that the incompatibility statute was designed to remedy the flaws in the 1901 law governing legal separation. Spouses who separated but could not divorce lived in a hazardous legal limbo where the temptation to establish extramarital sexual liaisons loomed too closely for the average and otherwise law-abiding New Mexican. To prevent the public corruption of "husbandless wives and wifeless husbands," the incompatibility statute allowed permanent separations to mature into spousal freedom.[19] In affirming the trial court's grant of a divorce, Justice Bickley pointedly distinguished incompatibility from the unacceptable option of divorce by mutual consent. Curiously, he rejected mutual consent while simultaneously noting that it was an approved method for ending inhospitable marriages among numerous peoples both past and present. According to Justice Bickley mutual consent divorce had received approbation from such thinkers as More, Milton, Selden, Lecky, Montesquieu, Bentham, and Mill, all of whom he listed in his opinion.[20]

The New Mexico jurisprudential pendulum achieved its highest liberal peak in the 1946 decision that reversed *Chavez* and outlawed recrimination as a divorce defense. Several years after his twenty-year marriage had effectively ended with a separation, Nick Pavletich sued his wife for an incompatibility divorce. Ellis Cacic Pavletich countered that Nick's adultery with Lucille Worrell should block his obtaining legal freedom. The true nature of the quarrel may be found in the 336-page transcript of the divorce hearing, much of it relating to disputes over property. District Judge Albert R. Kool granted Nick a divorce, rejecting the notion of recriminatory defenses because they fostered only "an intolerable moral situation as long as those parties live and are physically capable of the sexual act. . . . I think [that recrimination] is a cruel and inhuman law."[21]

Speaking through the author of the other *Chavez* concurrence, Justice Hudspeth, a supreme court majority agreed with Judge Kool that a spouse's adultery does not trump his or her otherwise valid divorce action. In a wide-ranging discussion Hudspeth reviewed the "slowly changing" views of recrimination around the world. He cited the idea of "divorce without fault" prevailing in Sweden, the Soviet Union, and Germany. He also discussed various legal authorities and included extended quotations from J. G. Beamer's influential essay "The Doctrine of Recrimination in Divorce Proceedings," which concluded that this peculiar divorce defense violated human experience and bred contempt for the law and the courts that administer it.[22] But Chief Justice Daniel K. Sadler launched a furious dissenting volley at his *Pavletich* colleagues. Incensed that incompatibility "brings us to the very border, if not into the actual domain, of trial marriage," Sadler argued for a retention of recrimination as a way to set limits to incompatibility. He feared that the new ground, "if freely employed," would effectively eliminate all others as the basis for divorce. Sadler stood fast against the sanctioning the grant of a divorce to a party who had triggered conjugal incompatibility by committing "a capital sin of the marriage relation."[23]

Recrimination's death had indeed been announced prematurely. Four years after *Pavletich* the departure of Justices Hudspeth and Bickley from the supreme court bench allowed Justice Sadler to eviscerate its earlier holding and resurrect recrimination in New Mexico. Myrtle I. Clark had pleaded her husband's adultery in response to his assertion of marital incompatibility. She contended that Robert's "insistence on his pretended right to engage in extra-marital affairs" was the sole cause of their incompatibility. The trial court refused to hear evidence about Robert's infidelity, since *Pavletich* had rendered such testimony irrelevant.[24] By a three-to-two vote, the supreme court remanded the case with instructions that the district court hear and evaluate the recriminatory evidence. The new *Clark* majority held that a divorce should be denied if it "shocks the conscience" of a trial court to reward a blameworthy plaintiff with undeserving freedom.[25]

Despite Justice Sadler's efforts, however, he could not destroy incompatibility. By the 1950s it became clear that the *Clark* limitation was ineffectual in slowing down divorce.[26] Trial courts were no more interested in the enforcement of recrimination than was the general public. As legal scholar Robert Earl Lee suggested, recrimination is "particularly pernicious because it arouses in the layman who learns of it a profound contempt for the law. And of course in this instance the layman is right."[27] By 1952, as Justice Henry G. Coors noted, incompatibility had become New Mexico's most commonly used divorce ground. After nearly two tortuous decades of development, incompatibility finally had shed the skin of fault. The *Clark* shock-the-conscience test was not overruled, but no court ever applied it. In the words of Justice Coors, all a plaintiff needed to demonstrate was "that a state of incompatibility exists regardless of whether it is anyone's or no one's fault."[28] No other relevant cases were decided in New Mexico until 1973. In two cases that year, the supreme court examined the history of incompatibility and recrimination "in the light of present social conditions." The court once again abolished the defense of recrimination in proceedings under the incompatibility statute, admitting the obvious in its understated confession that "this Court has not been entirely consistent in its views as to the validity and effectiveness of recrimination as a defense to divorce on the ground of incompatibility." [29]

The New Mexico experience with formal incompatibility confirms Professor Wadlington's observation that in most jurisdictions "the ingrained concept of fault is difficult for the judiciary to overcome." Nor was Wadlington alone; years before New Mexico's highest tribunal finally acknowledged its bumpy road to modern divorce, the United States Court of Appeals for the Third Circuit had remarked that New Mexico courts "have had difficulty in dealing with [incompatibility], even in the formulation of its definition and especially in deciding what recognition should be accorded to the defense of recrimination." [30] Nor was New Mexico alone in grappling uncertainly with formal no-fault. In Oklahoma evidence suggests that the practicing divorce bar, weary of the hypocrisy of manipulating the cruelty ground, convinced the legislature to pass an incompatibility statute in 1953. Three years later the Oklahoma Supreme Court rendered its interpretation of incompatibility. In a marvel of logical exegesis, the court concluded (in Professor Wadlington's delicious paraphrase): "that spouse X might be compatible with spouse Y even though Y was incompatible with X, and . . . under these circumstances no divorce should be granted." [31]

Incompatibility was not the only option that the formal legal system pursued to manage the divorce explosion; indeed, its adoption by the late 1960s by only six states and the Virgin Islands rendered this experiment rather limited. Another formal reform of the legal system, far more extensively applied, was the living-apart statute. The next section explores the range of this nonfault alternative and concludes that living apart laws were terrific failures because they ignored the demands of the popular culture.

The World of the Living-Apart Statutes

Many states took a different, time-oriented, approach to nonfault alternatives. In these jurisdictions "living apart" statutes recognized marital breakdown as a ground for divorce so long as it was evidenced by the parties' separation for a specified time. On first blush, since proof of the requisite separation was all that these statutes appeared to require, they appeared to provide a demonstrably simpler threshold than the incompatibility laws. In fact, however, some appellate courts again imposed a demand for an innocent plaintiff onto these statutes. More significantly, although legislatures continued to reduce the waiting periods that triggered applicability of these nonfault laws, divorce-minded wives and husbands still avoided them. Litigants vastly preferred to role-play their parts on the stage of a courtroom bound by the thoroughly corrupted but user-friendly rules of fault.

The tactical maneuvering between state legislatures and divorce clients resembled a B movie chase scene. The legislature would pass a living-apart statute with a lengthy waiting period. When very few divorcers availed themselves of the statute, the legislature would shorten the time period. By then, the divorce-minded were even more determined not to be stalled in their quest for ready divorce. The legislature would try again but never (until quite recent times) find its quarry. Twenty-three American jurisdictions enacted living-apart statutes before the passage of California's no-fault law in 1969. The first such statute was passed in Wisconsin in 1850, and two other nineteenth-century state legislatures enacted similar legislation. The bulk of the living-apart statutes date from the end of the Progressive Era and after.

These laws constituted a major theoretical inroad into the dominant fault milieu of family law. They allowed the parties to decide for themselves when a marital relationship had terminated, requiring only proof that a specified time period had elapsed in order to assure themselves and society that the rift was irremediable. Because the court proceedings were limited to technical issues of jurisdiction, venue, and proof of separation, the parties were spared the intrusion into their privacy that fault divorce proceedings mandated. Table 4 lists the period of separation required before the divorce filing in the living-apart statutes enacted in twenty-three jurisdictions before the passage of the California no-fault act.

Ostensibly, the theory behind living-apart statutes was that dead marriages deserved a formal burial. In 1929 the Supreme Court of Rhode Island articulated the rationale for these laws: "Any injury to the state from the dissolution of the family cannot now be cured by insisting on the continuance of a semblance of a marriage when the substance has long since disappeared."[32] But the living apart statutes did not authorize divorce upon marital breakdown. The catch to the laws is reflected in the "long since disappeared" phrase in the Rhode Island decision. A statute which required a multiyear separation before filing guaranteed that the departed ghost of the marriage would never return. It also assured that the statute would seldom be utilized.

Mid-twentieth-century legislators were in a bind. They knew, as both trial judges and the popular press repeatedly broadcast, that mutual consent was the operating principle in American divorce court. They were also troubled by the divorce rate, rising steadily in the teeth of restrictive and unchanging laws. Many state legislators endorsed what sociologist Ray E. Baber termed a "half solution" to the problem. They crafted statutes that on the surface would appeal to divorce-bound wives and husbands, particularly those more squeamish and less willing to engage in testimonial exaggeration or outright perjury. These laws would not require one spouse to malign the character of the other. They would appeal to marriage partners who had mutually agreed to terminate the association and sought to do so fairly and without needless blame.[33]

A nonfault basis, the removal of the need for vicious accusation, and the appeal of an honest divorce procedure: these were the carrots in the living apart statutes, which Baber also called "slow motion 'divorce by mutual consent.'"[34] There was only one stick, but it was a large one. In order to obtain these benefits, a couple would have to separate and then wait for five or eight or ten years. Despite their popularity with the legislatures, nonfault alternatives before 1970 never succeeded in capturing a significant market share of divorces. Appellate judges were at times skeptical about disentangling living apart statutes from the umbrella of fault and sporadically ruled that the party seeking the divorce must not be culpable in causing the separation.

But by far the major reason for the failure of the nonfault alternatives was that the divorcing public largely ignored them. The unappetizing waiting periods discouraged all but a very few. As William Seagle exclaimed in the *American Mercury*, Washington's law permitting no-fault divorce after eight years of separation was a wonderful idea, "but eight years is a long time in a world where life is short."[35] During the entire period under

Table 4. Living-apart divorce statutes enacted before 1971

Alabama
L. 1915, p. 370	5 years*
L. 1933, p. 142	2 years

Arizona
L. 1931, ch. 12, p. 20	5 years

Arkansas
L. 1937, no. 167, p. 630	3 years

Delaware
L. 1957, ch. 27, p. 40	3 years
L. 1968, ch. 296, p. 1064	18 months

District of Columbia
49 U.S. Statutes at Large 539 (1935)	5 years
79 U.S. Statutes at Large 889 (1965)	1 year

Hawaii
L. 1967, ch. 76, p. 75	3 years
L. 1970, ch. 116, p. 224	2 years

Idaho
L. 1945, ch. 125, p. 191	5 years

Kentucky
L. 1850, ch. 498, pp. 54–55	5 years

Louisiana
L. 1916, no. 269, p. 557	7 years
L. 1932, no. 31, pp. 222–23	4 years
L. 1938, no. 430, p. 1091	2 years

Maryland
L. 1937, ch. 396, p. 791	5 years
L. 1947, ch. 240, pp. 363–63	3 years
L. 1961, ch. 104, p. 95	18 months

Nevada
L. 1931, ch. 111, p. 180	5 years
L. 1939, ch. 23, pp. 16–17	3 years
L. 1967, ch. 278, pp. 805–6	1 year

New York
L. 1966, ch. 254, p. 266	2 years

North Carolina
L. 1907, ch. 89	10 years
L. 1921, ch. 63, p. 312	5 years
L. 1933, ch. 7; ch. 163, p. 143	2 years
L. 1965, ch. 6363, pp. 703–4	1 year

Table 4. (*continued*)

Puerto Rico		
	L. 1933, no. 46	7 years
	L. 1942, no. 62, p. 582	3 years
Rhode Island		
	L. 1893, ch. 1187, p. 237	10 years
South Carolina		
	L. 1969, no. 170, pp. 172–73	3 years**
Texas		
	Rev. Civ. St. 1925, art. 4629, p. 1268	10 years
	L. 1953, ch. 91, p. 366	7 years
	L. 1967, ch. 288, p. 699	3 years
Vermont		
	L. 1941, no. 43, pp. 53–54	3 years
Virginia		
	L. 1960, ch. 108, pp. 121–22	3 years
	L. 1964, ch. 363, p. 572	2 years
Washington		
	L. 1917, ch. 106, p. 353	8 years
	L. 1921, ch. 109, p. 332	5 years
	L. 1965, Ex. Sess., ch. 15, p. 1700	2 years
West Virginia		
	L. 1969, ch. 49, p. 329	2 years
Wisconsin		
	L. 1866, ch. 37, p. 40	5 years
Wyoming		
	L. 1939, ch. 106, p. 168	2 years

*Alabama's unique living-apart statute allowed relief to a wife who had been separated from her husband for five years and had not received support from him during that time. In 1919 (L. 1919, p. 878), the period without support was reduced to two years, and it remained at two years when the legislature lowered the separation period to two years in 1933 (L. 1933, p. 142). Despite the element of nonsupport, the Alabama Supreme Court decided that the divorce provision did not require proof of marital fault but merely reflected the fait accompli of a broken marriage. Barrington v. Barrington, 206 Ala. 192, 89 So. 512 (1921). In 1948 the court reaffirmed the nonfault character of the law by upholding a divorce awarded to a woman who bore a child from an adulterous relationship. Gardner v. Gardner, 34 So.2d 157 (1948).

**In order to enact its living-apart statute in 1969, South Carolina needed first to amend the state constitution. L. 1969, no. 77, p. 74, noting amendment of 1895 Constitution, art. 17, sec. 3.

study, Rhode Island had a provision in effect which allowed the trial court, in its discretion, to award a divorce to parties separated for ten years.[36] The state supreme court's approval of this technical deviation from fault did not trigger a rush upon the courthouse, nor could it have been so intended.[37] In fact, even states that repeatedly sliced their waiting period found little increase in takers. North Carolina's first living-apart statute, passed in 1907, required a ten-year separation. In 1921 the legislature halved that time period. Twelve years later the living-apart phase was reduced to two years. Finally, in 1965 only a one-year separation was required. Washington State's period of anticipation fell from eight years in 1917 to five years in 1921 to two years in 1965. In Maryland, the statutory procedure required a separation of five years in 1937, three years in 1947, and eighteen months in 1961. But no matter what the numerical prestidigitation, so long as the state's divorce code included cruelty as a divorce ground, none of these nonfault statutes were widely used. Why not?

Statutes providing for living-apart divorce were not aimed at facilitating divorce. On the contrary, they were efforts to stall the divorce traffic. Legislatures provided this kinder, gentler alternative to fault divorce in the hope that division-minded couples would wait out the statutory separation period, rather than hurtling pell-mell into court on a fraudulent ticket of fault. When vastly increasing numbers chose to enlarge the scope of fraud and perjury in order to obtain quickie fault divorces, the legislatures lowered the bait of the living-apart statutes. But no manner of conservative reform sufficed to curb the rush. True, a handful of long-dead marriages were formally buried under these statutes. But it strains human reason to believe that many couples desiring a divorce would plan on waiting for the bell to toll the eighth, or fifth, or even the third year of separation.[38] Given the fact that 80 to 90 percent of all divorces were uncontested, few couples chose to wait. The cases that dot the state appellate reports illustrate no-consent divorce, where the stumbling block resulting in litigation generally was the lack of an accord on property and future financial issues. Reported divorce cases were always unrepresentative of the general patterns of American divorcing.

North Carolina's experiment in living-apart jurisprudence provides a case study of this nonfault alternative. Because North Carolina did not allow divorce on many of the usual grounds, such as cruelty, desertion,

Table 5. Absolute divorces in North Carolina, by ground, 1958–69

Year	Number	Living apart	Adultery
		Ground	
1958	5,261	5,039	198
1959	6,271	6,032	219
1960	5,990	5,788	184
1961	6,355	6,142	204
1962	6,788	6,540	213
1963	7,227	6,974	229
1964	7,107	6,889	209
1965	11,069*	10,896	161
1966	11,320	11,268	47
1967	11,909	11,864	42
1968	12,385	12,339	40
1969	12,795	12,761	31

Source: Robert Earl Lee, *North Carolina Family Law* 1 (4th ed.) (Charlottesville, Va., 1979): tables 1 and 1A, at 220–21.

*Effective July 1, 1965, the period of required separation was reduced from two years to one. N.C. Laws 1965, ch. 636.

drunkenness, or neglect to provide, its living-apart statutes took on increased importance for divorce-minded couples. Paul H. Jacobson's statistical monograph listed adultery as the divorce ground in only 7 percent of North Carolina divorces in 1948, while 91 percent were based on the separation statute.[39] North Carolina was the Reno of living apart. Of the 13,300 divorce decrees issued nationwide in 1948 on separation grounds, nearly 6,000 were obtained in North Carolina.[40] The statistics displayed in table 5 confirm the overwhelming popularity (if only by necessity) of the living-apart provisions in later years.

Living Apart in North Carolina

Irene and John Cook were married on March 22, 1900. By August of that year, their wedded bliss had ended. A lengthy separation began, to be punctuated in the following decade by two extensive lawsuits in different counties, each reaching ultimate resolution in North Carolina's supreme court. During the course of the litigation, Irene persuaded a Wake County jury to convict John for abandonment in her action for limited divorce, and John sued Irene for absolute divorce in Alamance County.[41]

John Cook premised his suit upon the 1907 statute providing for divorce upon a ten-year separation.[42] Irene contended that John's suit was barred because the Wake County verdict had found him guilty of a marital offense, which thus prevented him from assuming the status of the innocent plaintiff in his divorce action. Key to Irene's position was her argument that a living-apart action must be based on mutual consent.[43] But the formal legal system was still rigidly opposed to mutual consent. On the recrimination issue the supreme court narrowly ruled against her. Speaking for the three-to-two majority, Justice William A. Hoke found nothing in the statute "to indicate that the right conferred is dependent on the blame which may attach to one party or the other." John's abandonment of Irene five months after their wedding was simply irrelevant to the action for absolute divorce.[44]

Justice Hoke regarded the statute's public policy basis to be the "assumption that it is not well for persons in these circumstances to be absolutely deprived of all right to marry again." A ten-year separation was evidence enough that the spouses were beyond reconciliation.[45] In a concurring opinion pointedly directed at the two dissenters, Justice George H. Brown reiterated Justice Hoke's reasoning in sepulchral language, claiming it impossible to imagine legislative intent "that the married life of the parties should be opened up and the dead skeleton of an unhappy past be resurrected and displayed in all its nakedness. Cui bono? . . . Why dig up from their graves the buried memories of broken lives? It is better to let the dead past bury its dead and not disturb the remains. Such was evidently the wise and humane purpose of the Legislature."[46]

Dissenting Justice Platt D. Walker matched Justice Brown's fervor, if not his necrological metaphors. Walker maintained that the living-apart statute should be read in the context of the overall divorce law, which permitted the awarding of divorces only to "the party injured." The legislature thus intended that the living-apart statute "work no wrong or oppression to the faithful and blameless spouse." Irene had steadfastly kept

her marital vows, while John had "unlawfully, unjustly, and cruelly abandoned" her and had thus forsaken his entitlement to the prescribed divorce
procedure. In an opinion whose logic strained the limits of the imagination, Walker warned that the court's holding would serve as a "precedent
for any evil-minded husband to desert or abandon his wife for the very
purpose of benefitting by the statute after ten years of his wrongful
separation."[47]

By 1919, Justice Hoke's interpretation of the living-apart statute had
been interred, and recrimination was exhumed. The litigation between
Robert and Susan Sanderson was factually similar to the *Cook* imbroglio.
Could Robert be found guilty of cruelty toward Susan and nevertheless
obtain a divorce after ten years? The answer from *Cook* II would be yes,
but Justice William R. Allen, a *Cook* II dissenter, convinced his colleagues
that a recent legislative revision of the statutory code should reverse the
result. The reenactment of the divorce law by the legislature contained no
change at all. But Justice Allen asserted that in its recent readoption of
the divorce law framework with both a "party injured" preamble and the
living-apart statute, the legislature had signaled a desire to reverse *Cook* II
and limit the applicability of the living-apart law to blameless petitioners.[48] That this revisionist legerdemain was a subterfuge for overturning
Cook II was made clear in Allen's strongly worded conclusion, which
echoed Justice Walker's earlier dissent: "It would be a harsh and cruel rule
to . . . permit a husband to drive a loving and faithful wife from his home
and refuse to permit her to return for ten years, and then reward his conduct by granting him a divorce."[49]

The preeminent importance of financial obligation was apparent in the
next attempt to interpret the living apart statute. After fourteen years of
marriage, A. R. and Saphrony Ann Lee separated in 1910 when Saphrony
was committed to a state hospital for the insane. Chief Justice Walter
Clark defined the injured party as the spouse "wronged by the action of
the other" and declared that the separation contemplated by the living
apart law had to commence by mutual consent. His wife's insanity prevented A. R. from clearing either of these judge-made hurdles. The chief
justice concluded with the money issue: Saphrony "is still entitled to support from her husband."[50] Another case involved Fay and W. J. Sitterson,
married in 1913. In 1915 W. J. was convicted of murder and sentenced to

twenty years in prison. Although he was pardoned in 1925, Fay had not seen or heard from him for ten years at the time she filed her action for divorce on the ground of living apart. Her personal blamelessness was, however, insufficient to overcome the new jurisprudential obstacles the supreme court had devised in the quest for theoretical empire-building. The court denied Fay her divorce because her marital separation had been involuntary, as she could not show that her husband had committed murder in order to effect the conjugal separation.[51]

Justice Walker's doubts that the North Carolina legislature could remove the requirement that a divorce plaintiff be the "injured party"[52] were put to the test in 1931. The legislature passed a new statute allowing for a divorce "on application of either party" after five years' separation, so long as no children had been born to the marriage and the plaintiff had resided in the state for the five years.[53] The supreme court hinted in 1933 that the new "either party" statute had removed the "injured party" requirement.[54] The issue was squarely presented the following year, when a trial judge, a disciple of Justice Walker, declared the "either party" statute unconstitutional "insofar as it gives the person who commits the wrong the right to take advantage of his own wrong." On appeal, the supreme court reversed the trial court, stoically observing that "the statute gives and the statute takes away."[55]

But the surprising serenity of the supreme court lasted precisely two years. In three cases decided in 1936, the court, now comprised entirely of devotees of Justice Walker, decided that the "either party" statute required a voluntary separation by mutual consent. A husband could not abandon his wife and then shield his immorality behind the facade of the "either party" language.[56] The apogee of recrimination was reached in 1938, when the supreme court closed the courthouse door to a husband who had the temerity to seek a divorce after he had been convicted and imprisoned for abandonment, nonsupport of his wife and two children, and contempt of court. The court rewarded his audacity with a jeremiad denouncing his "criminal and unlawful acts," which rendering shameful his seeking "to procure an advantage" through the divorce court.[57]

The court's high dudgeon extended to the legislature, whose neutral language had misled some into believing that the phrase "either party" meant what it said. After a rhetorical bow to the legislature's supremacy over the judiciary in matters of public policy, the court asserted its hegemony over interpretation: "It will not be assumed that any statute enacted by the Legislature was intended to override or depart from principles of public policy founded on good morals unless the language of the statute clearly and unequivocally indicates such an intent."[58] Moreover, whenever the legislature reenacted a law or used the same terms in a new statute, the court would presume that the legislature "in passing the later law knew what the judicial construction was which had been given to the words of the prior enactment."[59] Justice A. A. F. Seawell later summarized the North Carolina judiciary's view of the deferential relationship between these not-so-equal branches of government: "The history of divorce on the ground of separation discloses a number of statutes on the subject, interlaced with judicial interpretation and respectful legislative response."[60]

During World War II the supreme court flip-flopped on living-apart divorce in a brace of cases whose facts cast the "villain" in an extremely favorable light. Temporarily thrown off balance by their human sympathies, the justices changed their mind about the statute's reach, only to reverse themselves again a year later upon subsequent litigation in the same appeal.[61] In 1940 C. M. Byers told his wife Sara Sherman Byers that he would not live with her any longer because of her drug and alcohol abuse. C. M. left the family home, in the words of the supreme court, "in a condition to afford ample comfort and protection to [Sara] and the children." Although the couple did not enter into an agreement on spousal and child support, Sara received from her husband "unlimited credit . . . at grocery store, meat market, oil fuel dealer, dairy products dealer, druggist, doctors, dentists, laundry, dry cleaner, jeweler, florist, and all other dealers of the necessities and comforts of life in the City of Charlotte."[62] At C. M.'s suggestion, Sara went to two different hospitals for treatment as an alcoholic and drug addict. During the six months while she was hospitalized, C. M. lived in the home to take care of the children, moving out again upon Sara's return home. C. M. also paid his wife's hospital bill of nearly $1,400.

In deciding this case the supreme court faced a dilemma of its own making. Prior case law set out a requirement of mutual consent, which was not here met, despite C. M.'s exemplary conduct. But the court noted that in the most recent reenactment of the living-apart statute, the legislature had changed the phrase "separation of husband and wife" to "the husband and wife have lived separate and apart." Seizing on this minuscule alteration of the formulary, the court divined legislative intent to discard the judicial gloss on the word *separation* by the omission of that precise term in the new statute. Because the mutual consent requirement was part of the rhetorical baggage shipped with "separation," it could now be jettisoned in favor of the new terminology, which the court found "descriptive of a factual situation less amenable to interpretive changes."[63]

What about C. M., whose divorce had been denied by the trial court for want of mutual consent in the separation? The solicitous justices ordered him a new trial, remarking that while a husband may not obtain an advantage based on wrongful behavior, he clearly "is not compelled to live with his wife if he provides her adequate support."[64] But the new trial was a disaster for C. M. The jury found that he had failed to provide adequate support for Sara and the children, and that he had offered "such indignities to [her] person . . . as to render her condition intolerable." In round two in the supreme court, Sara became the victim and C. M. the villain. "One in flagrante delicto," thundered Chief Justice Walter P. Stacy, "is not permitted to recover in the courts." C. M. should have known better, the chief justice insisted: "One who plants a domestic thornbush or thistle need not expect to gather grapes or figs from it."[65]

The remaining North Carolina history may be quickly told. Although described by a commentator as "a rare combination of silliness, futility and brutality," the recrimination defense continued to receive the blessing of the supreme court for decades. In 1978 the legislature finally ended the charade by amending the divorce statutes specifically to abolish recrimination in living-apart divorce cases.[66] As with the New Mexico history, the reforms crafted by North Carolina legislators were subject to the erratic reading of state appellate courts unable or unwilling to shake loose the tar baby of fault. The formal legal system thus traveled uncertainly down the road from fault to nonfault. In the popular arena, on the other hand, the reforms were largely bypassed. A Maryland study, for example, found that the 6,430 absolute divorces issued in 1945 included 4,733 on the ground of desertion but only 319 based on the living-apart law. The reason was simple: the separation statute required a five-year wait, desertion only eighteen months. Maryland did not allow divorces for cruelty, so divorce filings gravitated into the desertion column. In the study's understated conclusion, "Plaintiffs are tending to shift the grounds alleged in order to use the more liberal . . . ones."[67]

These intramural matches between appellate courts and legislatures may have been a sideshow to the bulk of divorcing Americans, but they set the tone for further formal revisions of the divorce process. The next chapter examines the permutations of the most popular divorce ground, cruelty, as well as the gendered course of individualism that presented women with cultural responsibility—and blame—for the steamroller of American divorce.

FOUR

THE CASE OF THE
ALL-TOO-CONSENTING ADULTS

A sham battle against the little man who isn't there.

Paul W. Alexander, "The Follies of Divorce:
A Therapeutic Approach to the Problem"

In 1949 Judge Paul W. Alexander regaled readers of the *Ladies' Home Journal* with the story of the Nevada bill proposing divorce by slot machine. Upon arrival in the desert oasis, divorce customers would purchase a special key to a combination "juke box, time clock and slot machine." Insertion of the key in the device for forty-two consecutive days would automatically record the required residency period. On the final day, the divorce seeker would deposit two hundred silver dollars. Then "lights would flash. Wheels would spin. The juke-box section would give forth the first two lines of 'America.' As the music died away, a pretty divorce decree would pop out of a slot . . . complete with multicolored ribbons, the imprint of the the great seal of Nevada, and the signature of the district judge." But the bill died. Even the "Gambling Gomorrah" had its limits.[1]

New York, known as the "Poor Man's Reno,"[2] featured the nation's most restrictive divorce law, virtually unchanged from the one drafted by Alexander Hamilton in 1787 which allowed marital dissolution only upon proof of adultery.[3] Wags remarked, however, that New York had two divorce grounds, adultery and perjury.[4] Unable to rehearse the facile fables of cruelty recited in most states, New Yorkers specialized in hotel perjury: A couple bent on divorce arranged for the husband to be caught in the act of sitting beside a scantily clad corespondent when the wife, a process server, and a private detective armed with a flash camera burst into the hotel room. The corespondent, process server, and detective all were retained by the wife's counsel (whose fees were often paid by the husband) to play their scripted roles both in the hotel and later in the courtroom.[5]

New York trial judge Henry Clay Greenberg admitted to the readers of the *American Magazine* that the great bulk of Empire State divorces were obtained fraudulently, "and almost everybody in the courts knows it." Indeed, almost everybody in the state knew it, including the many thousands who read or heard about the New York *Mirror's* titillating series entitled "I Was the 'Unknown Blonde' in 100 New York Divorces!"[6] Judge Greenberg estimated that three-quarters of the adultery cases were staged, with the average performance of these productions lasting eight to ten minutes. Divorce judges felt bound to cooperate with the fraud, "caught in a system which, whatever the hypocrisy, is popular with a large segment of the bar and the public."[7] The wry flavor of New York divorcing at midcentury was captured in an exchange between *Time* magazine and a Brooklyn matrimonial lawyer. The periodical had reported on the characteristics of New York divorce jurisprudence, noting: "Occasionally, the pajamas are green instead of pink, but there are always pajamas and the woman is always blonde. Discontented New York wives shrink from the hoary tale, but the state law which permits divorce only on grounds of adultery leaves them no alternative. Chief sufferers are referees in divorce proceedings, forced to hear over and over the same old story of raid, surprised husband, pajama-clad blonde." But attorney Joseph Horowitz took issue with *Time's* description. In his experience handling divorce trials in New York, Horowitz informed *Time's* readers, "never has Madam X of the story been a blonde, never has she worn pajamas, never has a wife shrunk from the hoary tale. She has been 'brown-haired,' 'red-haired,' 'light-haired,' 'dark.'

She has worn a 'blanket,' 'black lace step-ins,' 'dancing tights,' 'panties,' 'white nightgown,' or 'nothing.' New York wives have not shrunk—most of them have laughed out loud."[8]

Trial judge Paul Bonynge admitted that he and his colleagues confirmed "thousands of divorces annually upon the stereotyped sin of the same big blonde attired in the same black silk pajamas."[9] But the variations in the color of the professional corespondent's hair and underclothes accentuated the uniformity of the perjury. New York, in short, had reversed the presumptions of the formal system. Despite the accusation by one investigative grand jury in 1948 that "widespread fraud, perjury, collusion and connivance pervade matrimonial actions [and] exude a stench and perpetuate a scandal,"[10] the rare judge who refused to accept the faked hotel evidence would "not be long hearing divorce cases."[11] Indeed, many divorce counsel complained that judicial referees hearing divorce testimony were less willing to grant relief in those few cases which presented a scenario other than the hotel frame-up. "They find the truth harder to believe."[12]

Many New Yorkers uneasy about hotel perjury resorted to an alternative legal subterfuge: annulment. Marriages could be annulled for misrepresentations about virtually any aspect of the conjugal relationship, including age, profession, character, disease, education, loyalty, mental incapacity, and property. At the end of World War II, Empire State jurisprudence allowed over 150 grounds for annulment.[13] Only California harvested as large an annual annulment crop as its cross-continental rival. From 1946 to 1950, for instance, more than two-thirds of all annulments in the United States were awarded in New York and California.[14] Perjury was the common coin of connubial freedom. In this Gresham's law of divorce, false testimony displaced the true because the effective lie was more valued by all sides. As Paul Alexander quipped, "The smoothest perjurer is soonest rewarded." The Michigan divorce judge who opened morning hearings in uncontested cases by intoning, "Let the perjury begin," understood the strictly symbolic character of the courtroom rituals.[15]

The pervasiveness of this bureaucracy of farce was illustrated in a 1949 experiment conducted by the Cleveland *Press*. Reporter Leonard Hammer submitted a bogus divorce petition in the name of Richard Campbell, the newspaper's makeup editor, and his wife. Hammer notarized the petition with a stamp conveniently left around the courthouse and inserted it into a pile of similar documents on Judge Samuel Silbert's desk. No proceedings were held in the case, and no evidence was ever presented. Nevertheless, six weeks later Judge Silbert—who handled up to fifty divorce cases a day—entered a decree divorcing the Campbells. When the ruse was exposed, Judge Silbert cited the participants for contempt and fined the newspaper one thousand dollars. The Campbells were refused a marriage license in Cleveland and had to drive to Indiana to get married again. In a system which operated on the presumption that all couples willingly consented to divorce, the Campbells stood out because they were only pretending.[16]

The Ritualized Dance of Divorce

Had the fault system for divorces succeeded in restraining the divorce rate, comprehensive family courts might not have emerged. But by the mid-twentieth century the traditional norms against divorce survived as a relic honored only by some religious conservatives. In 1952, for instance, Mary Lewis Coakley stoutly preached that the divorced who "succumb to the temptation to remarry" will go to hell.[17] The Catholic Church was most outspoken in this campaign. In a 1949 church-sponsored radio drama broadcast by the National Broadcasting Company's New York affiliate, the spurned wife of a philanderer rejected divorce in terms that encapsulated the Catholic Church's moral argument: "I know that divorce is an evil thing. I know that every divorce, like each wave of a treacherous tide, undermines the foundations of the citadel of marriage itself. I cannot be a hypocrite and deny my own wedding vows in order to marry again, because I would thereby make it easier for a hundred other girls to follow my example."[18] The Catholic Church had drawn its line in the sand. In the larger culture, however, the footprints of all those stepping from the altar to the courthouse and then back to the altar had virtually obscured that line.

No lobby for discontented spouses arose—nor could one have been easily imagined—to campaign for more realistic divorce. But such a special-interest group would have been superfluous. As two generations of readily divorced Americans had shown, legal absolution for a broken marriage could easily be purchased with a modest amount of pious perjury. When the required penance of social ostracism disappeared between the two World Wars, the divorce court lost its menacing aspect and took on the bland coloration of a registry.

Divorce changed as marriage changed. As sociologist Paul H. Landis reminded readers of the *Forum* magazine shortly after the end of World War II, the "companionship family," which "prizes romance and its ethereal happiness," was replacing the "institutional family rooted in the traditions of child-bearing, joint economic activity and filial duty." The definition of the ideal family limned by sociologists conveyed this change simply by omitting any reference to social responsibility. A successful family was one in which "husband and wife utilize their resources to work out a satisfactory mutual relationship." No third parties, divine or governmental, need apply.[19] So pervasive was this new understanding of marriage that when a Catholic prolocutor suggested that marriage should not be "primarily concerned with the happiness of the parties," he admitted that his view of marriage as a hell-or-high-water proposition would be seen as "ridiculous" by some.[20] No overriding communitarian purpose distracted couples from the focus on satisfaction. Even the emphasis on couples was somewhat overinclusive: once happiness usurped duty as the mainstay of marriage, the guideposts for satisfaction became increasingly self-centered.

With Americans viewing delight in marriage as the end, rather than the means, many thousands of spouses eschewed the work of relationship for the pursuit of what Philip Wylie termed the "'one and only' myth." Movies, pulp magazines, television soap operas, advertisements, and virtually the entire repertoire of popular music projected a "romantic complex creat[ing] expectations of a standard of psychic living which cannot be realized in most marriages." John McPartland found postwar Americans simultaneously raunchy and prudish, "the most sensual and profligate of peoples, worshippers of breast and thigh," while at the same time "a monogamous and chaste people to whom virginity is so sacred that it cannot be mentioned on our radios." McPartland concluded that "we raise our young in this never-never land where sex is bright and gay but doesn't exist."[21]

The state of marriage itself was oddly but roundly ignored by most media, which concentrated on the passion and pathos of romance and courtship. Once Cinderella married the Prince, neither was heard from again. Romantic comedies on the screen ended with "a kiss, blackout, marriage." In the popular culture of the 1940s, the wedded state lay in the merry miasma beyond the altar, an aesthetic limbo as much terra incognita as Hamlet's "undiscover'd country from whose bourn / No traveler returns." David L. Cohn suggested to the *Atlantic's* readers that marriage was "presented to the young by their elders, the movies, and slick magazine fiction, as a perpetual Christmas Eve with Tiny Tim passing double Martinis and saying 'God bless you, every one!'" In the pointed words of two contemporary sociologists, "the quiet pleasures of conjugal happiness" constituted a "denial of the romantic faith, which tells us that we should continue to burn with the same pure, gemlike flame for the rest of our lives."[22]

The burgeoning divorce rate in the 1940s indicated, however, not a disparagement of marriage, but its opposite: "modern couples demand more from marriage than their ancestors did."[23] After the Depression, Americans hankered after the married state in record numbers. During the 1940s the percentage of the divorced population increased from 2 to 3 percent, while the married cohort grew from 60 to 66 percent of the population.[24] World War II magnified the popularity of the marital state, even before American participation in the hostilities began. Samuel Tenenbaum noted the large increase in marriages during the summer and fall of 1940, as the Selective Service Act was debated and passed. The Japanese attack on Pearl Harbor "set off a frenzied rush to the altar," while the tense psychology of wartime created a "pathological interest in sex" as part of its heightened emphasis on adventure.[25]

War conditions took their toll on marriages, replicating in a far broader dimension the American social experience of the First World War. Tenenbaum, a New York City reporter-turned-psychologist, observed that war made husbands cynical and wives independent. The long separations made necessary by the conflict raised sexual temptation beyond the level of many to resist. Wartime was rushed time. As America raced through military preparation, a similar telescoping occurred within courtship rituals. Consequently, as historian D'Ann Campbell has observed, World

War II divorces "typically involved young couples who had not been acquainted very long and who had only a poor opportunity to know each other before the husband was shipped out. Immaturity was a basic factor, often leading to infidelity." Marital vows were breached on both the home front and the front lines, of course, but the feared promiscuity of the war years was the stateside woman's, not her soldier husband's. This skewed perspective was compatible with contemporary sociology, which equated women's drive for equality with moral degeneration. As a 1940 text put it: "The greater social freedom of women has more or less inevitably led to a greater degree of sexual laxity, a freedom which strikes at the heart of family stability."[26]

In the aftermath of the war, one Newark, New Jersey, judge heard twenty divorce cases in six weeks involving adultery alleged against soldiers' wives. Crowded dockets transformed divorce courts into express lanes: a Chattanooga, Tennessee, Bar Association report described a 1945 court session in which twelve divorces were granted in seventeen minutes. A *Newsweek* report on "Divorce: The Postwar Wave" highlighted Chicago jurist Edwin A. Robson's record-breaking stretch of hearing two thousand divorce cases in the last four months of 1945. Robson responded to the divorce craze by installing a nursery adjacent to his courtroom, to tend the children of these exploding wartime unions.[27]

These dramatic changes served notice that a culture tolerant of divorce abounded in postwar America. Charlton Ogburn, vice-chair and counsel for the Interprofessional Commission of Marriage and Divorce Laws, expressed his dismay that the American public "has remained rather apathetic in the face of the disturbing character of the divorce evil: the increasing number of divorces and the laxity of the courts in hearing and granting divorces, especially in undefended cases often based on fraud and collusion in violation of the statutes." But Ogburn was mistaken. Far from apathetic, the public usually supported the right to divorce even if it was not actually agitating for it. Maxine B. Virtue's observation that the "present cultural mores generally disapprove of the spouse who does not cooperate when asked for a divorce" more accurately suggests the flavor of the postwar popular culture.[28]

Despite the routine of divorces, the fault system for adjudicating them continued to provide an endless subject for exposés that were not so much damning as gawking at the human zoo. A 1945 *Life* magazine picture spread on divorce in Los Angeles remarked that mental cruelty "includes anything from a husband's reading too much to his disliking the way his wife cooks steak." Some cases resembled Rowena Laird's, who claimed her husband was rude to her friends and received a sympathetic murmur from the bench: "Better luck next time." Similarly, Anna MacGillevery's complaint stemmed from her husband's insistence that she wear lipstick. Her plea for autonomy was rewarded with a divorce. But not all the divorce stories substituted conjugal ennui for the statutory ground. Neva Krebs testified that her spouse stayed out at night, beat her up, and once tried to choke her.[29]

One story bore the marks of its Hollywood origin. The caption for two glossy pictures of recent divorcée Corinne Sylvia posing for Los Angeles newspaper photographers noted that she obtained her divorce by showing that after her husband persuaded her to vacation in Texas, he failed to send her the money to return to southern California. As Groucho Marx wisecracked, "Hollywood brides keep the bouquets and throw away the grooms." In Michigan, readers of the *Saturday Evening Post* learned, the dominant divorce standard specified "extreme and repeated cruelty." But this enhanced requirement could be met, during the average six-minute divorce hearing, by proof that the husband criticized his wife's clothing or refused to speak to her mother.[30] In Illinois, which also required a showing of "extreme and repeated cruelty," divorce court protocol demanded that the wife testify that her husband had slapped her precisely twice. The *Saturday Evening Post* sent John Bartlow Martin to observe Chicago divorce trials. Martin reported that the key questions and answers were always scripted, as follows:

Q. "During the time of your marriage, how did you treat your husband?"

A. "Good."

Q. "How did he treat you?"

A. "Bad."

Q. "Calling your attention to [specified date], what, if anything, occurred?"

A. "He struck me."

Q. "Calling your attention to [second date], what, if anything, occurred?"

A. [Same response.]

Q. "Did you give him any provocation or reason for striking you?"
A. "No."
Q. "Did this leave any marks or bruises?"
A. "Yes."
Q. "Cause you pain and suffering?"
A. "Yes."

This scenario was typically followed by a stipulation regarding the property settlement, the wife's waiver of alimony, and a request that the husband pay the wife's counsel fees. The wife's testimony was then rapidly corroborated by two family members or friends. The entire hearing took eight minutes. Uncontested divorce litigation thoroughly deserved Paul Alexander's scorn as "a sham battle against the little man who isn't there."[31]

The English Metamorphosis of Divorce "Cruelty"

Across the Atlantic, English society similarly experienced the transformation from an institutional marriage to one based on companionship. As both marital expectation and life expectancy increased, so did the perceptions of failure. The observation that couples now "have a much longer time in which to discover how unhappy their marriages are" reflects but one truth about the greatly increased rate of divorce in the twentieth century.[32] Marriage no longer functions as the door to a variety of economic, social, and educational services. The focus has shifted to the riskier ground of individualized happiness.[33]

The English legal system had not always accommodated the dogmas of individualism. Before 1937 only proof of adultery could liberate one spouse from the marital bonds.[34] In that year Parliament extended the grounds to include cruelty, desertion for three years, and incurable insanity after five years' confinement.[35] Matrimonial fault was the element that survived each legislative revision. Public debate over A. P. Herbert's 1937 bill focused attention on several developments in British society, including the gradually changing role of women and other new strains on traditional marriages.[36] Herbert had popularized his cause through his widely read novel *Holy Deadlock*, which recounted the routine circumvention of divorce laws by fraud, collusion, and perjury. Moreover, the Church of

England hinted that it was reconsidering its prerogative to speak for the nation. During the debate on the Herbert bill, the archbishop of Canterbury acknowledged that public policy in a democracy must allow religious organizations to impose their order upon their own members but should not let those groups, including the Church of England itself, set public policy for the whole state.[37]

Public reaction to the abdication crisis, coming on the heels of the Herbert bill debate, underscored the nation's upheaval in its view of marriage. The prospect of King Edward VIII's marriage to an American double-divorcée was widely perceived as unpalatable to the British government and people. The king accordingly abdicated the throne in order to marry Wallis Simpson. That Simpson had been the petitioner—and thus the innocent party—in her two divorces was of no consequence, for as Herbert had made clear in *Holy Deadlock*, purity of process did not characterize divorce proceedings. But despite the legal turbulence, an Anglican commission confidently pronounced on the eve of World War II that traditional marriage "is an institution of the natural order which is taken into and sanctified by the Christian Church."[38]

Significant social changes exploded on the British scene after World War II. The spread of education and the postwar increase in the average Briton's standard of living claimed responsibility for their share of the disturbance. But the most important factor in the disequilibrium of postwar Britain was unquestionably the social and economic emancipation of women. The percentage of married women workers in England more than trebled between 1931 and 1961, from 10 percent to 32 percent.[39] The burgeoning of the divorce rate immediately after World War II paralleled the American peak and proved to be as transitory as a similar statistical phenomenon experienced by both countries in the wake of World War I. But the newly altered gender relations appeared more durable. As noted sociologist Max Rheinstein asserted, "The rise in the rate of divorce . . . [coincided] with the change in the social position of the female half of the population" and accentuated the trend from institutional to companionate marriage.[40] A royal commission reported in the 1950s that in light of these changes, "women are no longer content to endure the treatment which in past times their inferior position obliged them to suffer. They expect of marriage that it shall be an equal partnership; and rightly so. But the working out of this ideal exposes marriages to new strains. Some husbands find it difficult to accept the changed position of women: some wives do not appreciate that their new rights do not release them from the obligations arising out of marriage itself and, indeed, bring in their train certain new responsibilities."[41]

Several postwar developments echo this awareness of unease at abrupt social transition. The 1947 Denning Report advocated greater use of counseling services in preventing divorce by urging couples toward a happier marriage experience. Two years later the Royal Commission on Population recommended that contraceptive advice be made available to married women. It recognized that repeated unplanned pregnancies were often symptomatic "not of a joyous sex life but of sexual coercion and distaste [which] could be associated with the instability rather than the stability of marriage."[42] The unsuccessful effort undertaken by the Morton Commission in the 1950s to examine and revise the entire structure of English marriage and divorce law reflected deep social fissures. Robert S. W. Pollard, chair of the Marriage Law Reform Society, noted in 1951 the common opinion among "responsible adults" that if a divorce is necessary, "it should be by agreement and without rancour." Under the current state of the law, Pollard added, this conviction led to the commission of collusion and perjury.[43]

The Morton Commission Report was roundly criticized for failing to come to a consensus. But public opinion was as fractured as the commission was deadlocked. Savaged on one side for attempting to preserve the Victorian family code in an age of choice, the report's refusal to elevate the status of divorce was vindicated in the minds of many by Princess Margaret's renunciation of Group Captain Peter Townsend on the ground that a divorced man was an unsuitable spouse. "Mindful of the Church's teaching that marriage is indissoluble, and conscious of my duty to the Commonwealth, I have resolved to put these considerations before all others."[44] The princess's stand provided a symbolic victory for the moral authority of the Church of England. In the 1950s, as Oliver R. McGregor observed, it appeared that the royal commission and the Church of England "had put paid to divorce law reform for at least a generation."[45]

Nonetheless, other signs indicated the friable nature of the church's stand. As the archbishop of Canterbury was to remark years later, Anglicans in the postwar period "frequently displayed an uncertainty about

A misogynistic undercurrent of post–World War II America can be seen in this series of illustrations accompanying articles by a psychoanalyst who claimed that the modern American wife "consumes her husband's self-confidence, his male superiority, his independence—and her own chance of happiness." (Figs. 8–10 by Howard Williamson for *Collier's*, October 30, 1948; figs. 11–13 by Jefferson Machamer for *Collier's*, December 7, 1946)

The "engineering" wife entertains
definitely for profit—not for fun

8.

The husband of the "career" wife
must learn to play second fiddle

9.

10.

Women deliberately project upon
potential or actual suitors an
impression that is not an accurate picture of their total nature

Their greater instability equips women for violence that is furiously vengeful and spectacular

11.

12.

Women feel it necessary not to improve on nature but to disguise it

The psychic mechanism of women is so constituted that the continuous guilt feeling stirs up a subconscious craving for punishment

13.

the identity of their Church and confusion about the proper direction for its development."[46] In its 1948 Lambeth Conference, for instance, a church committee appointed to consider the issue of marriage observed that "public opinion in favour of permanence in marriage has gravely declined, and divorce is ceasing to carry a public stigma."[47] While the church resolutely defended indissolubility, it acknowledged that social cohesion on this issue had disappeared. In 1955 the archbishop of Canterbury acknowledged the crevice in the wall supporting both law and morality by emphasizing the church's role in dealing "as little as possible in legalities and courts and as largely as possible in terms of moral and spiritual truth." But even while carving out differences between the church's discipline and the state's laws, the archbishop conceded that some second marriages (with the first spouse still living) have, "by every test of the Holy Spirit that we are able to recognise, been abundantly blessed."[48]

The Church of England did not yield its views on the indissolubility of marriage. But it reassessed its prerogative to speak for the nation, redefining its relationship to the state in many areas where previously the ecclesiastical law had held sway. Without abandoning its commitment to moral authority (vis-à-vis its membership), the church's shifting focus reflected a deeper concern with social, rather than moral, welfare.[49] The changing response of both church and state to modern sexuality also reflected a gradual evolution to norms of facilitating individual choice. The General Principles of the National Marriage Guidance Council in 1948 supported lifetime monogamous marriage, condemned sex outside marriage, and expressed wariness about birth control even within the marital union. The archbishop of Canterbury was quoted as condemning contraception even within the conjugal union "when misused to enable selfish and irresponsible people to escape the duties and disciplines of marriage and parenthood."[50] By 1958 the same paragraph had been changed to encourage contraception within marriage as a contribution "to the health and happiness of the whole family."[51] By 1968 the statement of principles had been eliminated, replaced by a bibliography of psychotherapy and sex literature. On issues of homosexuality, abortion, and illegitimacy, the Church of England took an active role during the 1950s and 1960s as a catalyst for permissive change.[52]

These social transformations were reflected in the broad expansion of divorce grounds by the judiciary. British courts transmuted the original requirement of legal cruelty that there be an infliction of physical harm or reasonable apprehension thereof into a rule that intolerable behavior—as defined by the offended spouse—warranted divorce. Unaffected by statute (for Parliament never defined cruelty), judicial policy evolved from protecting the petitioner from serious hurt to evaluating whether the marriage as a whole had deteriorated beyond the point of salvage. Some decisions increased the range of actionable cruelty to the limits of a further perimeter: an undefended allegation of cruelty represented, for many wives and husbands, simply their decision to abandon one marital venture and obtain license to assay another.

Relentless pressure from beleaguered spouses yielded this legal metamorphosis, which represented a sea change in the institution of marriage. In this sense the judicial imprimatur served, not to initiate, but primarily to acquiesce in social changes effected by dissatisfied wives and husbands themselves. The evolution of cruelty as a divorce ground in England substantially paralleled the American experience. In both countries the malleability of connubial cruelty allowed it to eclipse other fault grounds as the favored escape hatch for unhappy wives and husbands. From its start in merely trammeling the excesses of spousal savagery, legal cruelty evolved into a relatively painless method for terminating mutually undesired marriages.

After World War II, English courts reflected the elevated expectations of marriage—and the drastically lowered threshold of divorce—in declaring that cruelty encompassed "slovenly boorishness around the house,"[53] drunkenness,[54] indecent exposure,[55] inflicting excessive punishments upon a child of the parties,[56] and even treasonable activities.[57] The continuing tensions over sexual standards and gender identity were reflected in the decision that a man who cross-dressed before his wife and her relations committed matrimonial cruelty.[58] Similarly culpable was a husband whose wife consented to sodomy with him upon his representation that it was a normal practice.[59] A woman whose behavior led her husband to believe that she was engaged in lesbian activity—even though no such activity was proved—also crossed legal cruelty's forbidden line.[60]

The capaciousness of the cruelty ground may be seen in a contrasting pair of cases which also illustrate the boundaries of the cultural stereotypes portraying tight-lipped men and shrewish women. In *Atkins v. Atkins*,[61] a husband was granted a divorce because of his wife's nagging. The court reasoned that "dropping water wears the stone. Constant nagging will become completely intolerable, and although in the course of married life you may be able to point to no single instance which could possibly be described as . . . 'a row', yet nagging may be of such kind and so constant, that it endangers the health of the spouse on whom it is inflicted."[62] But if *Atkins* validated barbed loquaciousness as actionable cruelty, resolute taciturnity was held against a man in *Launder v. Launder*,[63] in which a wife prevailed on the ground of cruelty because her husband sulked and refused to talk to her.

Cruelty subsuming incompatibility reached its comic apogee in the 1963 decision in *Lines v. Lines*.[64] A wife petitioned for divorce on the grounds that her husband "persistently required her to tickle the soles of his feet."[65] The suit was undefended. A skeptical court appointed a queen's proctor to serve as amicus curiae to assist with legal argument. Aided by the counsel representing the public interest, the trial judge concluded that even though the husband had not intended to harm his wife, his persistence in demanding that she tickle him adversely affected her health and satisfied the ground of matrimonial cruelty. As a group appointed by the archbishop of Canterbury in the 1960s reported, the axis of legal divorce had shifted: "In practice the courts have already gone a considerable way towards transforming judgements theoretically founded on the matrimonial offence into what are virtually judgements on the state of the marriages in question." The church group added that recent court rulings strongly suggested that the "essence of 'cruelty' consists not in the animus of the respondent but, quite simply, in the emergence, through the conduct of the respondent, of a situation that the petitioner ought not to be called upon to endure."[66]

On both sides of the Atlantic, the doctrine of matrimonial cruelty had expanded to the horizon, pushing aside all other legal grounds. Anglo-American judicial policy had evolved from responding to the horrendous beating of the petitioner to "enabl[ing] the courts to dissolve marriages which have to far deteriorated that they no longer serve the interests of the parties or of society."[67] In the struggle for control of marriage, wives and husbands had triumphed over the state. The question remained which of the spouses would prevail in the internecine conflict that followed the demise of the marriage as an institution.

The Threat of Gendered Emancipation

Men and women evolved toward greater individualism at a distinctly different pace. Women's solo efforts continued to receive more criticism, and conservative critics of the perceived regression of society targeted women's liberties as the loss leader of cultural degeneration.[68] Blaming women for societal ruptures was also a common theme of hackneyed humor. In a 1953 law school address on the interprofessional approach to family problems, a college professor asked his audience to recall that "the good Lord made the Heaven and the Earth and Man in six days and rested. Then he made women and neither man nor God has rested since." He also alluded to the movement for "Women's Sufferage, the chief effect of which seems to be men suffering." Seriously intended essays often scored the same points. In a series of widely read articles in *Collier's* just after World War II, Ralph S. Banay sedulously argued the case that women's refusal to accept their biological destiny resulted in increased female criminality and schizophrenia.[69]

Dr. Banay, the research director in social deviations at Columbia University, had formerly been the chief psychiatrist at New York's Sing Sing Prison. Interpreting the drive for female emancipation in psychopathological terms, he claimed that women's "Stone Age" emotions—harboring a natural proclivity for sadism and masochism—stemmed from a nature no more sophisticated than that of "preadolescent children." Women's developmental jejuneness constituted for Banay a recapitulation of pre-adamite courtship rituals. He observed that women's "almost instinctual fascination with danger and horror would seem to be a vestigial remembrance of the thrill and danger of the ancient hunts in which women were captured and subdued."[70] In "The Husband Really Pays," Banay vigorously attacked what he considered the overly generous allowance of alimony to women. He saw the consequences of divorce as grossly uneven: women reveled in placing men in the "penal servitude" of alimony, while men endured the fallout of deeper alienation and ostracism after divorce.[71] Real women were repelled by the concept of female equality, Banay asserted, since "most normal women reveal in their dreams and fantasies that they wish to be swayed, overwhelmed and mastered by their men."[72] These desires for subordination further replicated the immutable tendencies of the species. Within modern marriage women's "emotional cannibalism" caused them to assert their independence by "devour[ing] their husbands." Banay divided troublesome women into three types. The "engineering" wife allowed her spouse no voice in running the household. The "prima-donna" wife pursued her obsession with her own ambition and pleasure. But the "competing" wife caused the greatest havoc. Her insistence on her own career and refusal to "live her ambitions vicariously . . . reduces her husband to the role of economic and emotional midget."[73]

Banay's sexual pogrom did not go unchallenged. A flurry of articles and letters to the editor attacked Banay for "purposely distort[ing] women's desires and aims" and called upon *Collier's* to "secure competent psychiatric therapy" for the psychiatrist himself. One letter writer guessed that Banay's misogynous razor had been sharpened on his own romantic misadventures: "Poor, dear Dr. Banay! I bet she was a pip!"[74] Yet the tenor of attacks on modern women revealed Banay as outspoken but not outdated. The editors of *Collier's* remarked that the hundreds of letters generated by Banay's initial article divided on exclusively gender lines in praising or panning his sentiments. Banay's call for severely limiting alimony received support from male correspondents who agreed in questioning why the husband should "pay alimony so his former wife can live on Easy Street."[75]

Attacks on alimony often achieved a vituperative tone entirely out of kilter with alimony's economic impact. That this displaced sexual hatred was not limited to men indicated that sometimes both sexes feared the shifting nature of marriage in the postwar era. Alimony served as the white-hot focus of a much larger cultural argument, one that has not yet been satisfactorily resolved. Many men—as well as a not insignificant number of women—perceived alimony as a windfall for recipients and a crushing burden on those forced to pay. Nationwide statistics showed, however, that alimony was decreed in only one-quarter of divorce cases, and that most awards were modest and often included sums for child support. In 1952 Chicago jurist Edwin Robson noted that wives in the Second City waived alimony in 93 percent of the cases. Five years later Divorce Commissioner C. Clinton Clad reported in the *Saturday Evening Post* that Los Angeles alimony awards averaged $35 per month, a figure which he asserted was in line with awards across the country. In Manhattan a study of alimony awards early in the decade showed that 60 percent of alimony awards were for less than $40 per week, and 14 percent were for less than $20.[76] But the public preferred to imagine the "ex-chorus girl blithely collecting $500 a week for the rest of her life from the unfortunate man who had the dubious privilege of [having been] her husband for six months." The popular vision of huge alimony assessments, Divorce Commissioner Clad wrote, owed its provenance to Park Avenue and Hollywood on the brain. "Almost daily one reads that this socialite got a multimillion-dollar property settlement and that movie star is asking for several thousand a month alimony. However, these cases are terribly rare. . . . In the run-of-the-mill cases, particularly if there are children, the woman rarely receives an adequate award." Still, tabloids outsold transcripts: Dan Hopson, Jr., observed that the "news value of the large divorce settlement produces the American myth of the 'bleeding' husband and the successful peroxide blond who now can vacation in Miami."[77]

The brouhaha raised by many men over alimony was also ironic since most support payments represented negotiated settlements, rather than orders imposed by a judge overcome at the sight of damp eyelashes daubed at by a clutched handkerchief. In a world in which the supply and demand of divorce fluctuated rather freely, the amount of support generally represented the "comparative eagerness of the spouses to dissolve the marriage." When the husband was the partner more desirous of the split, the wife could drive the support figure higher, as her price for cooperating. Conversely, when the wife was the moving party, the support tally was "often just as little as the husband's attorney feels she can be given without having the court question the validity of the agreement." Both the custody of children and their support were similarly subject to bargaining.[78]

Most commentators were uninterested in the facts, however, preferring to relate individual horror stories of long-suffering men languishing in alimony jails or too impoverished to remarry, while their bloodthirsty ex-wives feted themselves on the spousal dole.[79] In his New York *Herald Tribune* column, Art Buchwald parodied this trend by inventing a magazine feature article headlined, "How I Invested My Alimony and Made a Million Dollars."[80] Although it also read like parody, the subheading of one abolitionist proposal earnestly described alimony as a "medieval hangover [which] robs men, turns women into drones, promotes greed and damages innocent lives."[81]

Perhaps one reason why many men hated to pay money to their former spouses related to the broad sentiment that women were not capable of handling money wisely. American culture deemed the making of financial decisions to be man's work. A glimpse into this aspect of the sexual division of labor is provided by a 1954 advertisement placed by the Northwestern Mutual Life Insurance Company in *Time*. The full-page ad featured a photograph of "Miss Catherine B. Cleary," identified as vice president of the First Wisconsin Trust Company. The caption above the picture asks, "Are wives realistic when it comes to family security?" The body of the ad quotes Cleary's observations that in many families "the buying of life insurance is considered the man's responsibility. He often feels—I wonder how wisely—that his wife should not be asked to think about such things." Cleary criticized this attitude since the wife, in her opinion, best knew the daily money needs of the family. "I only wish," she lamented, that "more husbands would count her in as the partner she should be in planning the family security program."[82]

The partnership image was far from Alexander Eliot's mind as he advised women to "resist the degrading temptation to suck blood from a man who loved you once." In response to his article, a representative of United States Divorce Reform, Inc. congratulated the *Saturday Evening Post* for its devotion to the cause of alimony reform. Similarly, Sally L. Underhill praised Eliot for denouncing the "licensed extortion practiced by women too lazy to earn their own living."[83] During the long process of converting California from a traditional divorce state to the first exclusively no-fault American jurisdiction in 1969, the only allegations of sex-based inequality were made by divorced men who "charged that husbands were victimized and subjected to financial ruin by wives in divorce proceedings."[84] Not only did United States Divorce Reform, Inc. address the issue of gender equality at the California legislative hearings (the only organization to do so), it also attempted to qualify an initiative for the 1966 California ballot which would have removed jurisdiction over divorce and ancillary matters from the courts, placing issues such as alimony and property distribution in the hands of an "Administrative Department of Family Relations."[85]

Alimony reform became a cause célèbre for divorced men and for the women who married them. Fathers United for Equal Rights spawned the Second Wives Coalition as a separate sister organization. A lobbying group calling itself The Other Woman, Ltd. sponsored a fund-raising advertisement pitched at divorced men. The copy read: "Send us $1 to help get your ex-wife a job. Or a husband." A cartoon appeared underneath, depicting an ex-wife munching chocolates as she watched television.[86]

Rebuttals were more muted. "D.P." claimed not to know any women living on alimony but many who supported children without any help from their ex-husband. For Chicago judge Thaddeus V. Adesko, alimony was a losing proposition all around, "not enough for her and the kids, and . . . too much for him to pay." Indeed, the tail of the dismal payment record wagged the dog of the awards themselves. A field study of Kansas divorces reported one judge's sense that since alimony "is almost impossible to collect[,] there is not much reason to grant it." Even as well-informed an expert as family law specialist Henry H. Foster, Jr., crafted a skewed balance in his presentation of the issue: "Unless one is a zealous feminist he must be shocked by the number of unrealistic and unfair alimony awards just as he should be dismayed by the chronic breakdown in their collection." Such a slant is not surprising in an age where a joke nervously held that alimony represented "the cash surrender value of a husband."[87]

As if to stress that "alimony drones" were unrepresentative of their sex, the popular journals continued to allude to the feminine passion for submission. Woman's quest for dependence supposedly reached all the workaday corners of her life. Margaret Case Harriman considered it a "pretty canny observation" that "woman's best reason for getting married is to have somebody around the house to explain newspaper items to her and to tell her how to vote." Women were self-sufficient for life's major concerns, but day-to-day hassles required "something in trousers . . . [to] put that mysterious male power to work" and get things done.[88] In "A

Woman's Career," a song originally written for his 1948 Broadway musical, *Kiss Me, Kate*, Cole Porter echoed this sense of woman's instinctual need, a frailty that she "never, never will lose." No matter how much a woman achieves in her career, "her life is a failure, at least in her heart / If she can't hold her man."[89]

Margaret Harriman's observations and Cole Porter's lyrics symbolized a tactical hegemonic retreat on the issue of gender equality. American culture by and large retained its suspicion of women's refusal to remain boxed. Girls flaunting their lack of discipline, wives emasculating their husbands, mothers unsexing their sons: these accusations positioned woman once again as the storm center of cultural change. Large segments of America, both male and female, felt that pushing the limits of women's economic opportunities and social outlook carried too many risks. But how could the clock be turned back?

One avenue of hope for the triumph of the nostalgic dream over the unrooted future pointed to divorce reform. Marital breakdown was the lightning rod in the sex-driven cultural storm. In many ways woman's worst sin was leading the charge to the divorce court. As Harrison Smith concluded, "We are trying to find a scapegoat for the failure of marriage, the awesome tide of divorce and annulment, and there woman stands, the obvious center of all of man's emotional disturbances."[90]

The conservative reforms of incompatibility laws and living-apart statutes had failed to stem this "awesome tide of divorce." It also had become abundantly clear that the fault ground of cruelty was less a barrier and more a tunnel for divorce. The formal legal system next turned to a plan composed of equal parts of inducement and coercion, offering reconciliation and the abolition of divorce grounds as the bait. The following chapter explores therapeutic divorce and the alternative family courts devised on the juvenile court model.

FIVE

THE DECEPTIVE PROMISE OF
THERAPEUTIC DIVORCE

> Now, damn it, shut up. I'm telling you—
> you love each other.
>
> *Harriet F. Pilpel, "The Job the Lawyers Shirk"*

The fault system was a sieve. None of the official legal reforms had affected the swelling divorce rate at all. The regime of fault had not only failed to preserve the nuclear family, it had become the engine of transformation into the post–World War II age of divorce. Once conservative reformers identified fault itself as the rate-determining step for the rise in divorce, they proposed radical surgery in an effort to reverse what they perceived as an ominous decline in the stability of the American family. In looking for a way to disassemble the fault system in order to render divorces more difficult to obtain, they found a quite serviceable—if somewhat surprising—model at hand: the juvenile court.

A product of the Progressive drive to merge governmental activism with therapeutic ends, the juvenile court occupied what Andrew J. Polsky has described as the "shadowy ground between legal tribunal and social agency."[1] As the immediate but much more potent successor to the House of Refuge and reformatory movements, the juvenile court transformed legal institutions to further its goal of adjusting the personalities and behaviors of the predominantly lower-class children who swamped its caseloads. The ultimate goal of the new court and its vigorous social service adjunct, the juvenile probation department, was to produce a radical transformation in the values and lifestyle of their clients.[2] Child reformation, as so defined, was rarely achieved. But the juvenile court was created—and persists—as a paradigm of professional cross-fertilization. Key advocates of administering therapeutic divorce through family courts, such as Ben B. Lindsey and Paul W. Alexander, served as juvenile court judges for many years. They sought to expand the power of this coercive social experiment to families whom they viewed as socially irresponsible. Alexander worded the issue so as to make the connection clear: "Since the problems in a divorce case are so much more social than legal, why isn't it logical to take the embattled spouses out of the antiquated old divorce mill with its creaking legalistic machinery and put them into a socialized court, as we have done with the juveniles?"[3]

America after World War II was the land of the experts, and "socialized" courts for marital woes fit hand-in-glove with the powerful emphasis on scientific guidance of everyday problems.[4] Many legal and social science experts viewed most divorce seekers as "sick" and even "mentally ill" couples whose freedoms should be curtailed because of the adverse social consequences of their contemplated action.[5] They believed in a strong link between divorce and future juvenile delinquency for the children of the severed union, who almost by definition were doomed to be neglected as a result of their parents' breach of the familial bond. As Lynne Carol Halem has noted, this "etiological relationship between divorce and childhood crime . . . provided a rationale for modeling the family tribunal after the juvenile courts."[6]

Postwar America experienced the acceleration of the transition of the family from the institutional to the companionship form. While the quest for family togetherness embodied the ideal of happiness, the individualistic demands of a romance culture often undermined family unity. Both in Great Britain and in the United States the range of actions deemed sufficient by the courts to satisfy the cruelty ground for divorce continued to expand beyond any imaginable outer limits. The particular tensions

felt by women as wives and mothers became a lightning rod for significant cultural dissatisfactions, as the vituperative attacks on the system of
alimony showed. Issues of crime, social deviance, and divorce thus merged,
against the backdrop of the uneven diffusion of social science concepts
into the legal profession. Seen through a haze of often-unacknowledged
class bias, a single solution emerged: therapeutic divorce, administered by
family courts composed of equal parts of sheriff and social worker, counselor and judge.

"Without Guilt or Sin"

Although family courts had been proposed before World War II, very few
had been established. Maverick judge and social radical Ben Lindsey did
his share in widely disparate venues. After the Ku Klux Klan drove him
from the domestic relations bench in Colorado, Lindsey reemerged in
California, where he won election to a judgeship in 1934 and provided the
leadership that resulted in the establishment of the Children's Conciliation Court of Los Angeles in 1939.[7] In Milwaukee a "pre-divorce" court
with a Department of Conciliation opened its doors in 1935.[8] Surprisingly, however, the family court that was best known, due entirely to the
energy and charisma of its founding judge, was located in Toledo, Ohio.
Judge Paul W. Alexander fired the movement for family courts from the
1940s to the 1960s. Hailed as the "father of family law,"[9] he most lucidly
and persistently articulated the philosophy of therapeutic divorce, and his
life's work greatly influenced the evolving understanding of marriage and
the law for the remainder of the twentieth century.

Paul Alexander was a rebel in a robe. He believed in the rehabilitative
power of the judicial system, and he bitterly criticized the divorce process
because it rewarded perjury and punished forgiveness, thus reversing
common sense. Unlike radicals who wanted the law to reflect unalloyed
individualism and free choice in marital partners, however, Alexander
held that a judge's main role was to reintroduce warring couples to each
other under a flag of truce. Each divorce petition represented an opportunity for the state to reunite the parties. During the parley social science

experts—the rehabilitation professionals, as Alexander viewed them—would pressure the couple to reconcile.

After practicing law for nearly a quarter-century in his hometown of Toledo, Alexander in 1936 was elected to the domestic relations and juvenile bench, on which he served for three decades. He converted the Toledo court into a national showplace for the implementation of his family court ideas. Although he never achieved his complete reform program, Alexander was widely recognized as the pioneer of and godfather to the therapeutic divorce movement.[10] Alexander kept a carved ship's model on the wall behind his desk. Over it appeared the legend: "Who doth not answer to the rudder shall answer to the rock."[11] Alexander's lifelong ambition was to steer. His professional attainments were many: at various times he headed the National Council of Juvenile Court Judges, the National Conference of Juvenile Agencies, and the Legal Section of the National Conference on Family Life. He also served as trustee of the National Probation and Parole Association, and he chaired the American Bar Association's Interprofessional Commission on Marriage and Divorce Laws.[12]

Alexander realized that couples engaged in an uncivil war would not willingly participate in a process aimed at frustrating their goal of secession. Quite aware that the fault regime offered no check on the divorce rate, he proposed a conservative revolution in liberal clothes: the elimination of all divorce grounds and their replacement with a therapeutic process, divorce "without guilt or sin."[13] Divorces were to be granted upon the breakdown of the marriage. But who determined whether a marriage was sunk or shipshape? Not the parties, whose impulsivity rendered them incapable of understanding their true condition. Alexander believed that troubled wives and husbands manifested their confusion and helplessness by the act of filing a divorce petition, which he deemed "an application . . . for the remedial services of the state."[14]

In Alexander's view the central paradigm of the old divorce court was erroneous. The fault system's call for an "innocent" complainant and a "guilty" defendant did not reflect the complex psychological makeup of conjugal relationships. In family life the question of guilt, relocated from criminal law, was a clumsy barometer of the state of the marriage. Although he worried about the quotidian fraud perpetrated upon the judicial system,

Alexander's main concern lay with the immoral consequences of a system of divorce grounds. When traditional adversary procedures are "employed to resolve intrafamilial conflicts," he observed, they "tend to fan the flames." He would replace courtroom dogfights with a "non-adversary or conference type of procedure in determining issues and prescribing remedies." [15] Marital warfare would end in a therapeutic armistice: as the oft-quoted title of one of Alexander's articles phrased it, "Let's Get the Embattled Spouses out of the Trenches." [16]

While many critics viewed the system of divorce grounds as too conservative, Alexander perceived the fault regime as too liberal. When a litigant in a traditional court procedure proved that her or his spouse had been unfaithful, or had behaved with actionable cruelty, or in some states had failed to provide adequate support, the court had no choice but to grant a divorce. Even if the judge believed that the marriage could be saved; even if the children would suffer terribly from the dissolution; even if, in fact, the marriage had not broken down, the divorce decree must issue. Alexander considered this mandatory award of a divorce upon proof of specific grounds to be the worst corruption of family law in America. [17]

He agreed with the liberals that divorce grounds were a wretched substitute for marital breakdown. He proposed to eliminate all grounds. But Alexander would take an eraser to the statutory code in order to give the court discretion to deny divorce even in cases of adultery, cruelty, or non-support. As a sociologist wrote in support of Alexander's theories, the concept of divorce justice should satisfy the real need of troubled families: not a ruling on the lawfulness of conduct, but "having the family members *brought into a working relation with each other*." [18] In place of the controlling guilt-or-innocence dichotomy, Alexander and his allies substituted the paradigm of mental illness. Divorce seekers were sick. They had come to the robed marriage doctor, whom society had equipped with the right tools and consulting specialists to decide upon the appropriate treatment. The injured person certainly should not self-diagnose or prescribe the needed remedy because expert guidance was essential: "though pain drives [the patient] to demand amputation of his shattered leg, the surgeon won't amputate if the leg can be repaired." [19] Moreover, those in conjugal crisis generally were unaware both of the opportunities for expert assistance and of their particular need for professional relief. Since divorce was symptomatic of illness (the divorced were "spoiled and stunted in devel-opment"),[20] the ultimate aim was to improve the procedure so as to re-move the pathology. As John H. Mariano emphasized, "We do not pass laws against disease; we strive to eradicate disease."[21]

Troubled marital partners were impulsive, pursuing divorce out of an "immature" and "infantile" inability to cope.[22] Proponents of therapeutic divorce repeatedly stressed the vulnerability and uncertainty of those poised, as it were, at the precipice of divorce. The working hypothesis of therapeutic divorce was forcefully stated by Nester C. Kohut: "A substan-tial number of marriages alleged by the parties and supposed by the at-torneys and divorce courts to be broken, lifeless or irreparable, are not in fact completely or irreversibly broken."[23] Kohut, a marriage counselor, sociologist, and lawyer, was the director of Save the Marriage, Inc. He argued that incompatibility and voluntary separation need not lead to divorce. Assertions of cruelty should not be taken at face value, and de-serting spouses should be tracked down. All in all, Kohut felt that Ameri-can society had a "tendency to over-sympathize . . . [with] a distraught spouse."[24]

The belief in divorce as liberating was seen as a manifestation of men-tal instability and an unresolved oedipal complex. In the words of John S. Bradway, "The domestic sufferer often is content, consciously or other-wise, to 'kill' his family."[25] Equating divorce with personal freedom indi-cated a neurotic deviation which, if unchecked, could lead to the destruc-tion of a critical social institution. The aberrant mental state of the divorce-minded was repeatedly underscored. A Richmond, Virginia, chan-cery judge advised matrimonial lawyers to remember that they were "not advising a client who is in a normal state of mind. . . . Anger and jealousy create a sudden psychosis." The client in the grip of hatred and hurt pride was "mentally ill."[26]

Despite Alexander's benevolent utterances calling for the avoidance of guilt and sin, he aimed to shift the debate from procedural rights in di-vorce cases to "selfishness, sinfulness, [and] immaturity." He believed that "tactful, gentle and persistent persuasion can induce even the most prideful or willful or belligerent spouse to talk frankly and freely." Once these miscreant spouses released their neurotic hold on the obsession of divorce, Alexander believed, they would be open to the desirability of reconciliation.[27] Through the method of therapeutic divorce, society carried out its obligation to ensure that only the truly broken marriages were legally dissolved. All others—and the expectations were high that a majority of present divorces would be in this category—could be restored to health. The family court, not the impulsive couple, would decide when the marriage was beyond repair. Clearly unsalvageable unions would be terminated quickly and quietly, without a public trial and the necessity of proving grounds. But the marriages that science and modern jurisprudence had brought back to health would redeem themselves through reconciliation. "Even though a couple has diagnosed its own case as hopeless," wrote a church group supportive of therapeutic divorce, "the judge would be able to draw upon the help of a body of counselors representing religious, social, psychiatric and legal insights which might point the way to reconciliation."[28] That the family court was a vessel in the command of the therapeutic state was rendered plain in that the power to dissolve unions, which several decades of litigious activity had operationally shifted to the individual couples, would now be reestablished as the prerogative of the government.

The reliance on expert intervention to alter the dynamics of failing marriages also led Alexander and his allies to criticize living-apart statutes. Laws allowing for divorce after a set period of separation were "clinically unjustifiable" because they "presuppose that distraught couples are the best judges as to the viability of their marriage."[29] They were also inappropriate because they circumvented the family court's therapeutic approach.[30] Living-apart provisions were similar to fault grounds in their ready amenability to proof. Once a couple established the requisite separation period, the trial judge was obliged to grant the divorce, even if she or he believed the couple could yet be reconciled.

Unhappy with the approximately four hundred thousand annual separation agreements that dealt only with matters of custody, property division, and support and did nothing to lessen the "rate of marital carnage," Nester Kohut proposed alternative "Therapeutic Separation Agreements." These documents epitomized the reach of therapeutic divorce concepts, "demonstrat[ing] how the separation agreement can be constructed so as to serve as a therapeutic instrument, using experience from the field of the behavioral sciences."[31] In contrast to the "mundane economic" focus of most separation agreements, these "therapeutic" instruments would emphasize the positive aspects of separation, that is, the opportunity and obligation to obtain counseling and plan reconciliation. Kohut imagined that even separating parties still "desire to preserve their marital bond intact." With the "passage of time" and "professional marriage counseling," the parties' "feelings or perspective" toward the separation might change. The spouses agreed to do "whatever is necessary" to try to save their marriage. The agreement contained specific provisions for counseling, including the dates when the parties would "review in earnest the status of their marital relationship by meeting . . . with or through their respective attorneys, marriage counselors or clergymen." A specific clause providing for future conciliation was essential.[32]

However, just as couples should not separate without the guiding hand of legal and behavioral experts, so too Kohut believed that beleaguered spouses should not attempt "dangerous . . . unprepared reconciliations." The beneficent apparatus of law and social science was especially needed if the parties wished to end their separation, since generally marital partners were "incapable and ineffective in resolving their differences by themselves." Distressed wives and husbands who signed such agreements pledged to "steadfastly refrain" from a precipitous reconciliation, especially if "for the sole purpose of satisfying sexual desires." The therapeutic agreements aimed to help afflicted couples make "a success of their separation" by reconciling, but only under professional supervision.[33]

Nor were incompatibility statutes acceptable to the advocates of therapeutic divorce. None of the states providing this ground had established adequate mechanisms to investigate the assertion of incompatibility. Even though some appellate courts had tethered incompatibility to notions of fault, the easy pathway to consent divorce allowed by the fault regime discouraged the use of this divorce alternative. Moreover, therapeutic divorce champions believed that apparent incompatibility inhered in every marriage, "and its emergence is not so much a signal to quit as the indication that the task of mutual adaptation is about to begin."[34] As with living-apart statutes, the divorce ground of incompatibility failed because it bypassed the essential therapeutic commitment and allowed marriages to end without expert consultation. In the postwar era, Christopher Lasch observed, "enlightened opinion . . . identified itself with the medicalization of society; the substitution of medical and psychiatric authority for the authority of parents, priests, and lawgivers, now condemned as representatives of discredited authoritarian modes of discipline." Alexander regarded therapeutic divorce as an overdue "medicalization" of one of society's most pressing problems.[35]

The Social Control Origins of the Family Court

The lessons learned by the merger of legal compulsion and social science expertise in the juvenile court were not lost on those who sought to expand the court's jurisdiction to the whole range of failing families. As early as 1917 the National Probation Association adopted a resolution recommending the organization of "Family Courts" on the juvenile court model. Such courts should discourage "legal formality and delay" while encompassing "ample probation departments" as well as "psychopathic labs sufficiently equipped to conduct the necessary scientific investigations."[36]

During the interwar period the reformers' faith in social science experts increased as their trust in the traditional legal system eroded even further. The new institution they dreamed of would dispense with the "traditional furnishings of the usual court room," disregard "customary legal procedure," and even discourage lawyers from participating at all. A completely revamped court needed a new name: "Family Court" won out over more colorful appellations, such as "Bureau of Family Adjustment" and Ben Lindsey's utopian and antibureaucratic term, "House of Human Welfare."[37]

Many attributes of the envisioned family tribunal were borrowed directly from the earlier court's renovations. Juvenile court judges almost immediately had redesigned the courtroom to deemphasize legalism. Adopting an extremely loose chancery procedure, the children's court bypassed traditional legal rules. As for the antipathy toward lawyers, Minnesota juvenile court judge Grier Orr exulted that in his courtroom "lawyers do not do very much . . . and I do not believe I can recall an instance where the same attorney came back a second time; he found it was useless for him to appear."[38] In Quintin Johnstone's estimation, lawyers "are generally so uninformed on juvenile court methods and juvenile care facilities that they can perform no important function in delinquency cases." In discussing the ideology of the juvenile court, David J. Rothman noted that disregard for the amenities of common law disposition was a positive value for the reformers. He remarked that in "almost every anecdote that judges or other proponents recounted about the workings of the court, a gentle and clever judge persuaded a stubborn or recalcitrant offender to 'fess up,' to tell the truth. Obviously this represented, not a violation of the individual's right against self-incrimination, but the first step of the delinquent toward rehabilitation."[39]

The same impatience for procedural niceties characterized the advocates of therapeutic divorce, who frequently pooh-poohed concerns about the use of coercive procedures in family courts. The sainted end of preserving the central institution of American life justified the tainted means of dishonest therapy and devious social control. The reformers justified their deviation from the canons of Anglo-American litigation standards in two ways. First, they soft-pedaled the coercive aspects of therapeutic divorce, insisting on such oxymorons as "gentle judicial coercion." Second, they argued that since the traditional legal canons had failed to save marriages, the family court represented a new and necessary beginning in American domestic relations.

Authority in family courts would lie, not in the musty tomes of precedent, but in the fresh face of science. The divorce petition was to be "interpreted as an expression of social difficulty which calls for expert help."[40] In the operation of the family court, Judge Alexander proposed handing the scalpel to therapeutic professionals, thus jettisoning not only the party-driven adversary process but also the reliance on case precedent and judicial review. No possible guidance could be derived from the rule elucidation and factual exploration of prior cases: therapeutic divorce would deal with each case as a new individualized reclamation project. By the same token appellate review would be rendered superfluous. Either the parties would have received the divorce they initially requested, or they would have reconciled. The work of a family court could not be appealed.

Although judges would still preside over the new court, their internal command would be markedly circumscribed. An enlightened judge, proclaimed a New York City magistrate in 1934, "must know how absurd it is for any human being to substitute his own opinions and assumptions for the professional findings of experts. . . . When knowledge in fields other than the law is necessary to reach an intelligent decision, only those who are expert in them should be permitted to have a deciding voice." In the words of a modern student of the twentieth-century expansion of state power, this "casual attitude toward therapeutic power suggests . . . the impact of science-as-ideology."[41]

Confidence in the benevolent power of experts, whether in social science, medicine, or psychology, characterized the American attitude toward all social problems. Scientific techniques were believed to inhabit "a world that was beyond popular passions." The new reliance on science trumped traditional mores in fields as far apart as child rearing and constitutional interpretation. Benjamin Spock's *Baby and Child Care* reflected an elevation of scientific sense over customary nostrums. And the Supreme Court's citation of social science studies in its 1954 decision declaring school segregation unconstitutional reflected at least a bow toward this power. Alexander's family court was fundamentally of a piece with a culture in which experts "took over the role of psychic healer."[42]

The family court and therapeutic divorce movement blossomed quickly, bloomed brightly, then died abruptly. This curious chronology may best be understood in the context of a broader pattern of fitful integration of law and the social sciences. The drive for family courts garnered support so long as its call for a merger of law and psychology remained novel, exciting, and unexamined. Therapeutic divorce rapidly lost momentum when its premises were finally held up for review, and American society realized that it did not wish its judges to act as marriage counselors or its psychologists to have judicial power.

Calls for interdisciplinary cooperation pervaded legal texts, law reviews, and bar association journals beginning in the decade of the Second World War. "The temper of the times," an Ohio trial judge observed, "is unquestionably favorable to emphasizing the sociological aspects in domestic relations cases. Members of the bench and bar must guide the application of this trend." Sidney P. Simpson and Ruth Field stressed the "necessity for functionalism in the law, a functionalism which must be implemented by the findings of social science." Charles H. Leclaire assessed the goal of the enterprise as improving the "entire marriage-family-divorce-sociological-legal relationship." Prophets of disciplinary colle-giality broadcast the identical message dozens of times.[43]

The clamor for interdisciplinary collaboration grew so vociferous, how-ever, that it emphasized the distance to be covered as much as the hunger for professional fusion. Alexander acknowledged that the law "has tradi-tionally shown considerable reluctance to stray off its own reservation." For all of Karl Llewellyn's advice that "it pays to be neighborly," coopera-tive efforts were unimpressive in scope or number.[44] Robert Kramer, a participant in the 1959 Institute of Family Law conference at Duke Uni-versity, gauged the scholarly outpouring with a skeptical eye: "Scarcely a year passes where a learned journal of sociology or law, or whatever field you pick, fails to carry a brave article with a manifesto that what we need is interdisciplinary research." Yet, Kramer concluded, very few joint proj-ects were attempted. Four years later a former president of the Russell Sage Foundation admitted the rarity of "planned cooperation" between behavioral scientists and lawyers but insisted that a "good start has been made."[45]

In his provocative "Why Lawyers Are Dissatisfied with the Social Sci-ences," Samuel M. Fahr provided a philosophical and methodological ba-sis for the interdisciplinary unease. Although he addressed the particular tension between law and social science in criminology, his remarks had broader application: "Fundamentally the social scientist is culturally ori-ented, and a man of statistics; whereas the lawyer tends to look at matters from the standpoint of an individual client. On the other hand, and herein lies the paradox, most social scientists seem to focus on the criminal and not upon his act; whereas the traditional approach of the law has been to concentrate upon the act."[46] Communication between the disciplines was arduous enough; cooperative projects proved intensely difficult to orga-nize. Alexander's plea that law and the social sciences "get off our high horses, and bury our interprofessional jealousies" was greeted with only lip-sync affirmation.[47]

A similar pattern of exploration and retrenchment can be seen in the treatment of social sciences within legal education. The ideal of a law casebook developed by Christopher Columbus Langdell and James Barr Ames in the late nineteenth century continued to dominate until the middle of the twentieth. Among domestic relations casebooks, this "pure" approach, devoid of all information but that contained within appellate opinions, represented the norm. These texts, usually labeled "Cases on . . ." or "The Law of . . . ,"[48] contained no noncase materials[49] and consisted simply of a selection of cases,[50] thematically arranged.[51] These texts distilled the orthodox formalism of family law.

A rival approach developed at Columbia University in the late 1920s, as a result of extensive law faculty studies in legal education, which in turn had been influenced by sociological jurisprudence and legal realism. Columbia law professor Albert C. Jacobs and University of Michigan sociologist Robert C. Angell produced a report on family law teaching which called for a research-based sociological approach. In 1933 Jacobs produced the first domestic relations casebook on this new model, in which the cases were liberally interlaced with sociological materials.[52] While subsequent editions of Jacobs's domestic relations text retained a flavoring of sociological materials, the movement for integration passed by the somewhat static originator, so that by the 1950s Jacobs's tome was referred to as "a reasonably traditional law book." That decade saw the integration of law and social science emerge as the "slogan of the day."[53]

But integration may not have passed the epigrammatic stage. An article in the 1950 *Journal of Legal Education* noted that the interdisciplinary focus "has been attempted only in some of the 'progressive' schools." Elsewhere, the paucity of faculty expertise and student interest had stalled the effort. Indeed, the 1961 edition of Jacobs's once-revolutionary casebook shifted from a law-and-society focus to one of legal craft, with the result that sociological studies, although "enlightening," had to "yield place to technical matter."[54] A "second explosion" of social science information in casebooks was presaged by Fowler V. Harper's idiosyncratic *Problems of the Family* in 1952. Harper split his text roughly in half between legal materials and those drawn from anthropology, sociology, and psychiatry.[55] The full flush of a new consciousness in domestic relations texts arrived with the 1960s, accompanied by the widespread, if belated, realization that a family law practitioner "must be something of a psychologist, psychiatrist, sociologist, and negotiator."[56]

This background helps us understand the ambivalent relationship between law and science in the middle decades of this century. While American society steadily yielded increasing acreage to the claims of science, the legal profession sported a more complex attitude, "simultaneously skeptical and unbelievably gullible" about the authority of social science and the nature of the accommodation required of the law.[57] This mixed legacy left a large imprint upon the history of the family court and the revolution in divorce law.

Honest and Dishonest Divorce

National attention was focused on therapeutic divorce by the Report of the Legal Section of the National Conference on Family Life, presented at the White House in May 1948. Paul Alexander had been joined in developing the report by Reginald Heber Smith, the grand old warrior of the legal aid movement. Smith had popularized their findings a few months earlier in a widely cited article in the *Atlantic*. In "Dishonest Divorce," Smith did not mince words about the scope of the problem: "In the whole administration of justice there is nothing that even remotely can compare in terms of rottenness with divorce proceedings." He asserted that divorce had spun crazily out of sync with society and must be controlled by a greater reliance on creative use of legal authority. "The law," Smith reminded his readers, "is the most powerful instrument for social control that civilization has been able to evolve." The weight of the law should, however, support the agendas of nonlegal experts, for the questions of broken marriages and divorces were primarily social, economic, medical, and spiritual in nature. Smith pointed out that the investigations necessary to determine marital viability could not be accomplished in a legal system in which practically all divorces were uncontested.[58]

Therapeutic divorce reformers often railed against the fault regime for allowing one spouse to present, pro forma, the prearranged verdict agreed to by the parties. Under the premises of the adversary system, the absence of one party simply made it easier for the other to satisfy the burden of proof. Because therapeutic divorce operated under entirely different suppositions, the attendance of both parties should be required in order to facilitate the mandatory investigation and counseling.[59] Judges should be "unshackled" and allowed to order social intervention more aggressively, since the law "steadily demonstrates a vital capacity to regulate life in many of its aspects and activities." As N. Ruth Wood argued in a 1949 article in the *Virginia Law Weekly*, the divorce reforms were intended, not to make divorce easier or more difficult, but "to substitute truth for deception . . . and to give the courts real opportunity to prevent marriage failures by conciliation and treatment, rather than to restrict them to the punishment of such failures by divorce."[60]

Belief in the impulsivity and loss of judgment of would-be divorcers justified the use of coercion, an ever-present element in therapeutic divorce. Since, in Alexander's words, couples in conflict suffered from an "utter lack of insight" into the factors underlying what they—often mistakenly—believed to be an irreparable marriage breakdown, they needed the firm hand of a benevolent family court to help them "think straight." While most therapeutic-minded judges aimed to reduce to a minimum the lawyer's role as an advocate in family court, Alexander took a different tack. Attorneys had an "indispensable" role as an "effective ally of the court in 'selling' the best plan to his client."[61] Traditional advocacy, in Alexander's view, must be subordinated to the call for therapeutic adjustment. The new ideology constrained not only the court and its social science experts but even private divorce lawyers, shifting their loyalty to a new client, the state-ordered marital unit.

To this end several proposals were made embodying radically nontraditional views of the nature of advocacy and of the divorce hearing itself. Domestic relations expert John S. Bradway suggested a shift away from proof of fault grounds to broader social questions. At a divorce trial, the issues to be tried would include the following questions:

> 1. Why are these particular spouses unable to live amicably together as normal married people do?
> 2. Will the parties be sufficiently better off in any demonstrable fashion after the divorce than they were before?
> 3. How will the process of granting a divorce affect the security to which other members of the group may be morally entitled?
> 4. Will some other solution than a divorce decree be more adequate to the particular problems?[62]

Another proposal replaced not only the nature of the issues to be tried but also the composition of the jury. Raphael Lemkin argued that divorce cases should be tried by a panel containing experts from the behavioral sciences as well as "lay people with experience in family life." The emphasis on the lawyer's reorientation toward social work culminated in Bradway's proposal that the legal profession develop a new specialty, the "family lawyer," whose client would be the family as a whole, not any of its members.[63]

At a 1952 conference on divorce law at the University of Chicago, Alexander defended his use of compulsory referrals for therapy in family court cases by analogy to juvenile court practice. Children did not always willingly attend juvenile court and often had to be taken into custody by police. Despite that coercive beginning, juveniles often benefited from social casework. The same procedure could work with divorce-minded adults. As Alexander had earlier phrased it, with his customary directness, "We suggest handling our unhappy and delinquent spouses much as we handle our delinquent children."[64] He dreamed of transforming the divorce court "from a morgue into a hospital."[65] This change would require a substantial revision of philosophy and personnel. The philosophical milieu would copy the jurisprudence of the juvenile court. The staff of the new family courts would expand to include psychiatrists, clinical psychologists, social and psychiatric caseworkers, and marriage counselors.

But the most dramatic metamorphosis would have to occur within the judiciary. Case law specialists on the domestic relations bench would be replaced by judges trained in and sensitive to a whole array of the social and medical sciences, from community organization to psychiatry. Traditional standards of judging, in which the offense precedes rehabilitation, would be replaced by canons requiring rehabilitation in an effort to prevent the commission of the offense of divorce. Advocates of therapeutic divorce saw little conflict between coercion and therapy. In Alexander's view the promise of a divorce procedure freed from guilt and sin was worth the price of some judicial compulsion in the direction of the preservation of the bedrock institution of American society. The ultimate coercion, of course, was the vast increase in the power of the court. Petitioners would not even be able to apply for a divorce without the court's consent. Thus, divorce by party consent (the de facto popular system) would end. Moreover, a divorce decree would be granted only if the social investigation, plus the court's own inquiry, "compelled the conclusion that the marriage could no longer be useful to the spouses, the children, or the state."[66]

England also experienced a therapeutic divorce movement in the 1950s and 1960s, with all its Alexandrian components. Indeed, the calls for social work intervention and away from formal legal grounds sounded much the same on both sides of the Atlantic. A noted English law professor remarked on the broad agreement that divorce courts "have an investigatory function entirely absent in ordinary civil cases." And a London magistrate and barrister expressed the impetuousness of divorce seekers in terms virtually identical to those of his American cousins: "A high proportion of those who wish to break up their home do so on impulse; by social help and organization . . . a large number of such people find out that their problems can be put right without breaking their marriages."[67]

In a 1960 address to the Family Law Section of the American Bar Association, Sir Eric Sachs, a high court judge, explained the reconciliation program promoted by the English bench. At the magistrate's court level, probation officers intervened to attempt a reconciliation, often working with the Marriage Guidance Council, a nationwide voluntary organization.[68] The vice chair of the Divorce Law Reform Union, a marriage law society founded in 1906, presented a different program at the same conference. Stephen Keleny called for a "new equitable gloss" to be superimposed on the existing fault grounds, allowing the courts discretion to dissolve marriages that had absolutely broken down. This novel equitable tool would have, however, two edges. Fault grounds would be bypassed, but the new divorce regime would display the pennant of a revived morality. For the court to grant a divorce under the proposed dispensation, it had to be convinced of the "petitioner's worthiness."[69]

The discretion to grant new divorces brought with it the corresponding power to deny old ones, even where the fault grounds had been satisfactorily established. Recognizing the porous texture of fault and the reality of mutual consent, Professor Kahn-Freund insisted that "there are situations in which the court must be able to say 'no' though both spouses want a divorce."[70] On both sides of the Atlantic, courts were gearing up to say no in different ways. Some saw more than a nominal conflict between the canons of marriage therapy and the directive strategy of the new family court. This clash is clearly viewed in the histories of some experiments in counseling and conciliation.

"Gentle Judicial Coercion"

Convinced of the purity of their goal and the benevolence of their methods, the advocates of the therapeutic state proposed to sacrifice personal autonomy on the altar of divorce reform. Sociologist Eugene Litwak, for instance, saw no role conflict in the operational methodology of the family courts. The "basic premise of law as therapy," he observed, "is that people seek divorce because of serious emotional problems. Therefore, any legal procedure seeking to control divorce should provide that the spouses see a therapist."[71] But were therapy and compulsion compatible? An examination of the workings of the Los Angeles Conciliation Court affords an opportunity to examine this issue in context.

The conciliation court was the brainchild of Ben Lindsey.[72] Ever the heterodox, Lindsey believed in automatic divorce for childless couples (who should practice birth control until they were certain they wanted children) but was quite chary of granting the privilege after the family had expanded. He once told a divorce-seeking couple that his court was "concerned with the right of your children to you, rather than your right to your children."[73] The conciliation court was designed to work as a "pre-divorce" tribunal. A wife or husband who found their marriage in jeopardy could file a petition for a conciliation hearing. No divorce petition could then be filed for thirty days. In the meantime, the court clerk notified the other spouse of the conciliation hearing. If he or she ignored the notice, the court could compel attendance. From that point on, however, participation was voluntary, although the pressure of early intervention was aimed to induce reconciliation. In the words of a reporter studying matrimonial litigation, the Los Angeles Conciliation Court represented the "farthest any American court has gone in the direction of forcing couples to attempt a reconciliation before they may get a divorce."[74]

Lindsey, who was seventy years old when the California legislature adopted his plan for the conciliation court in Los Angeles, never served on it. The court achieved its period of greatest influence under the leadership of Judge Louis H. Burke in the 1950s. Key to Burke's operation was his development of a comprehensive "Reconciliation Agreement" to be signed by the couple. As described by one of Burke's successors, the agreement contained twenty-five pages covering "practically every facet of married life." Appended to the basic agreement were up to eight special form agreements covering particularized items such as the presence of third parties in the home, stepchildren, an agreement for one of the spouses to attend Alcoholics Anonymous, or the termination of an extramarital romantic liaison.[75]

The original appointment letter, signed by the judge, contained an admonition to the summoned party: "We trust you will keep this appointment voluntarily, and avoid the necessity of requiring the Court to issue a subpoena."[76] If the court succeeded in persuading the couple to attempt a rapprochement, it would draw up a reconciliation agreement containing a series of specific commitments about the couple's future behavior. The terms of this contract (which included abundant sermonizing by the court) provide a snapshot not only into the heart of therapeutic divorce but also into a social system which the reformers were desperately trying to recapture. Couched in the rhetoric of therapeutic divorce, the Los Angeles reconciliation agreement is a fascinating cultural document which at one level points backwards toward the idyllic image of conservative utopia, while its very terms reveal the seeds of family conflict that are about to burst any hope of restoring the institutional family.

A typical reconciliation agreement opened with the couple's admission that their marriage "has become sick" and that they "should go to a professionally trained person for help."[77] After these ideological mea culpas, the parties formally agreed "that they will not accuse, blame or nag each other about things which have happened in the past." A reiteration of the gendered social order followed. The wife agreed that housework, meal-preparation, child care, and maintainance of the "inside of the home" were her responsibilities. The husband took charge of financially supporting the family, in addition to caring for the "outside of the home."

Despite a gesture toward the existence of working women, noting that in those cases the husband "must share to a larger extent in the work of the home," the task of sustaining the traditional domestic order fell on the wife.[78] Women who refused a dependent role were "robbed of their full dignity." The inequality of the burdens is apparent in the paragraph labeled, ironically, "Husband's Role in the Family":

> It will always be true in marriage that the greatest giving will be required on the part of the wife. Through pregnancy and child-raising

she loses the independence which the man continues to retain. When today we find a woman who is reluctant to face the loss of such independence it is generally because she does not trust the man to be loving, confident and considerate, particularly at the time when she must, of necessity, depend solely upon him. Generally speaking, a good woman is happy to go through a great amount of sacrifice for her husband and family, as long as his step is firm, his love tender and his faith in her and in himself is strong.

Other provisions in the agreement commanded a mutual effort to share interests and hobbies, respect for the privacy of each other's mail, and avoidance of gambling, excessive drinking, and sarcastic language. The couple promised to make new friends among other married couples, so as to remove themselves from the unhealthy influence of their former circles of single friends. Conceding the importance of religion, the couple agreed to attend church regularly and to recite a family prayer daily. The document included rules for mealtimes, social occasions, personal appearance, and relationships with relatives. The husband accepted his responsibility to take his mate out for social activities, within the constraints of the family budget, at least once a week.

Clauses relating to child rearing blended the sublime with the banal. After a preface pointing out that there are "no dull moments in parenthood," the parents acknowledged that their child is "the handiwork of God" and pledged to think and speak of the child as "our" child, never as "my" child or "your" child. The enormity of the task of child rearing was brought home by the declaration that an "estimated . . . 80 percent of what a child is, or turns out to be, is attributable directly to his parents." Numerous specific rules on discipline preceded a discussion of a sound family relationship based on obedience through love.

Wife and husband agreed to moderation in sexual intercourse, which was spelled out as "twice a week" under "normal conditions," not spelled out. The agreement contained a primer on the importance of "'lovemaking' as a prelude to sexual intercourse," because of the different physiological proclivities of each sex, which were explained in detail. Oblivious to the findings of Alfred Kinsey, the agreement limited its discussion to sexual stereotypes, contrasting a man's sexual susceptibility to the "slightest stimulation" with a woman's slow "passion side." For a woman, the agreement asserted, "physical union . . . is out of the question until her physical desire is sufficiently aroused and her glandular processes have prepared her body for such union." Unless a woman "has been properly prepared," sexual intercourse will not bring her "to the necessary climax and consequent release of nerve tension." The husband was warned that "repeated acts of intercourse which do not result in satisfaction for the wife become unpleasant." For her part, the wife agreed "not to act like a patient undergoing a physical examination." Conjugal sexuality thus reified the gendered universe. A wife was dependent on her husband for the financial support of herself and the children, for her social life, and also for her sexual satisfaction. Her sexual duty before conception consisted of refraining from behaving as if she were on an awkward gynecological visit.

Financial planning was not neglected. The wife was designated the family treasurer. Each party agreed to a set amount of spending money each week, whose purpose was specified. The wife's "pin money" could be spent on cosmetics and the beauty parlor, while her spouse would allocate his "pocket money" for snacks and golf expenses. The agreement's final page contained a rare paean to married love, remarking that "wise couples will not suffer their mutual attachment to become casual and commonplace under the spell of monotony, or to languish with neglect, or to degenerate into mere selfish passion." On the contrary, enlightened wives and husbands "will realize that in this life they possess nature's most valued treasure—the loyal love of a human heart."

Unlike the customary method for regulating contracts, which relies on party implementation, the court's contempt power directly enforced the terms of the reconciliation agreement. Indeed, the wife and husband acknowledged that violation of the agreement's specifications might subject the offender to imprisonment and a fine. Moreover, the agreement could not be rescinded by the parties. It remained in force until further order of the court. Judge Burke claimed he used the contempt powers "very carefully." In the first biennial period, for example, twenty contempt proceedings were instituted, resulting in jail terms for seven husbands and three wives. In addition to punishment for breach of the reconciliation agreement, the court occasionally placed restraining orders on paramours or relatives who interfered with the harmony of the family unit.

In one instance reported in the *Saturday Evening Post,* Burke jailed a husband and his lover for five days after they had spent a night together. Since the husband's inamorata had endorsed the reconciliation agreement, agreeing to stay away from the husband, the judge felt justified in incarcerating both adulterers. "After that," remarked a divorce counselor in Judge Burke's court, "people took these agreements seriously."[79] The threat of coercion hung heavy over the proceedings. As a court counselor elaborated to a wife unsure whether to believe her unfaithful husband's promises to reform: "Your husband has agreed to promise in writing that he will never consort with the lady again under penalty of going to jail. This is how sincere he feels about it. For a man of his standing, the penalty of jail assures you that his promise is not one that has been lightly made."[80]

Did the "gentle judicial coercion" work? The statistics are virtually undecipherable and the methodological problems likely insurmountable.[81] How was reconciliation to be measured? Did failure to file a divorce suit for one year signify that the parties had reconciled? The primary problem was that, even dealing with a population in which one partner (at least) had expressed an interest in staving off the breakup of the marriage, the therapeutic divorce advocates were unable to show that their coercive gentleness succeeded. Robert J. Levy, serving as the reporter for the Special Committee on Divorce of the National Conference of Commissioners on Uniform State Laws, went further, stating that the "prevailing opinion seems to be that court-connected conciliation services are a waste of time and money."[82]

The Uneasy Union of Marriage Counseling and the Law

The profession of marriage counseling emerged in the 1930s but for years was plagued by the paucity of marriage counselors as well as by the proliferation of mountebanks. As late as 1949 an article in *Woman's Home Companion* remarked that marriage counseling was "a new idea for most of us" and proceeded to outline its rudimentary principles, while advising its female readership to beware the "thousands of quacks" employed in the field.[83] The same issue carried an article conveying the British viewpoint. The piece by David R. Mace, the general secretary of the National Marriage Council in England, reflected the striving for exclusivity typical of budding professions in its complaint over the unauthorized practice of marriage counseling: "The average woman would never think of doctoring her neighbor's tooth or offering to represent her in a lawsuit. But she will cheerfully and with great confidence embark upon the treatment of her neighbor's marital problems."[84]

The apprehension about marital counseling fakery grew to enormous proportions during the 1950s. In addition to the *Woman's Home Companion*, *Good Housekeeping* and *Cosmopolitan* warned consumers about "flamboyant" advertising, impossible guarantees of success, exorbitant fees, and the sharp tactic of insisting that the client sign up for a specific number of sessions in advance.[85] The *American Psychologist* estimated that 25,000 quack counselors earned more than $375 million in 1953, and the report was still being trumpeted ten years later in the *Saturday Evening Post* as "A Growing National Scandal."[86]

The demand for marriage counseling, from any source, appeared to be expanding faster than the supply in the 1950s and 1960s. A national study reported that while 42 percent of all Americans who sought professional mental health help in 1957 needed assistance with a marital problem, only 4 percent went to a marriage counselor. Clergy, physicians, psychologists, and lawyers were contacted far more often, probably reflecting the lack of professional marital counselors.[87] The rapid spread of an organization modeled on the twelve-step program for recovering alcoholics manifested the surging need for marital help. Divorcées Anonymous was the creation of Samuel Starr, a Chicago domestic relations lawyer who had found that "in practically every case" divorced persons "were sorry for the step they had taken."[88] Chapters of Starr's organization sprung up in many localities throughout the country, providing nonprofessional divorce counseling. The work of Divorcées Anonymous consisted primarily of divorce survivors relating the horror stories of their own experiences and proposing problem-solving alternatives to sinners on the brink. The guilt of those who had sinned was the key weapon in converting those about to fall into temptation.

These years also saw the propagation of the notion that divorce lawyers were pseudo-counselors, whose first goal should be the reconciliation of the troubled couple. John Mariano was the leading exponent of the view that attorneys should overcome their "litigious predisposition" and practice "therapeutic listening" to deal effectively with their divorce-seeking clients. Mariano advocated "juristic therapy," a listening technique for attorneys which served as "the infallible X-ray needed to guide the analyst out of the emotional neurosis into which the psychoneurotic spouse had fallen." [89]

Mariano's therapy was directive. In his view the attorney's client was not the individual but the marriage itself. Although Mariano subscribed to the broad goal of maintaining the individual as a "wholly integrated personality," he insisted that a psychoanalytic lawyer should aim at developing a "juristic evaluation which justifies maintaining the marriage." [90] Although Mariano maintained that members of the bar should avoid practicing "psychiatry without a license," the line between prescribed and proscribed therapeutic activity was difficult to fathom. The matrimonial attorney overheard shouting at the couple in his office, "Now, damn it, shut up. I'm telling you—you love each other," undoubtedly believed in his heart he was engaging in appropriate lawyerly therapy. And according to Mariano's directive guidelines, he was. [91]

Edward Pokorny, Detroit's longtime statutory divorce proctor, once achieved a reconciliation by ordering a couple to embrace and shoving them at each other. On another occasion a wife's mother interrupted a conference between Pokorny and the couple by taking a toy baseball bat and beating her screaming daughter on the rear end until Pokorny and the husband restrained her. "Curiously enough," Pokorny related, "that reconciled them." These circus tales do not a program make, although Pokorny's office claimed a 35 percent reconciliation rate. [92] Disputes over the mission of therapy lay at the heart of the conflict over the merger of counseling and the courts. In Utah the state-sanctioned marriage-counseling experiment came under fire from Judge Aldon J. Anderson, chair of the Judges' Advisory Committee on Marriage Counseling Services. Anderson testified before the State Legislative Council that an unbridgeable gap had opened between the courts and the marriage counselors. Utah's judges wanted the therapists to practice "directional counseling," in the belief that couples would benefit from explicit instructions. Since the marriage counselors had rebelled at that oxymoronic construction of their role, Judge Anderson recommended shutting down the whole project. He concluded that courts were no place for mental health programs.[93]

New Jersey's experience reveals another facet of coercive conciliation. In 1956 the state supreme court's Committee on Reconciliation proposed that "Family Counseling Services" be established under the jurisdiction of the chief probation officer. Aware of the unsavory implications of that juxtaposition for couples under marital stress, the committee at the same time recommended that the chief probation officer's title be changed. That same iron-fist-in-velvet-glove approach characterized New Jersey's attitude toward the voluntariness of conciliation. Initially, one of the parties was expected to seek help voluntarily, but if the efforts of the judge and the court staff to persuade the couple to seek the assistance of the Family Counseling Services failed, that "refusal should be met with an order requiring submission to the agency."[94]

No concerns were voiced as to the consequences of expanding state power over private lives. The end of reconciliation simply overwhelmed any queasiness as to the coercive means. Paul Alexander's philosophy found its articulation in the committee's rationale: "Compulsion in so personal a matter . . . may provoke resentment and tend to frustrate efforts to bring the parties together. But where neither spouse has sought conciliation before seeking to dissolve the marriage by court action, should it be assumed that the situation is hopeless and allow the litigation to proceed in ordinary course? Or should an attempt be made by mandate as a condition to institution of the suit?"[95] Following precedents in California and England, the New Jersey legislature adopted the committee's recommendation and established quasi-mandatory marriage counseling as a concomitant of divorce actions in two districts for a three-year period beginning in September 1957.[96] Within three years the experiment was abandoned as a massive failure. Of 2,293 cases referred to the divorce counselors, only 57 had been reconciled, a failure rate of 97.3 percent.[97]

A few commentators believed that marriage counseling served a purpose in demonstrating the futility of reconciliation in particular cases and thus assisting in the couple's adjustment to divorce.[98] This conversion of marriage counseling to divorce counseling was far from the minds of the family court advocates, but it demonstrates the difficulty of limiting any profession to the preset rubric of an interdisciplinary project. Marital counseling's unruliness—as viewed from the perspective of the advocates of therapeutic divorce—showed its practitioners' greater sensitivity to its clientele than to any commitment to reconcile the irreconcilable.

Therapeutic divorce was a quintessential cultural paradigm, combining the manager with the therapist, archetypes which together "largely define the outlines of twentieth-century American culture."[99] But in the 1960s therapeutic divorce reached a crossroads. Despite the reformers' prodigious efforts, most family courts were still hamstrung by what they perceived as an antiquated legal system which preserved the shell of the adversary process and at the same time prevented the complete absorption of divorce into the therapeutic project. Some observers believed that the movement had run its course without achieving any major breakthroughs; others felt that the critical mass would be reached in England or California, and reform on therapeutic grounds would spark the long-awaited revolution in preserving marriage. The last chapter details the final thrust of therapeutic divorce, a series of turns which nearly realized success in both England and California, only to fail completely when the final shape of the reforms finally conceded the overwhelming triumph of unrepentant individualism.

14. Men on "Alimony Row" in 1941 thank Chicago judge Rudolph Desort for releasing them after each had served six months in jail for failure to pay alimony and child support. (The Bettmann Archive)

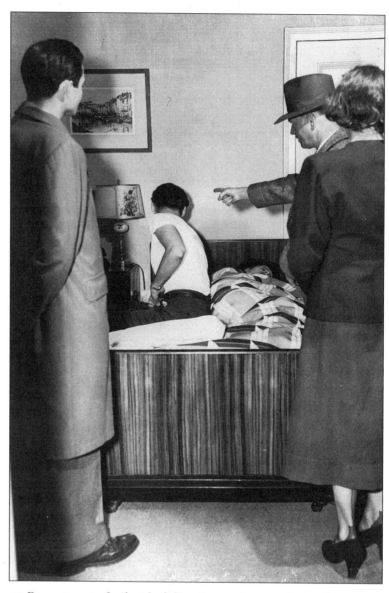

15. Reenactment of a "hotel adultery" scenario: a professional core-spondent plays the role of the "other woman" in bed, while a detective and other witnesses stage a raid on the complicitous husband sitting on the bed. (The Bettmann Archive)

16. Marilyn Monroe as she appeared in court in 1954 to divorce Joe DiMaggio. The hearing on Monroe's pro forma claim of "extreme cruelty" lasted less than 10 minutes. (The Bettmann Archive)

17. Noted "therapeutic divorce" advocate Judge Paul W. Alexander takes the oath of office in Toledo. (Family Court Center, Toledo, Ohio; Toledo *Blade*)

18. College professor Paul Henson, chair of Fathers United for Equal Rights, protests the unfairness of alimony payments in Maryland in the 1970s. (The Bettmann Archive)

19. The elusive promise of pain-free divorce is renewed in this freshly divorced couple's car. (The Bettmann Archive)

SIX

THE TRIUMPH OF NAKED DIVORCE

Love, the quest; marriage, the conquest;
divorce, the inquest.

Helen Rowland, Reflections of a Bachelor Girl

In codifying its laws in 1872, California provided for the full panoply of fault in divorce grounds: adultery, extreme cruelty, willful desertion, habitual intemperance, willful neglect, and conviction of a felony.[1] The only statutory deviation from culpability came in 1941, when the legislature authorized divorces in cases of incurable insanity. In the 1950s and 1960s, on the eve of the most dramatic reform in American divorce law, the Golden State calmly reflected the major trends in national divorce patterns. Its divorce rate, though higher than the national average, was on a par with its western neighbors. California had not experimented with incompatibility or living apart statutes, but its supreme court had practically gutted recriminatory defenses.[2] In typical ten-minute court hearings, 95 percent of divorce complainants blithely related their prefabricated stories of how their spouses' "extreme cruelty" had destroyed their marriage. This statutory requirement could be met by the plaintiff's mere assertion that her spouse was "cold and indifferent," which caused her to become "nervous and upset."[3]

Although Marilyn Monroe's 1954 divorce from Joe DiMaggio elicited a deluge of publicity, it employed the minimalist legal procedure common to the vast majority of cases. Monroe's page-and-a-half complaint alleged that she had suffered "grievous mental suffering and anguish" at DiMaggio's hands. Her lawyer casually told the press that the extreme cruelty charge was mere boilerplate and could refer to anything as "common as political differences." At the divorce hearing Monroe testified that DiMaggio "wouldn't speak to me for five to seven days at a time—sometimes longer, ten days." She also complained that the former Yankee Clipper told her "Stop nagging me!" and would not permit her to have many visitors. Their marital relationship, she told the court, consisted largely of "coldness and indifference." After fewer than eight minutes of such testimony, the court granted her a divorce on the grounds of her spouse's "extreme cruelty."[4]

According to Herma Hill Kay, a leading figure in the no-fault movement, by the 1960s "it was impossible to make divorce easier in California than it already was."[5] California appellate justice Macklin Fleming confessed with wry humor that he had been "probably one of the few lawyers in California who ever succeeded in losing an uncontested divorce." He recounted the story of one couple who decided to get divorced and retained his services. Fleming filed the complaint in the wife's name and obtained a default judgment against the husband. However, on the day of the court hearing, the wife found herself unable to utter "anything mean about her husband or about the extreme cruelties our complaint alleged he had inflicted upon her." Fleming still believed he could have obtained a divorce, despite the total absence of proof, but unfortunately the judge "didn't approve of divorces and went no further in granting them than the letter of the law demanded." Fleming lost his undefended case—in which he represented both sides—and promised himself never again to take a divorce case to court "unless the wife was prepared to swear she would cut out her husband's heart with a steak knife and serve it to her children for Sunday brunch."[6] Fleming's hyperbole underlined his frustration at failing to persuade his client to mumble even the meager words of mild regret that would have passed the jurisprudential test of "extreme cruelty." Given this ease of divorce, it was not surprising that when Governor Edmund G. Brown appointed a commission in 1966 to begin a "concerted assault on the high incidence of divorce in our society and its often tragic consequences,"[7] many panicking California couples rushed to the courts in order to get divorced before the anticipated legal tightening.[8]

Across the Atlantic, the Church of England wielded its declining moral authority as best it could in favor of one last stand against divorce. Under the auspices of the archbishop of Canterbury, the church's plan called for a full-service family court, with a coterie of social science experts ready to conduct a comprehensive "inquest" on every allegedly deceased marriage.[9] Heavily influenced by the report of the archbishop's group, California's reformers proposed a similar mix of coercive therapy and legal hurdles to divorce.

Those Californians who anticipated that the reformers would try to raise the legal threshold correctly read the tea leaves of therapeutic divorce. But those who plunged into divorce as if to beat the clock lacked confidence in their dissolution-minded cohorts. Informal divorcing under cover of the fault system had outflanked the conservative reforms throughout the century in both England and America. In this final sally the contradictions inherent in compulsory conciliation combined with a rejection of the hefty price tag for family courts to yield a divorce paradigm in new clothes. The Anglo-American no-fault revolution was dressed in the raiment of the therapeutic salvation of marriage. But the result was naked divorce.

Objections to Utopia

In 1953, at a symposium on the interprofessional approach to family problems, maverick law professor Quintin Johnstone warned the participants that despite the popular appeal of family courts, their spread faced strong opposition. Johnstone listed the objections: the high cost of the super-staffed tribunals, lawyers' distrust of social workers and resentment at the potential loss of fees in a nonadversary procedure, the moral and ethical opposition of some members of the bar and some religious groups to compulsory counseling, and the sense that courthouse attempts to reconcile parties already committed to divorce came too late.[10] Although he was mocked at the time, Johnstone turned out to be prescient.

The opposition to compulsory conciliation first came from psychiatrists who objected to directed counseling. Believing the norms of their profession compromised in the quest for preserving marriages, some protested. As Thomas French explained, it was not a psychiatrist's business "either to try to save a marriage or to try to destroy it."[11] Far from dovetailing with the reformers' premise that divorcers were impulsive and childish, the canon of individual empowerment began with the opposite presumption, that psychotherapy assisted adults to walk their own road to personal independence.

Over and again, the advocates of reform acknowledged the tension between therapeutic divorce and other norms of therapy, only to fall back on a mélange of ideological hope and anecdotal experience, clumsily cobbled together with reference to the effectiveness of the juvenile court in dealing with recalcitrant children. Emily Mudd, the director of the Marriage Council of Philadelphia, responded to Dr. French's concerns by arguing that a skilled psychiatrist could assist couples in generating the motivation to reconcile.[12] Insisting that treatment could begin with reluctant patients, Mudd noted that since "the most prevalent reason for divorce is the lack of maturity of one or both partners . . . how can we expect the most childish and immature voluntarily to seek help?"[13] Sarah Schaar, head of the legal department of Chicago's Jewish Family and Community Center, stressed her "very definite feeling" that compulsory counseling worked. Paul Alexander remarked that just as police herded juveniles into court, so courts should steer couples into counseling. He expected "respectable case work" from this procedure. New York City judge Anna M. Kross responded to Dr. French's remarks in asserting that she had "yet to find the person who, in the final analysis, is not willing to accept help."[14]

Dr. French was outgunned in this exchange, and his views remained in the minority for years. In 1961 the ABA's Family Law Section Subcommittee on the Conciliation Court reported the continuing controversy about the propriety of strong-armed conciliation. While noting that many social workers found the tactics repugnant or ineffective, the committee insisted that "experience has proved that what might be termed 'gentle judicial coercion' plays an important role in effecting reconciliations."[15] Ultimately, however, the contrary views prevailed, resulting in a sharper distinction between the role of judges and that of behavioral scientists. While perhaps not entirely subscribing to Thomas Szasz's view of compulsory counseling as "moral Fascism,"[16] the mental health and legal professions began to demarcate their boundaries more clearly. Counseling took place away from the courthouse. Judges did not pretend to practice social work. This cleavage reflected a return to the recognition of the antipodal natures of judging and counseling, and it sounded the death knell for Alexandrian family courts.

"Bob-Haired, Flat-Heeled Social Workers"

Paul Alexander enjoyed telling the story of the older judge who thoroughly disliked the notion of merging social science and law: "[He] told me that I was wasting the taxpayers' money in hiring those bob-haired, flat-heeled social workers; that their reports were illegal and that I would get myself in trouble if I used them." That older judge was not the only member of the legal profession who feared that family problems would become the "domain of impractical, theoretical and inexperienced social workers."[17] Lawyers' attacks on the family court ranged from petty dislike of social workers and peevishness over the loss of fees should divorce clients reconcile to serious concerns that compulsory counseling unconstitutionally burdened an individual's right to privacy.[18] Juvenile courts already had become "social workers' courts," and some lawyers worried about the shift to "social information with its seemingly alarming potentialities for destrucion of traditional concepts of adversary litigation."[19]

The divorce bar frequently complained about loss of legal fees should family court judges and their social work contingents successfully reconcile their divorce-bound clients. As might have been expected, Judge Alexander weighed in on the side of the social scientists, deriding attorneys' reluctance to support conciliation and attributing it to venality. For matrimonial lawyers, Alexander carped, "divorce is their rent, their stenographer's salary, their baby's shoes, sometimes their solid gold Cadillac."[20] Professional rivalry surely fueled the bar's antipathy to the amalgamation of law and social work.[21] But distrust of any system of organizing knowledge and action which sought to displace the traditional role of client advocacy provided a strong motivation for many barristers. While their recalcitrance was sometimes phrased as an insistence "that the law remain pure,"[22] often a clannish repugnance emerged, as in the churlish opinion of many judges and lawyers that psychiatrists, social workers, and marriage counselors were a "dubious or even evil influence on our society."[23]

"'Social workers' courts" were also expensive, although no consensus was reached on the affordability of family courts until the late 1960s. One side of the argument pointed to the enormous cost of a professional staff.[24] The other acknowledged the price tag but asserted that great savings to the court system and to society would flow from decreased rates of divorce and juvenile delinquency.[25] On balance, however, the most telling criticisms addressed the central concerns of power in society and the different approaches of law and social science to the resolution of issues of authority. In an oft-cited 1956 article, Professor Max Rheinstein asked rhetorically if American society was "ready to concede to the state that same grave power as in criminal law of transforming the personality structure of a citizen simply because he has failed to make a success out of a marriage with some other individual?"[26] The therapeutic divorce advocates were ready, but American society was beginning to retreat from that outer limit.

The "Fairyland of Benevolence"

The rejection of the family court ideal was of a piece with the reconsideration of the juvenile courts in the 1960s. Following up on the early criticism of Paul Tappan and others, Charles W. Tenney, Jr., described the yawning gap between the magnanimous ideals of the juvenile court and its shoddy performance to date. Writing in the 1969 *Annals of the American Academy of Political and Social Science,* Tenney called the juvenile court myth a "fairyland of benevolence."[27] The trampling of children's rights proved to be the dark side of ostensible compassion, as the United States Supreme Court declared in two 1960s cases, *Kent v. United States*[28] and *In re Gault.*[29]

The problems with the juvenile court were legion, beginning with deficient staffing and funding. A 1963 survey found that 25 percent of juvenile judges had no legal education; in fact, 20 percent had no college education. One-third of the judges reported that no probation officers or social workers were attached to their court and between 80 and 90 percent had no available psychologist or psychiatrist.[30] Appointment as a juvenile court judge, a shining honor at the outset of the experiment, had skidded in prestige by midcentury to the embarrassment of serving on what was nicknamed the "diaper squad."[31] The effort to banish lawyers from the court had largely succeeded; but the exclusion resulted in the invisibility of juvenile issues in legal academia. The juvenile court had been born in 1899, but not until 1967 was the first casebook published on the subject.[32] The confidentiality of juvenile court proceedings exacerbated the lack of public and professional attention devoted to these issues. In many ways these once-revolutionary courts had slipped into the backwater of the law. The deeper dilemma was structural: a recipe combining the powers of a criminal court with the resources of a social agency yielded an undigestible stew. Judge Alexander insisted that the Bill of Rights did "not readily fit into the picture of the juvenile courts" and complained that the court itself was not receiving a "fair trial." But in the words of contemporary critic David Matza, the juvenile court "masquerades as a civil court despite its tell-tale dealings in penal sanction." In the 1960s the mask was lifted.[33]

The renewed emphasis on rights in the *Kent* and *Gault* decisions reflected a sense that the project of socialized justice had been tried and found wanting. The Supreme Court attributed the "highest motives and most enlightened impulses"[34] to the originators of the juvenile court, but it observed that "studies and critiques in recent years raise serious quesions as to whether actual performance measures well enough against theoretical purpose to make tolerable the immunity of the process from the reach of constitutional guarantees applicable to adults."[35] The history of the juvenile court, the justices declared, "has again demonstrated that unbridled discretion, however benevolently motivated, is frequently a poor substitute for principle and procedure."[36] Law professor Henry H. Foster, Jr., crisply summed up the import of *Gault*'s insistence on procedural due process for juveniles with his remark that the Supreme Court "refuses to believe that kangaroo-court procedures are therapeutic."[37] The juvenile court's insistence on a social evaluation of the child in lieu of legal evaluation of the offense had resulted in a functional presumption of guilt and the application of punitive sanctions under the guise of treatment.

Judge Alexander blasted the adversarially oriented juvenile court lawyer who "possesses no social conscience or is constitutionally contentious or vainly legalistic or mentally myopic, [and who] seems impelled to earn his fee by putting on a show for his client." Social work professor Tom A. Croxton also called for the juvenile court bar to trade its adversariness for a role as a "participant decision maker," part of the "dispositional team," including behavioral scientists and the court, all sharing the aim of reha- bilitating the child.[38] But Law professor Thomas A. Coyne called for the return of adversarial lawyers to the juvenile court in order to reestablish the balance between the court and the juvenile. Finally, in 1970, the Supreme Court insisted that the adult criminal law standard requiring proof beyond a reasonable doubt applied during the adjudicatory stage of juvenile proceedings. The juvenile court was, in short, ordered to act more like a court and less like an omnipotent and irresponsible social agency.[39]

Contempt for juvenile court processes was not limited to the bench and bar. Social personnel dealing with juvenile delinquency were also critical of the unproductive yoking of therapeutic discourse and a legal setting. Andrew Polsky aptly summarized their perspective:

> A legalistic outlook warped the court's understanding of its clients: while science might disdain rigid categories and simple labels, a judicial institution found them indispensable. Further, given that according to the therapeutic ideal a client had to participate voluntarily in the treat- ment relationship, it did not seem possible to treat youngsters under the court's direction. Juvenile offenders certainly grasped the cold fact that they were subject to legal discipline. And this led them to dismiss clinicians associated with the court as an annoyance or to manipulate them to secure lenient treatment.[40]

The reconstitution of juvenile justice paralleled the disintegration of support for the Alexandrian family court idea. Even though William M. Kephart asserted in 1955 that he could not recall a single article attacking the family court in law journals, social science publications, or daily newspapers, the plethora of kudos had not produced comprehension. At the end of the decade, Alexander was still heard protesting that "very few people understand what a family court is or how it operates."[41]

But perhaps most people understood too well. As the failure of the court-supervised Utah marriage counseling experiment illustrated, the blend of judicial compulsion and therapeutic independence satisfied no one, least of all the baffled and frustrated clients.[42] Family courts may have been invented to "solve" the predicament of troubled families, but the solution usually was preordained to be enforced reconciliation. That American divorce practices remained unyielding in the face of this double bind should, in retrospect, have come as no surprise. Courts, as Charles Tenney observed, "do not solve problems; they resolve issues."[43] The peremptory and blunt tools of a court's legal equipment render it generally ill suited to devise answers to broad social or psychological questions.

Recognition of this limitation was, of course, at the heart of the therapeutic divorce advocates' call for an infusion of social science experts into the heart of the court's decision making. But the expectation that social casework would catalyze judicial operation did not count on the converse impact. As courts became socialized, counseling assumed a judicial demeanor. When criticized, the system pulled apart again. These spasmodic movements played out a Heisenberg principle of therapeutic divorce: even when the position of the family court could be identified, its momentum carried it elsewhere. Moreover, many family courts were socialized in name only; understaffed, underfunded, and overwhelmed, they processed domestic cases on an assembly line indistinguishable from the procedure in standard-issue civil courts with divorce jurisdiction. Sociologist Ray Baber sketched the weary scene at such courts during this era:

> Judges without special training, too few probation officers or officers with little or no qualification for their work, and a lack of technically trained specialists such as psychiatrists frequently make of the court a poor imitation of what it could be. It is depressing to sit and watch cases pass in array before the judge—cases in which the trouble has been developing for ten years, yet which are disposed of in ten minutes by a judge whose remarks to the persons before him show no understanding of their problems. A tired officer will lay a few record sheets

before the judge before he hears the principals and whisper a few words to him in recommendation. Often these are based upon an extremely brief contact with the principals.[44]

Baber's lugubrious account seems impossible to reconcile with Alexander's energetic rhetoric. But perhaps that was the problem. Max Rheinstein declared that he would willingly support an open-ended and powerful family court regime if "all the courts . . . would be staffed with Paul Alexanders." Judge Alexander may have appeared everywhere, but he only sat in Toledo.[45]

From the outset the therapeutic divorce venture also had been plagued by underfunding. The 1948 White House Conference had focused national attention on the report prepared by Alexander and Reginald Heber Smith, presenting their new approach to divorce reform. The report was adopted by the 1948 and 1949 conventions of the American Bar Association, both of which expressed the desire that President Truman appoint a national commission. But despite his "wholehearted concurrence in the objectives of the Conference," Truman did not act, and the ABA was forced to establish its own commission in 1950. Hopes that government or private foundations would fund research were dashed, with the single exception of Maxine Virtue's 1956 field study of metropolitan divorce courts. Max Rheinstein, as a member of the ABA's Interprofessional Commission, succeeded in persuading the University of Chicago's Comparative Law Research Center to conduct several seminars, which resulted in the publication of some essays on the subject. All in all, it was an anticlimactic yield from such a melodramatic beginning. But even more anticlimax lay ahead.[46]

The proponents of therapeutic divorce had always championed integrated family courts to deal with all domestic issues, from delinquency to dissolution. But the constitutionalization of juvenile court procedure effected by the Supreme Court in the 1960s highlighted the fact that the adjudication of juvenile delinquency—even by a "socialized" court—was a function of criminal law. The more that therapeutic divorce proponents coupled the essence of the family court to the rehabilitative philosophy of the juvenile court, the more that divorce-minded couples were reminded of the obloquy expressed by the Alexandrian judgment that divorce was largely impulsive and that irresponsible divorce was a crime against society. Alexander's determination that the family court should "have ample authority for dealing with people who seem to understand only the language of authority" made it clear that he viewed divorce as a form of law enforcement.[47]

But divorce and crime proved to be oil and water. The steeply rising divorce rate among the middle class in the 1960s swept into the issue millions who believed that the criminal law and the juvenile court were largely state measures for the control of the lower class. While one family court judge wondered if "placing juvenile matters in the same court with husband-and-wife cases will have a debilitating effect upon the long-developed specialized approaches of the juvenile court," many couples considering divorce worried about the spillover in the other direction.[48]

The linkage of divorce and crime was also a product of institutional cross-fertilization. In 1959 the National Probation and Parole Association proposed a model family tribunal in its Standard Family Court Act. The plan was developed in cooperation with the United States Children's Bureau and the National Council of Juvenile Court Judges. Court services available in the model court would include both probation officers and marriage counselors.[49] The frequent cry of therapeutic reformers that divorce bred juvenile delinquency would be answered by the development of comprehensive family courts, equipped with an equal measure of arrows and olive branches. The message could hardly have been clearer: if you fail the marriage counselor, you will deal with the probation officer. Paul Alexander's axiom had forshadowed this precise rationale: "Who doth not answer to the rudder shall answer to the rock."[50]

The "Inquest": Divorce in the English Style

In Great Britain the Church of England had always served as both rudder and rock on family issues. The epigrammatic force of the adage "The Church of England is the Tory Party at prayer"[51] had substantially weakened by the second half of the twentieth century, but it had not entirely ebbed. In 1962 an important book on English divorce practice could still assert that "the law of the Church is the rock on which much of our modern law has been built."[52] On the introduction the following year of a parliamentary bill permitting divorce upon seven years' marital separation, the archbishop of Canterbury protested so stridently that the effort to introduce no-fault divorce was withdrawn.

Yet before the end of the decade, England, led by its church, had revolutionized divorce law and substantially influenced the course of reform in the United States. The English Divorce Reform Act of 1969 was intended to eliminate the hypocrisy of the fault system, with its expansion of the cruelty ground beyond all reason, while more effectively preserving marriages. It soon became clear, however, that what Parliament had approved was only a halfhearted therapeutic divorce measure, which had unequivocally failed. The entropy of divorce-minded wives and husbands could not be contained.

In 1951 Eirene White had introduced a private member bill in Parliament proposing a "marital breakdown" standard for divorce, one that could be met when the couple had been separated for seven years. The friction sparked by her proposal caused White to withdraw the bill in exchange for the government's agreement to establish a royal commission to study the issue. The Royal Commission on Marriage and Divorce, chaired by Lord Morton of Henryton, considered a prodigious amount of evidence, heard from 67 organizations and 48 individuals, conducted 102 meetings, labored for four years, and produced a report in 1956 containing more than four hundred pages. In the end, deeply fractured, it settled nothing.

The Morton Commission stalemate revealed the Church of England's power as "the most influential opponent of change in the matrimonial law."[53] The archbishop of Canterbury strongly argued against any reform, and his views largely prevailed, since no legislative change could be premised on such a divided report. The church's Memorandum to the Commission insisted that only the fault regime validated true moral principle. Awarding a divorce to a guilty party would reek of injustice. The church earnestly maintained that Eirene White's bill would supply the motivation for unscrupulous interlopers to form illicit liaisons with married persons, incited by the knowledge that the faithless spouse would be free to marry the paramour in seven years.[54]

In 1963 Leo Abse attempted a parliamentary revival of the proposal for divorce upon seven years' separation. But in the House of Lords, the archbishop of Canterbury opposed a separation ground as a subterfuge for promoting divorce by consent.[55] Abse's bill failed. However, in the course of the debate, the archbishop expressed his dissatisfaction with the existing law and the lax procedures in divorce courts: "If it were possible to find a principle at law of break down of marriage which was free from any trace of the idea of consent, which conserved the point that offenses and not only wishes are the basis of the breakdown and which was protected by a far more thorough insistence on reconciliation procedure first, then I would wish to consider it."[56]

In the spirit of therapeutic divorce, the archbishop intended any new marital breakdown standard as a tool for tightening, not liberalizing, divorce procedure. Some conservatives always had maintained that a single act (or even repeated incidents) of adultery or cruelty did not necessarily destroy the marriage.[57] But the marital fault system always had granted divorces upon proof of transgression, without further inquiry into the state of the marriage. This regime had once been prized not for its subjective virtue but for its stark objectivity, for staking out some line of demarcation between allowable and unforgiveable conduct. Now that line had crumbled.

The archbishop hinted in the House of Lords debate that the law should go further: require that divorce-minded spouses not only prove their partners' guilt but also establish that the marital relation had terminated irrevocably because of that culpable action. The church would put its moral weight behind a new form of divorce, fault-plus. In 1964 the archbishop appointed a committee to explicate the church's position on marriage breakdown as a divorce standard. After two years of study, the group published *Putting Asunder: A Divorce Law for Contemporary Society*. Consistent with the concerns articulated by the archbishop, the group declared that a breakdown standard avoided the devil of divorce by consent and was not "incompatible with a covenant of lifelong intention."[58]

Echoing the reproaches of Paul Alexander and the family court movement, the archbishop's group launched a devastating attack on the hypocrisy and fraud of the marital fault system, scoring it "not only on moral and legal grounds, but on social and psychological [grounds] as well."

Putting Asunder called for fault to be dethroned as the divorce criterion and replaced by marriage breakdown.[59] Rejecting a menu approach to divorce legislation, the church group emphasized that fault and marriage breakdown were philosophically incompatible systems.

But *Putting Asunder* proved more audacious than previous approaches. It articulated a system of legal proof of breakdown by analogy to a coroner's inquest. As a coroner scrutinizes a corpse for clues to its demise, so courts should conduct an inquest on each allegedly dead marriage to determine whether resuscitation—a task normally beyond the capacity of a medical examiner—was possible. The primary consequence of this bold critique of and alternative to the existing divorce system would be a startling increase in judicial intervention in daily life. The courts would conduct an inquest to evaluate the moribund status of every marriage submitted for divorce. Thus, the pro forma procedure adopted in undefended petitions would have to be scrapped. Since over 90 percent of divorce petitions were unopposed, the escalating demands on the justice system would be astronomical. In fact, *Putting Asunder* suggested that, given the requirements of a divorce inquest, "an uncontested case could on occasion call for greater care and judicial skill than one that was contested."[60]

The extent of official intrusion into private life was also reflected in the drafters' call for "considerably expanded" pleadings in divorce cases. These would detail "the history of the marriage in question, the reasons alleged for its failure, any attempts made to achieve reconciliation, and all arrangements proposed for the care of any children, for the disposal of property, and for maintenance in general."[61] Establishing fault under the existing divorce law would not guarantee a decree, since a petitioner would still bear the burden of showing marital breakdown. Nor would a complainant in an uncontested case be assured that hers would be the only voice a judge heard. The archbishop's group recommended that the divorce court have "discretionary power to require the attendance of both parties."[62]

But the drafters were far from sanguine that all relevant facts would come to light if the fact-finding process was left to the parties and their counsel. Indeed, they felt that the lax process of the courts yielded a street standard of divorce by consent. Given the traditional reluctance of common law judges to engage in inquisitorial procedure, they recommended that, especially in uncontested cases, "provision should be made for the intervention, when needed, of counsel representing the public interest or the interests of children of the family."[63]

The penalty for failing to satisfy the enhanced breakdown standard was denial of the divorce decree. The court should refuse the decree where it felt the proposed maintenance was not adequate to the dependent spouse or children, or where the conduct of the petitioner in regard to the marriage was found to be such that in the court's judgment issuing a decree would be against the public interest.[64] Thus, in addition to raising the ante by inventing this fault-plus standard, *Putting Asunder* gave divorce judges carte blanche to keep the marital yoke in place in the "public interest."

The comprehensive therapeutic nature of the church's program was evident in its call for a massive infusion of forensic social workers "as part of immediate procedural reform." These new court officers would assist judges in verifying attempts at reconciliation, testing the reliability of assertions made to the court, and providing further investigative services.[65] *Putting Asunder* served, in short, as the Church of England's last trumpet call for conservative reform and a radical effort to reverse the flow of English divorces.

Despite the prominent reception of *Putting Asunder*, it soon became apparent that the church could acquiesce in but no longer command or withstand divorce reform. Within three months of the publication of the report of the archbishop's group, the government's Law Commission produced its own report, *Reform of the Grounds of Divorce: The Field of Choice.*[66] The Law Commission rejected the church's blueprint for an intrusive family court on the grounds of cost and impracticality. Moreover, the commission believed that a "detailed inquest into the whole married life would prove more distasteful and embarrassing" than present fault-based but cursory proceedings. Nor was the commission impressed by compulsory conciliation. Reconciliation efforts made mandatory would degenerate into wasting "the time of marriage guidance counsellors . . . on 'cock and bull' stories to the detriment of sincere applicants."[67]

In detailing its own breakdown scheme, however, the law commission chose to reconstitute the old grounds of fault, deeming them alternate methods of showing marital breakdown. Additionally, the dissolution of the conjugal relationship could also be premised on two new living-apart provisions. Divorce could be obtained upon irretrievable marital breakdown, which could be proved in one of five ways: adultery, cruelty, desertion for two years, separation for two years if the respondent did not object, or separation for five years.[68] With only minor changes these proposals became law in the Divorce Reform Act of 1969.[69] The English reforms maintained the shell of therapeutic divorce and greatly influenced the California no-fault law. In fact, had the Law Commission's proposals achieved their intended effect, the Divorce Reform Act truly would have achieved a radical conservative revolution. But the commissioners did away with fault grounds only to revive them as "elements" of the new breakdown standards. Theoretically, at least, proof of a fault element no longer would guarantee a successful divorce, for the court was specifically authorized to make an independent evaluation of the alleged marital breakdown.

Church and state each believed that the 1969 legislation had ushered in a new era of honesty in domestic relations. A stabilization of divorce rates was anticipated, and the bulk of the divorces that did occur were expected to fall into the two breakdown/separation categories. Both these suppositions proved wrong, however, and the Divorce Reform Act was quickly judged a failure. Most strikingly, divorce reform à la marital breakdown resulted in an even more explosive burst of cruelty petitions, from 17.7 percent of all cases in 1971 (when the 1969 act went into operation) to 41.4 percent in 1986. The continued proliferation of behavior-based petitions represented a desire for rapid terminations that outweighed the now-negligible stigma attached to fault divorces. From 1971 to 1986 the percentage of fault-based petitions ranged between 61.4 percent and 77.8 percent, despite the existence of two living-apart alternatives. In 1994 nearly two-thirds of divorces were granted on fault grounds.[70] Establishing spousal cruelty had remained as easy and popular a divorce ground as ever.

The 1988 Law Commission concluded that the Church of England had been right two decades earlier in insisting on the unpalatability of a blend of fault and nonfault grounds within a single divorce system.[71] But the earlier Law Commission that had written *Field of Choice* had also been correct in believing that marital breakdown was not justiciable.

Acknowledging that the 1969 compromise had been labeled in professional journals as "uneasy" and even "bungling," the 1988 Law Commission proposed finally to divorce fault from matrimonial law completely.[72]

What happened to the Divorce Reform Act of 1969? As the Law Commission belatedly acknowledged in 1988, the internal logic of a matrimonial breakdown system leads ineluctably to divorce on demand.[73] This eventuality is precisely what the archbishop's group worked to avoid. But once the church held the door open for divorce reform, the liberalization movement that had hitherto operated within the courts' trivialization of the cruelty ground emerged as the dominant force in family law. We next turn to the greatest American effort to install the philosophy and mechanism of therapeutic divorce. California followed the news from England closely, both in heartily proposing and in ultimately rejecting a comprehensive family court.

The Final Boomerang of Conservative Reform

In 1963, the same year in which Leo Abse's no-fault bill triggered the divorce reform process in Parliament, California assembly member Pearce Young initiated a study to identify issues and amass information "with a view towards developing a legislative program to strengthen family relations."[74] Young's initiative resulted in the establishment of legislative committees to consider measures dealing with family life, including reform of the divorce laws. At three public hearings held in 1964, a variety of legal, scientific, theological, and lay witnesses criticized California's divorce system, linking it to the increasing social and moral deterioration of society.[75]

Judge Roger Pfaff, who presided over the Los Angeles Conciliation Court, vigorously argued at one of the hearings for an extension of mandatory conciliation services throughout the state, claiming that nearly 90 percent of California divorces were "neither necessary nor justified . . . provided these people could actually have some counseling and were interested in saving their marriage." The committee members were quite favorably impressed by Pfaff's testimony.[76] In his message to the committee, Governor Edmund G. Brown emphasized that divorce "erodes the very foundation of our society." He made the connection between divorce and crime quite literally, telling the legislators that three-quarters of the juvenile delinquents and more than half of the inmates in penal institutions "come from broken homes." Free divorce was the villain for Brown, a Roman Catholic, and he called on the committee to "probe and expose the core of this growing social problem."[77]

No legislative proposals emerged from this first round of activity. But in the spring of 1966, Brown appointed the Governor's Commission on the Family, composed of two state senators, one assembly representative, five judges, six attorneys, two law professors, one social worker, four physicians, and one member of the clergy. The commission was assigned four tasks:

> 1. study the framework of laws relating to the family and suggest revision;
> 2. determine the feasibility of family life education courses for the public schools;
> 3. consider developing uniform national standards of marriage and divorce jurisdiction; and
> 4. examine the establishment of statewide family courts and recommend procedures for their most effective functioning.[78]

The governor's commission largely ignored the second and third assignments and concentrated its proposals on one integrated scheme, heavily influenced by the archbishop of Canterbury's group: no-fault dissolution of marriage, to be processed by a therapeutic family court. Not only did the commission quote at length from *Putting Asunder*, but its proposal linking the removal of fault to a transfer of domestic cases to an administrative and therapeutic—rather than purely adjudicative—body replicated the heart of the Church of England report.

The commission tied the removal of fault grounds in California to the operation of this powerful sociolegal agency, whose mission was to provide therapeutic aid to salvage a foundering marriage. A formal termination of the matrimonial union was sanctioned upon proof of marriage breakdown, but only after penetrating scrutiny and after the judicial process had given the parties every recourse in aid of conciliation. This final thrust of the therapeutic divorce movement is exemplified by Philip L. Hammer's discussion of the pitfalls and pluses of mandatory counseling in the evolution of the California experiment. Hammer acknowledged at the outset that "requir[ing] a psychiatric type examination and counseling of persons seeking dissolution of their marriage is a potentially significant interference by the state with the privacy and personal liberties of the individual."[79]

But, Hammer insisted, many situations warranted state interference: when one spouse opposed the dissolution, when minor children needed the state's protection, when the parties were having difficulty working out a rational distribution of property, when custody and support were unresolved, and when psychiatric intercession was needed for the "reduction of anti-social hostility and tension." The claims favoring state intervention in these instances "fairly clearly outweigh the interest of the individual in being free from inquiry by the state into the events of his private life."[80]

The rhetoric of therapy was in full flower in this proposed reform. The new legal lexicon banished even the word *divorce*. Candidates for "marital dissolution" would file not a "complaint" but a "petition of inquiry," reminiscent of Paul Alexander's tenet that a divorce complaint be considered "an application . . . for the remedial services of the state." The case would no longer be captioned "Wife v. Husband" but the seemingly less contentious "In re the Marriage of Wife and Husband." A stress on marital counseling, to be provided by a trained professional staff, would replace the former focus on adjudication and burdens of proof. The Sturm und Drang of the adversary system would become obsolete, the commission believed, since grounds for divorce would no longer be relevant.[81]

Upon the filing of the petition of inquiry, the court clerk was to schedule a conciliation conference. This initial interview was mandatory, and attendance could be compelled by court order. Subsequently, the court's counselor was to inform the judge whether the parties had decided to (*a*) become reconciled, (*b*) continue counseling, or (*c*) resume "their application for an inquiry into the marriage, with a view to its possible dissolution."[82] The legislative fantasy that listed two nondissolution alternatives first, as well as the condescending psychobabble in which the third option was expressed, perfectly illustrated the tendency of therapeutic divorce to mask the reality of marital breakdown and is of a piece with Judge Pfaff's fatuous assertion that nearly 90 percent of California divorces could be averted if only the couples understood the consequences.[83]

After the initial interview a minimum waiting period of 120 days was required before the formal dissolution hearing. During this time the counselor was expected to work with the parties and prepare a written report setting forth "the counselor's recommendations together with supporting facts as to the continuance of the marriage."[84] At the hearing the court could make the decision that the marriage had broken down irreparably. If so, an immediate order dissolving the union would follow. However, if the court was unable or unwilling to make such a finding, the parties would face a ninety-day continuance, during which time they were encouraged to utilize the professional counseling facilities of the court. After this last delay the court would order the marriage dissolved upon the request of either party.[85]

Each stage of the litigation manifested the continual pressure to convert a divorce action into a conciliation procedure. A determined couple could, of course, dodge the persuasive machinations and endure the delays—eight months or longer, particularly in a busy urban court—until they were granted a "dissolution." But the very process of stalling divorce-minded partners was an integral component of therapeutic divorce, premised as it was on the belief—which contrary evidence could not dislodge—that divorce was at heart an impulsive act.

Partisans of therapeutic divorce made a penchant of distinguishing between marital breakdown and divorce. But they never understood that a marriage usually dissolves in fact long before one of the spouses decides to request a decree. Commenting on the applicability of the English reforms to the United States, Monrad Paulsen remarked that it was "astonishing how a vision of the atypical case has dominated the discussion of divorce by consent. Debaters conjure up the vision of two insincere pleasure seekers ready for new adventures rather than the common case of a tragic, weary couple who have concluded at last that the pain should cease."[86] In a 1966 address to the Family Law Section of the American Bar Association, a Milwaukee family court judge humorously exemplified the reformers' illusion that delay is therapeutic:

They tell the story of a divorce-minded husband consulting an attorney in Milwaukee about starting an action for dissolution of the marriage. "Well, we'd start with serving and filing a summons only," the lawyer explained, "then sixty days must elapse before we can file the complaint, and another sixty days before the action can be tried. There would be a referral to the Family Conciliation Department to discuss reconciliation. Because there are minor children involved, there would have to be a preliminary hearing on temporary custody and child support and the court might order a custody investigation which might take an extra ninety days. If custody is in dispute, the judge would probably appoint a guardian *ad litem* to represent the minor and dependent children and he might need some time to prepare for the trial . . ." "Forget it," said the husband, "I can't stay mad that long." [87]

The governor's commission derived the standard for dissolution of marriage from two sources. The first was the opinion of Justice Roger Traynor in *DeBurgh v. DeBurgh*,[88] in which the California Supreme Court had diluted the recrimination statute to allow a trial judge to grant a divorce if, despite the existence of fault grounds on both sides, the legitimate objects of matrimony had been destroyed. The second source was the work of the archbishop of Canterbury's group, then recently published. Prior efforts at introducing therapeutic divorce had succeeded only in adding an ostensibly no-fault option to the statutory list of grounds. The framers of California's reform were anxious to eliminate grounds altogether, in order to have total control of the dissolution process. With this aim, the timing of the publication of *Putting Asunder* could not have been more fortuitous. The archbishop's group set forth a detailed rationale for a clean slate, as well as an argument for ending the perfunctory registration of undefended suits.

As the English proposal reasoned, the retention of fault grounds leads to needless divorces and "invests with spurious objectivity acts [whose] real significance varies widely." [89] Marital breakdown, on the other hand, theoretically was not subject to collusive prior arrangement and presented the issue of continuing the marriage in terms far more amenable to therapeutic intervention than did adultery or extreme cruelty, particularly when those fault grounds were so often understood to be faked.

Moreover, divorces would no longer be "undefended," as the emphasis was no longer on contesting charges but on conciliation, and the court could command both spouses to participate.

The governor's commission was more successful than the archbishop's group in substituting marital breakdown for a fault standard in the final legislation. But the California reformers retained the concept of individual blameworthiness when relevant to the determination of child custody and when specific incidents of misconduct were "determined by the court to be necessary to establish the existence of irreconcilable differences."[90] As explained by the commission's cochairs, the new court would be required to examine the "whole picture of the marriage," including spousal misconduct, which could be "completely explored."[91]

This large-mouthed exception to the ostensibly fault-free tenor of the proposal did not escape serious criticism. On one level this apparent aberration simply may have served to allow petitioners to place their marital breakdown in context, what lawyers call *res gestae*. But what would be the effect on the desired "conciliatory and uncharged atmosphere" of barring fault at the front door but allowing it to be "completely explored" when it entered at the rear?[92] Howard A. Krom argued that this revival of culpability undermined the purposes of the law in permitting "the prejudicial introduction of fault-oriented testimony whenever a spouse can convince the court that it would be necessary to establish the existence of irreconcilable differences." Krom pointed out that this two-edged provision "obviously creates an incongruity between the no-fault criteria for dissolution and the type of evidence needed to show that one is entitled to a decree."[93] As Lynne Carol Halem observed, contrary to the reformers' promise, this provision retained fault as an "integral component of the reform law."[94]

Although its language did not survive in the final legislation, one of the bills proposing divorce reform included a provision that in making its findings as to irreconcilable differences, the court should "be guided by, but not limited to, the statutory grounds and corresponding judicial decisions in effect prior to the effective date of this act."[95] Given this linguistic melange, the view that "fault concepts may be unavoidable"[96] in the new divorce procedure was quite reasonable, even if it turned out to be mistaken. Divorce may have been written out of the domestic relations vocabulary in California. But dissolutions were about to explode.

Therapeutic Divorce and the Cost of Privacy

The conservative aura of the reforms created the impression that the Family Law Act of 1969[97]—signed into law by Governor Brown's successor, Ronald Reagan—would truly escalate the hurdles facing dissolution-minded couples. Both law review commentary and appellate court interpretation reinforced the notion that California no-fault had closed the gates on divorce on demand. In the statute's first year, Charles W. Johnson suggested that a dissatisfied spouse seeking a dissolution must establish irreconcilable differences by presenting "substantial reasons" for not continuing the marriage.[98] Appellate affirmation was not long in coming. In 1972 the California Supreme Court noted that while the legislature had devised a no-fault, nonadversarial procedure, it "did not intend that findings of irreconcilable differences be made perfunctorily."[99]

The court pointed out that the legislature had rejected a proposal whereby the parties would be entitled to a divorce upon the processing of certain steps and the passage of a certain period of time. On the contrary, the Family Law Act placed the trial court in the role of "'an overseeing participant to do its utmost to effect a healing of the marital wounds.'"[100] In order to perform this critical task, judges must independently review evidence about the condition of the marriage. The supreme court specifically rejected the notion that the parties could consent to dissolve their marriage and then have that consent constitute the required establishment of irreconcilable differences.[101]

Even though the California reforms aimed to dethrone fault and eliminate the acrimony of the adversarial system, the state's highest court continued its long-standing concern with collusion. The supreme court worried about the parties' agreeing "that one of them would present false evidence that their differences were irreconcilable and their marriage had broken down irremediably." It never questioned how a trial judge was supposed to distinguish between genuine and ersatz matrimonial failure when both parties were determined to divorce. It merely ruled that it was the function of the trial judge, not the parties, to decide whether the evidence sufficed in order to allow for a divorce.[102]

In asserting a distinction between the will of the trial court and that of the parties seeking judicial sanction on their dissolution, the supreme court was ignoring large chunks of the history of twentieth-century divorce. With the trial courts acclimated to a generation or more of granting divorces upon the "pious perjury" of unchallenged extreme cruelty or hotel adultery, it should have been apparent that a general guideline that trial judges should make independent findings would be woefully insufficient to change the practice of divorce in California. But more legal flotsam was to follow before the appellate courts surrendered.

Soon after the *McKim* case was decided, a California court of appeals handed down *In re Marriage of Walton*,[103] addressing several challenges to the new law. The court determined from the legislative history that the irreconcilable differences to be proved by the plaintiff "must be substantial as opposed to trivial or minor." The defendant would always have the opportunity to prove the contrary proposition, and the trial judge had the discretion "to receive evidence of specific acts of misconduct." The court rejected a standard "based upon the subjective attitude of the parties" and insisted that the Family Law Act did not constitute a "license for dissolution of marriage by consent." The court concluded by emphasizing that the plaintiff had the burden of establishing the existence of "substantial marital problems which have so impaired the marriage relationship that the legitimate objects of matrimony have been destroyed and as to which there is no reasonable possibility of elimination, correction or resolution."[104]

But the vision of no-fault conceived by the reformers, that scrupulous trial courts—not impulsive couples—would determine the right to a divorce, never materialized. Trial courts under California no-fault simply refused to deny divorces under any circumstances. Even if divorce judges had been inclined, they could have performed no inquests or investigations into the death of the marriages presented to them. The California legislature had vetoed the reformers' creation of a system of statewide family courts. The reasons were twofold: concerns about the judiciary injecting itself into bedroom breakdowns buttressed fear of the stiff price tag for therapeutic divorce.[105]

Although some reformers, such as Herma Hill Kay, claimed that the proposed family court system would subscribe to the "careful protection of individual privacy in the counseling process," [106] their voices were overcome by those who feared the rise of a controlling bureaucracy whose clientele would be, not lower-class juvenile delinquents and their families, but the legislators' "colleagues, friends, and even themselves." [107] Concerns about timeliness and efficiency also led legislators to doubt that mandatory counseling was viable when initiated at the courthouse door.[108] Nor were judges keen on the many changes in courtroom practice that therapeutic divorce threatened.[109]

The cost estimates for supplying the requisite psychiatrists and social workers were daunting. The governor's commission admitted that "creating a professionally-staffed Family Court will not be an inexpensive undertaking." But it hoped that the benefits obtained, in terms of family case streamlining and prevention of "broken homes," would be worth the fiscal sacrifice.[110] This cost-benefit analysis of family saving was not new. Max Rheinstein had made virtually the identical point a decade earlier: "If the [family] court achieves what it is said it will, the cost of running it will easily be overbalanced by the saving of the cost of juvenile delinquency, alcoholism, and general dependency of abandoned wives and children." [111] But this argument faced its biggest hurdle in California, and it could not overcome the growing sentiment in both the legal and psychiatric professions that the sheriff and the therapist should not blend.

Exactly how "not . . . inexpensive" family courts in California would be was revealed in October 1967 when the analyst for the Joint Legislative Budget Committee calculated an additional yearly expenditure of $4,427,500. Worse news was to come, for this analyst's estimate was the lowest received by the legislature. The presiding judge of the Los Angeles Family Court Department testified that the cost for a statewide program could run as high as $10 million annually. The higher valuation was generally believed to be more accurate, and the legislature considered it an unacceptable burden on the public coffers.[112]

Contrary to the rhetoric of reform and the anticipation of the public, California's Family Law Act of 1969 resulted in the rapid expediting of

divorces, as a "perfunctory judicial acknowledgement of marital breakdown replaced the parade of witnesses and staged courtroom battles."[113]
As with previous divorce reforms, the legislative and appellate law systems pursued their goals of articulating policy norms and directing the
evolution of formal legal rules. The statutory language and the appellate
opinions were filled with the bravado of obstruction, a grandiloquent effort to render no-fault more cumbersome than fault. As before, neither
system succeeded in imposing its will on actual divorcing behavior.

Trial courts continued to pay little heed to case law or statute. They
found their roles as divorce registrars streamlined by the removal of the
necessity to play audience to the farces of fault that had been such a large
part of their former dispensation. But the familiarity of the legal land-
scape immediately after California no-fault was an illusion: the unintended consequences of reform were about to usher in a divorce revolution. No longer did conjugal dissolutions have to be bargained for in the
shadow of the formal law.[114] No longer did the parties have to negotiate at
all. The statutes enacted following the lead of California no-fault left the
legal system prostrate, thus eliminating the need for litigants to conspire
to outflank its formal requirements.[115]

Mutual consent, the fulcrum of marital dissolution for at least a half
century, had been abruptly shelved. Its statutory demise was accompanied
by the loss of the communitarian oil useful in lubricating most family
conflicts that end in divorce. The dismantling of the mutual consent regime
thus exposed the jagged razor of marriage demolition on demand. The
designers of therapeutic divorce had planned to promote reconciliations
and lower the rate of dissolution. Instead, their machinations yielded no-
fault divorce on demand, a stunning about-face which rejected the increased administrative control the reformers desired. That the passage
of the California statute resulted in boundless divorcing gives testimony
to the persistent if frustratingly formless doctrine, the law of unplanned
aftermaths. The divorce system's lubricity had now disappeared. These
radical changes in the formal legal system had stripped the process of its
cultural authenticity by artificially accelerating the tendencies toward a
socially atomistic and destructive form of individualism. Law permeates,
as E. P. Thompson reminded us, "*every* bloody level,"[116] and in this scenario law has had devastating social effects. No-fault, this new paradigm
in family law, constitutes nothing more elegant than naked divorce.

EPILOGUE

THE NAKED ARE SEARCHING
FOR CLOTHES

*I can divorce my wife of 26 years with less difficulty
than I can fire a secretary I hired last week.*

Randall Hekman, former judge

By 1977, seven years after the effective date of the California no-fault reform, only three states remained wedded to exclusively fault concepts in
marital dissolutions. That same year Riane Tennehaus Eisler reported
that since the enactment of the irreconcilable differences standard in the
Golden State, not a single divorce petition had been denied. Indeed, none
of the forty-four California domestic relations judges interviewed by
Lenore Weitzman in the mid-1970s could recall ever refusing a request
for a divorce under the new dispensation. Five years into the reign of no-
fault, the California legislature repealed the provision that had allowed
proof of specific bad acts to show the existence of irreconcilable differences. The legislature thus removed one of the few remaining exemplars
of the fault *mentalité* as it recognized that irreconcilable differences were
nothing more than a self-operated escape hatch from any marriage.
Naked divorce had triumphed.[1]

Six months after the effective date of California's divorce reforms, Iowa became the second state to gut its fault system and replace it with an "irretrievable breakdown" standard. A 1972 survey of twenty Iowa trial judges analyzed the 1,810 divorce cases they had heard within the previous year. Of that total, 1,599 had been uncontested, 211 contested, and in not one case had the prayer for a divorce been denied.[2] A Nebraska survey of nearly 10,000 dissolution cases in the mid-1970s similarly "failed to reveal a single instance in which it could be said with certainty that a divorce which was desired by even one of the spouses was ultimately refused."[3]

On one level it appeared that the divorce revolution constituted a U-turn to the past. *Plus ça change*: both legal culpability and the very framework of divorce grounds had disappeared. *Plus c'est la même chose*: the formula had changed, but division-minded wives and husbands did what they wanted. The legal culture, in this view, did not appear to differentiate divorcing in the 1970s substantively from the easy ways of a generation earlier. But this analytical insouciance was seriously misleading. A true jurisprudential revolution, in fact, had catapulted the informal law of divorce from "mutual consent," its operating gear for half a century, to the transmission of "divorce on demand." The consequences were staggering. As Herma Hill Kay, one of the principal proponents of California no-fault, pointed out in retrospect, "Divorce by unilateral fiat is closer to desertion than to mutual separation."[4]

The California state senate and assembly were not, of course, entirely responsible for the radical shift in the cultural paradigm. As John Dewey remarked much earlier in the century, "rugged individualists" tend to become "ragged individualists."[5] The hell-for-leather egoism that shattered the institutional family and whose baby boomer children flaunted themselves during the "Me" decade in the 1970s has resulted, a quarter-century later, in a bottomless concern with personal rights matched by a fervid disinterest in preserving relationships. American cultural traditions, sociologist Robert N. Bellah and his colleagues observed, "leave the individual suspended in glorious, but terrifying, isolation."[6] This cultural primacy of detachment has now been encoded into our divorce laws. In this sense culture has created law, been shaped by law, and, fundamentally, become law.

But no-fault laws in turn have generated dramatic outputs. No-fault enshrined in statute and practice what American culture had been only idly drifting toward in other aspects of life: a predilection for formal and radical autonomy. The reification of divorce on demand intensified the development of what Milton C. Regan, Jr., has aptly termed the "*acontextual self*," a creature "who stands apart from any social relationship in which he or she is involved."[7] The marital relationship has exhibited no immunity from this legal virus. The "happiness principle embedded in the no-fault ground has dealt a devastating blow to the durability of marriages."[8] And the dethronement of mutual consent in divorce law has fostered the loss of mutuality throughout American society.[9]

Nor should this result be surprising. "Law is more than a barometer of social change," historian Norma Basch has noted. It "has an autonomy of its own and is capable of asserting its influence over legislators, jurists, and the public."[10] The raw gender equality promoted by the passage of no-fault—and achieved with virtually no participation by organized women's groups[11]—initially was perceived by many women as a splendid enhancement of their status both in marriage and after. But second thoughts came quickly. Martha L. Fineman has argued that the no-fault "revolution" was exactly that: a 360-degree turn which brought us "back to where we substantively began."[12] The earlier focus on formal equality has been replaced by a feminist debate over the competing subjectivities within no-fault. For many women the formal changes in divorce law signified achievable freedom and societal validation for goals of self-actualization. But "what apparently escaped notice," commented Deborah L. Rhode, "were the inequalities in men's and women's status following divorce."[13]

The rejection of law's protectionist ideals has focused attention on the many ways in which social reality remains gendered. Feminists have focused attention on how women's "disproportionate assumption of 'private' domestic responsibilities has constrained their 'public' opportunities."[14] Mothers predominantly retain child custody after divorce, and employed women continue to receive grossly unequal compensation for their labor. Many agree with Mary Ann Mason's argument that, for women, the "concept of equality is a trap."[15] In jurisprudential terms feminism today is split between advocates of formal equality and champions of women's differences.[16] Although the current debate is more nuanced, it resembles the hefty disputations earlier this century between supporters of protectionist legislation for women in industry and staunch defenders of equal rights, including suffrage, for the sexes. The dilemma floods over academic boundaries: by the late 1980s, half of all single-parent families had dipped below the poverty line, and 70 percent of those families were headed by divorced or separated women.[17]

While 5 percent of American children lived exclusively with their mother in 1960, 25 percent did so in 1990. Seventy percent of incarcerated juveniles come from fatherless homes. Judith Wallerstein's study of the effect of divorce on children found that five years after the split, over one-third suffered from moderate or severe depression. Despite common assumptions about children's vaunted resilience, Wallerstein's field research continued to find serious adverse consequences in children ten and fifteen years after the parents' divorce.[18]

Barbara Dafoe Whitehead has called for a national "conversation about the family" to explore "cultural solutions" to the problems stemming from the excesses of divorce. Indeed, as Bellah and his coauthors noted, the current ideology of American individualism "has difficulty . . . justifying why men and women should be giving to one another at all." The conversation requested by Whitehead has started, but the early dialogue sets a cacophonous tone: juxtapose a *Newsweek* cover story on "Deadbeat Dads: Wanted for Failure to Pay Child Support" with Mary Frances Berry's *The Politics of Parenthood: Child Care, Women's Rights, and the Myth of the Good Mother*.[19]

Nor are women any closer to resolving the work/family dilemma: compare *Answers to the Mommy Track: How Wives and Mothers in Business Reach the Top and Balance Their Lives* with *Staying Home: From Full-Time Professional to Full-Time Parent*. *Answers to the Mommy Track* introduces readers to "women who are extremely dedicated to career goals but simultaneously demonstrate the great lengths to which they will go to be responsible to family commitments." *Staying Home*, dedicated by its authors "to our mothers, who stayed home for us," rejects any track for women but motherhood, which it claims has become the "most controversial career" for a woman.[20] This theme is echoed in Katie Kelley Dorn's *From Briefcase to Diaper Bag: How I Quit My Job, Stayed Home with My Kids, and Lived to Tell about It*. Although Katherine Wyse Goldman rejects the *Leave It to Beaver* family model in *My Mother Worked and I Turned Out Okay*, the defensive tone of Goldman's title may indicate a shifting in the wind.[21]

New challenges at times prompt old responses, and some have thought the unthinkable, calling for the return of fault as the sole criterion to end marriage.[22] Barbara Bennett Woodhouse has decried as unconscionable no-fault's brushing aside a spouse's history of physical and mental exploitation. She has advocated reintroducing the discourse of fault into the divorce law narrative as a way to "provide protection and compensation for victims of abuse of spousal trust," particularly women.[23] Stephen D. Sugarman has observed that the "rhetorical force" of a broadside against the no-fault system "can be enhanced if set in the context of an innocent and a guilty spouse." He has outlined several roles appropriate for reinvigorated fault, such as in cases involving "reprehensible conduct" or the allowance of a tort suit for the wronged spouse on top of the recovery obtained by application of the no-fault law.[24]

Others have suggested ways to pull back on the reins of no-fault, recognizing that divorce on demand "effectively disenfranchises the party who has not initiated the termination."[25] Allen M. Parkman has championed requiring mutual consent before granting a divorce, a step which he believes will force spouses to consider more deeply the benefits and costs of divorce to their families.[26] Elizabeth S. Scott has advanced "precommitment" restrictions, by which a couple could set out in an antenuptial agreement the conditions under which their marriage could be dissolved. These options might range from a legally enforceable commitment "'til death do us part,'" to milder obstacles to divorce, such as conditioning a decree on economic penalties or mandating a delay before the award of any divorce.[27] Under Scott's rationale a couple could decide that only marital fault—as they defined it—would render their marriage amenable to divorce proceedings. Bills introduced in statehouses in Illinois, Washington, and Indiana in 1995–96 proposed Scott's "covenant marriage" option for couples who desired to enter into connubial relationships impervious to no-fault divorce. These bills aimed, in the words of the Illinois measure, at differentiating between two types of state-sanctioned unions, a "marriage of commitment" and a "marriage of compatibility."[28]

The mid-1990s have seen a growing legislative effort to turn back the divorce clock. In the most widely discussed bid, Michigan state representative Jessie F. Dalman introduced an eleven-bill package designed to establish a two-tier divorce system. Couples without minor children could obtain a divorce upon consent. But if a family had minor children, or if one spouse objected to the dissolution, the party seeking a divorce would have to prove the marital fault of the other. The reinvigorated fault grounds, quite familiar to students of history, featured the unholy trinity of adultery, desertion, and extreme cruelty, which would have to be established by a "preponderance of the evidence."[29]

Similarly, in his 1996 Condition of the State address, Iowa governor Terry Branstad attacked no-fault for "transform[ing] marriage into an arrangement of convenience rather than an act of commitment." Branstad called for no-fault divorce to be replaced by laws that require a divorce court to find mutual consent or marital fault.[30] The Indiana Family Institute has proposed the Justice in Family Law Act, which would limit divorce to mutual consent or fault grounds. Micah A. Clark, the institute's associate director, attacked the excesses of Indiana's "irretrievable breakdown" standard, under whose banners a "whole generation of Hoosiers has placed its marital future in a law that favors the unfaithful, the uncommitted, the selfish and the immature."[31] In 1995 and 1996 measures to kill or at least wound no-fault were introduced in Georgia, Idaho, Hawaii, Pennsylvania, Virginia, Illinois, and Kansas.[32]

In a sense, of course, the concept of fault has never disappeared from spousal relationships, particularly at their breaking point. Studies confirm that issues of moral responsibility have retained their prominence in marital breakdowns.[33] In their study of contemporary divorce trends, Sarat and Festiner noted that despite the legal irrelevance of culpability, "clients continue to think in fault terms and to attribute blame to their spouse."[34] Social researchers Wallerstein and Blakeslee made the point bluntly: "What other life crisis engenders the wish to kill? In what other life crisis are children used as bullets?"[35] As a 1990s self-help bestseller characterized it, divorce is "often a long and painful process that never truly ends."[36]

Divorce has always been disturbing, and often traumatizing. This book has endeavored, not to deny the torment of marital breakup, but rather to argue that under the fault regime couples seeking to rebuild their lives through divorce tended to work through their anger in negotiating their exit from a failed relationship. The "blaming" ritual of the fault era may have had a cathartic effect even when the divorce had been prearranged. Under the current fault-free legal culture, divorce-minded spouses can wholly disregard their partners in demanding and securing a divorce. But society pays a steep price. Individuals have captured the flag of families, with the result that many "bitter divorce brawls . . . seem to be over social needs that right now can be experienced only in personal terms."[37] The marital dissolution is assured, but what were once quaintly termed the "ancillary" issues of children and cash are now subjected to the grinder of real, adverse, gut-wrenching litigation. No-fault has, in many ways, exacerbated the pain of marital dissolution.[38]

Nor should this book be seen, however, as a call for the return of fault. In the face of the overwhelming evidence presented of the farcical nature of American society's lengthy dalliance with fault-only divorce mechanisms, the conclusion that we should reinstall the "unholy trinity" in our divorce pantheon is untenable. Conditioning a divorce upon one spouse's epitomizing the other as adulterer, deserter, or beast not only provides a pathetic parody of the complex dynamic of intense psychological relationships but also grossly overestimates the power of law over culture. The mightiest law is that of necessity: couples who seriously desire to divorce will succeed.

But divorce law is not impotent: it can require that couples who divorce do so only after giving the matter serious reflection and after assuring that an economically disadvantaged spouse and all dependent children are treated fairly. Proposals that favor mutual consent, one- to two-year periods of separation, and mediation efforts incline in this direction. Bills to gut no-fault divorce and return to the scarlet-letter milieu of proving the unholy trinity of fault are nostalgic attempts to recapture what never was.

Throughout America naked divorce has gone too far. The astonishing suggestion that the criterion of culpability might stage a comeback in the divorce ring illustrates the fascinating contingency of history. This study has looped and spliced several story lines of culture and law in an effort to trace the history of the process by which twentieth-century Americans dissolved their marriages. The rival legal arenas at last have blended into one, and American culture has reached a dead end on divorce. A new legal and cultural matrix on marriage and divorce must now emerge.

NOTES

Introduction: The Rival Arenas of Divorce

1. See, e.g., Max Rheinstein, *Marriage Stability, Divorce, and the Law* (Chicago, 1972), especially chap. 14, "The Liberal Breakthrough, I: England and New York," and chap. 15, "The Liberal Breakthrough, II: California, the Commissioners on Uniform State Laws, and the Federal Republic of Germany"; Roderick Phillips, *Putting Asunder: A History of Divorce in Western Society* (Cambridge, 1988); William L. O'Neill, "Divorce as a Moral Issue: A Hundred Years of Controversy," in Carol V. R. George, ed., *"Remember the Ladies": New Perspectives on Women in American History* (Syracuse, N.Y., 1975), 127–43.

2. George E. Howard, *A History of Matrimonial Institutions* (Chicago, 1904); Nelson Manfred Blake, *The Road to Reno: A History of Divorce in the United States* (Westport, Conn., 1962); and Glenda Riley, *Divorce: An American Tradition* (New York, 1991).

3. Riley, *Divorce: An American Tradition,* 6.

4. Blake, *Road to Reno,* 226–43.

5. Lynne Carol Halem, *Divorce Reform: Changing Legal and Social Perspectives* (New York, 1980).

6. Rheinstein, *Marriage Stability, Divorce, and the Law,* 258; see also Riley, *Divorce: An American Tradition,* 162–63.

7. Phillips, *Putting Asunder,* 531, 561, 569, 615, 636. For an abridged version, see Phillips, *Untying the Knot: A Shorter History of Divorce* (Cambridge, 1991).

8. Herbert Jacob, *Silent Revolution: The Transformation of Divorce Law in the United States* (Chicago, 1988), 13, 54, 74, 166. Feminist theoretician Martha L. Fineman disputed Jacob's claim that no-fault reforms were revolutionary. Fineman believed that the statutory changes were "in fact *antirevolutionary*—operating to undermine the fledgling potential for freedom presented for women by newly won economic opportunities coupled with an ability to freely leave unsatisfactory marriages." Fineman, "Neither Silent, nor Revolutionary" (book review), *Law and Society Review* 23, no. 5 (1989): 947. For a fuller exposition of her views that the equality offered to women pursuant to no-fault laws was purchased at the cost of more profound equity, thus leaving women at a greater economic disadvantage, see her *The Illusion of Equality: The Rhetoric and Reality of Divorce Reform* (Chicago, 1991), 52, 174–75.

Fineman and sociologist Lenore Weitzman maintained that divorcing women had been awarded a significantly larger share of marital assets during the preceding fault regime of divorce law. Fineman, *Illusion of Equality*, 52–53; Weitzman, *The Divorce Revolution: The Unintended Social and Economic Consequences for Women and Children in America* (New York, 1985). This roseate view of the fault era is contradicted by law professor Stephen D. Sugarman, who agreed that women today do, on the whole, fare poorly in the division of marital assets at divorce. But he contended that they had been equally unsuccessful under the fault regime. Sugarman, "Dividing Financial Interests on Divorce," in Stephen D. Sugarman and Herma Hill Kay, eds., *Divorce Reform at the Crossroads* (New Haven, 1990), 130–65. The emerging consensus appears to describe divorce, in whatever form, as continuing to have enormously adverse economic consequences for women. See Jana B. Singer, "Divorce Reforms and Gender Justice," *North Carolina Law Review* 67 (1989): 1103–21; Jacob, "Another Look at No-Fault Divorce and the Post-Divorce Finances of Women," *Law and Society Review* 23 (1989): 95–115.

9. See, e.g., Mary Ann Glendon, *Abortion and Divorce in Western Law* (Cambridge, Mass., 1987), 65–80.

10. Lawrence M. Friedman, "Rights of Passage: Divorce Law in Historical Perspective," *Oregon Law Review* 63 (1984): 666, and *Total Justice* (New York, 1985), 134. See also Friedman and Robert C. Percival, "Who Sues for Divorce? From Fault through Fiction to Freedom," *Journal of Legal Studies* 5 (Jan. 1976): 61–82, and *The Roots of Justice: Crime and Punishment in Alameda County, California, 1870–1910* (Chapel Hill, N.C., 1981), 325. For a general discussion of Friedman's themes, see his *A History of American Law*, 2d ed. (New York, 1985), 582–88. Kermit L. Hall espouses a similar viewpoint in *The Magic Mirror: Law in American History* (New York, 1989), 300.

11. See W. F. Ogburn and M. F. Nimkoff, *Technology and the Changing Family* (Boston, 1955), 239; Charles W. Tenney, Jr., "Divorce without Fault: The Next Step," *Nebraska Law Review* 46 (1967): 62.

12. James G. Snell, *In the Shadow of the Law: Divorce in Canada, 1900–1939* (Toronto, 1991), 7.

13. Susan S. Silbey and Austin Sarat, "Critical Traditions in Law and Society Research," *Law and Society Review* 21 (1987): 171.

14. E. P. Thompson, *The Poverty of Theory and Other Essays* (New York, 1978), 96.

15. Friedman, *History of American Law*, 150–52; Robert W. Gordon, "J. Willard Hurst and the Common Law Tradition in American Legal Historiography," *Law and Society Review* 10 (1975): 44. See also G. Edward White, "The Appellate Opinion as Historical Source Material," *Journal of Interdisciplinary History* 1 (1971): 491–509.

16. Paul W. Alexander, "Public Service by Lawyers in the Field of Divorce," *Ohio State Law Journal* 13 (1952): 19–20.

17. J. Willard Hurst, *The Growth of American Law: The Law Makers* (Boston, 1950), 13; Robert W. Gordon, "Critical Legal Histories," *Stanford Law Review* 36 (1984): 70 n.34.

18. Clifford Geertz, "Ideology as a Cultural System" in Geertz, *The Interpretation of Cultures* (New York, 1973), 193, 216; David Gross, "Lowenthal, Adorno, Barthes: Three Perspectives on Popular Culture," *Telos* 45 (1980): 122, 125. For other definitions of culture, see Richard A. Barrett, *Culture and Conduct: An Excursion in Anthropology,* 2d ed. (Belmont, Calif., 1991), 54–76; Michael Kammen, *Selvages and Biases: The Fabric of History in American Culture* (Ithaca, N.Y., 1987), 125; Stuart Hall, "Cultural Studies: Two Paradigms," in Richard Collins et al., eds., *Media, Culture, and Society: A Critical Reader* (London, 1986), 33–48; Marc J. Swartz and David K. Jordan, *Culture: The Anthropological Perspective* (New York, 1980), 52. A good discussion of the difficulties of cultural definition is found in Elvin Hatch, *Theories of Man and Culture* (New York, 1973), 1, 336–358.

19. Lawrence M. Friedman, "Legal Culture and Social Development," *Law and Society Review* 4 (1969): 29. On legal culture, see Friedman's *The Legal System: A Social Science Perspective* (New York, 1975), 193–268; Stewart Macaulay, "Popular Legal Culture: An Introduction," *Yale Law Journal* 98 (1989): 1545–58; Jerold S. Auerbach, *Justice Without Law* (New York, 1983), 142.

20. Macaulay, "Popular Legal Culture," 1555 n.47. Some definitions of popular legal culture assume too cozy a symbiosis between commonplace legal nostrums and statutory revision. For instance, Friedman explains legal culture as the instrumentality by which popular norms are transformed into "legal dress and shape." Barbara Yngvesson modulates that theme by suggesting that popular legal culture consists of an ongoing cultural exchange between popular sentiment and formal authority. These reasonable definitions are often accurate, but this study attempts to show that on the issue of twentieth-century divorce the uncertain relationship between the people's law and that of the legislatures and higher courts resembled neither Friedman's funnel nor Yngvesson's dynamic. See Friedman, "Law, Lawyers, and Popular Culture," *Yale Law Journal* 98 (1989): 1579, and *The Republic of Choice: Law, Authority, and Culture* (Cambridge, Mass., 1990), 4; Yngvesson, "Inventing Law in Local Settings: Rethinking Popular Legal Culture," *Yale Law Journal* 98 (1989): 1692–93.

21. Mary Ann Glendon, "Marriage and the State: The Withering Away of Marriage," *Virginia Law Review* 62 (1976): 688. For historian Roderick Phillips the "most striking" paradox in the Western world is the "simultaneous popularity of marriage and divorce." *Putting Asunder,* xi.

22. William Seagle, "The Right to Consolation," *American Mercury* 2 (May 1924): 39–44.

23. Edward S. Martin defended Judge Ben Lindsey's notion of "companionate marriage" as describing an everyday truth: "People get married and if they are

not suited, they get divorced." Martin, "Race Wars and Marriage," *Harper's* 155 (Oct. 1927): 656.

24. Katherine F. Gerould, "Divorce," *Atlantic* 132 (Oct. 1923): 470.

25. Willing Rattray, "Divorce as Manners and Custom," *New Republic* 45 (Dec. 9, 1925): 80–82.

26. William L. O'Neill, *Divorce in the Progressive Era* (New Haven, 1967).

1. The Feminization of Divorce after World War I

1. The term *new woman* is a recurring trope in historiography. In *Bicycles, Bangs, and Bloomers: The New Woman in the Popular Press* (Lexington, Ky., 1990), Patricia Marks describes the adventures of the "new woman" of the 1880s and 1890s. Each generation seems to call its women new, and historians sensitive to their subjects should follow suit, all the while looking behind the label. See Harriet Abbott, "What the Newest New Woman Is," *Ladies' Home Journal* 37 (Aug. 1920): 160. On the social and sexual personae of the new woman from the 1870s to the 1930s, see Carroll Smith-Rosenberg, *Disorderly Conduct: Visions of Gender in Victorian America* (New York, 1985), 245–96.

2. Margaret Deland, "The Change in the Feminine Ideal," *Atlantic* 105 (March 1910): 287–302. The author of two divorce novels, as well as essays and poems, Deland focused on moral issues in personal relationships. Her unorthodox approach to safeguarding the conventional family idea may be seen in her extensive work with unmarried mothers, whom she and her husband brought in to their home to support.

3. Rheta Childe Dorr, "The Problem of Divorce," *Forum* 45 (Jan. 1911): 68–79.

4. "A Minister's Defense of Divorce," *Literary Digest* 44 (Jan. 13, 1912): 73–74; Anna Garlin Spencer, "Problems of Marriage and Divorce," *Forum* 48 (Aug. 1912): 188–204; Henry James, "Is Marriage Holy?" *Atlantic*, March 1870, 363. Abba Goold Woolson epitomized the Victorian perspective: "Whatever tends to deteriorate the marriage relation and consequently the home, tends to deteriorate the whole machinery of life, whether social or political." Woolson, *Woman in American Society* (Boston, 1873), 82.

5. David M. Kennedy, "The Family, Feminism, and Sex at the Turn of the Century," in Thomas R. Frazier, ed., *The Private Side of American History*, 2d ed., 2 (New York, 1979): 119 (originally published as "The Nineteenth-Century Heritage: The Family, Feminism, and Sex," in David M. Kennedy, *Birth Control in America: The Career of Margaret Sanger* [New Haven, 1970]); E. A. Ross, "The Significance of Increasing Divorce," *Century Magazine*, May 1909, 151.

6. Warren I. Susman, "Scarcity vs. Abundance: A Dialectic of Two Cultures," *Nation*, Feb. 16, 1985; Anna B. Rogers, *Why American Marriages Fail* (Boston,

1909), 16; E. B. Harrison, "A Woman's View of Divorce," *Nineteenth Century* 69 (Feb. 1911): 329–34.

7. Leo Lowenthal articulated the rationale for looking at culture through the lens of both popular and formal literature, arguing that such work is a "particularly suitable bearer of the fundamental symbols and values which give cohesion to social groups." Lowenthal, *Literature, Popular Culture, and Society* (Palo Alto, Calif., 1961), xi. The two most significant studies of mass magazines in the period under study are Theodore Peterson, *Magazines in the Twentieth Century*, 2d. ed. (Urbana, Ill., 1964), and Frank Luther Mott, *A History of American Magazines*, vol. 5, *Sketches of Twenty-one Magazines, 1905–1930* (Cambridge, Mass., 1968). On the powerful cultural voice of popular periodicals, see Alice G. Marquis, *Hopes and Ashes: The Birth of Modern Times, 1929–1939* (New York, 1986), 91–139; Joe Alex Morris, *What a Year!* (New York, 1956), 180–92; George E. Mowry and Blaine A. Brownell, *The Urban Nation, 1920–1980*, rev. ed. (New York, 1981), 19–23.

8. Jürgen Habermas, *The Structural Transformation of the Public Sphere: An Inquiry into a Category of Bourgeois Society*, trans. Thomas Burger (Cambridge, Mass., 1989), 172; Barton, "Do Too Many People Marry?" *Good Housekeeping* 82 (Feb. 1926): 19, 163–77. Bruce Barton, an advertising genius who created the archetypal housewife character Betty Crocker, later served in the U.S. Congress and became a nemesis to President Franklin D. Roosevelt. His nationwide fame came in the wake of his 1925 bestseller, *The Man Nobody Knows*, which had first appeared in serial form in *Woman's Home Companion*. A good sketch of Barton is presented in Warren I. Susman, *Culture as History: the Transformation of American Society in the Twentieth Century* (New York, 1984), 122–31.

9. Ethel Klein, *Gender Politics: From Consciousness to Mass Politics* (Cambridge, Mass., 1984), 35.

10. Department of Commerce, *Historical Statistics of the United States* (Washington, D.C., 1960), 139, 179.

11. Elaine Tyler May made this point in *Great Expectations: Marriage and Divorce in Post-Victorian America* (Chicago, 1980), 62.

12. Ibid., 47.

13. Anonymous, "The Aftermath of Divorce," *Harper's* 169 (Aug. 1934): 365–73; Ruth Hale, "Freedom in Divorce," *Forum* 76 (Sept. 1926): 333–38. Hale founded the Lucy Stone League, which advocated that women keep their original last names after marriage.

14. Gustavus Myers, "The Rapid Increase of Divorce," *Current History* 14 (Aug. 1921): 816–21; Clarence Darrow, "The Divorce Problem: A Plea for the Application of Rational Principles to the Question of Domestic Relations," *Vanity Fair* 28 (Aug. 1927): 31. In 1930 historian Preston William Slosson recorded the "blunt truth" that "almost any American man or woman who was tired of the marriage relation could have it dissolved at the cost of a little time and trouble."

The Great Crusade and After, 1914–1928 (New York, 1930), 143. In *Middletown*, a major social study of Muncie, Ind., Robert S. Lynd and Helen Merrell Lynd contrasted the casual newspaper reporting of divorces in the 1920s with a government official's remark forty years earlier referring to a compilation of divorce statistics as "the repulsive exhibit." *Middletown: A Study in American Culture* (New York, 1929), 122.

15. Dorothy Dix was quoted in Lynd and Lynd, *Middletown*, 128; Robert Grant, "Domestic Relations and the Child," *Scribner's* 65 (May 1919): 525–30. Grant served as Boston probate judge for thirty years, from 1893 to 1923. As such, he had no divorce jurisdiction but ruled on questions of ordering husbands to provide support for separated wives. The prolific author of both fiction and nonfiction on family and legal issues, Grant recorded his perception of "many signs that the American woman has become enamored of the doctrine that wives who find their husbands uncongenial ought to have a divorce for the asking, in order to be free to marry some one else." Grant, "A Call to a New Crusade," *Good Housekeeping* 73 (Sept. 1921): 42–43, 140–44. Nor was such a characterization unusual for Grant. In two divorce novels Grant "depicts the woman as permitting her desire for social and economic position to triumph over all other urges, even that of mother love." James H. Barnett, *Divorce and the American Divorce Novel, 1858–1937* (New York, 1939), 105.

16. Quoted in David A. Shannon, *Between the Wars: America, 1919–1941*, 2d ed. (Boston, 1979), 159.

17. Rollin Lynde Hartt, "The Habit of Getting Divorces—II: Its Growth since the War," *World's Work* 48 (Sept. 1924): 519–24.

18. Mrs. Raymond [Margaret Dreir] Robins, "President's Report," National Women's Trade Union League, *Proceedings* (1917), v, quoted in J. Stanley Lemons, *The Woman Citizen: Social Feminism in the 1920's* (Urbana, Ill., 1973), 20; W. L. George, "Women in the New World: Is There a Change in Morals?" *Good Housekeeping* 76 (Feb. 1923): 78, 145–47; Benjamin P. Chass, "Alarming Increase in Divorce," *Current History* 22 (Aug. 1925): 789–92. See also Emily Newell Blair, "Where Are We Women Going?" *Ladies' Home Journal* 36 (March 1919): 37, 85. On the mobilization of women during the First World War, see Slosson, *Great Crusade and After*, 58–60.

19. Beatrice M. Hinkle, "Women and the New Morality," *Nation* 119 (Nov. 19, 1924): 541–43. Hinkle, who had divorced in 1915, generally focused in her writings on issues of sex and dependency. See her "Marriage in the New World," in Hermann Keyserling, ed., *Book of Marriage* (New York, 1926), and "Women's Subjective Dependence upon Man," *Harper's* 164 (Jan. 1932): 193–205. Hinkle and Charles R. Dana established the first psychotherapy clinic in the United States, in the medical college at Cornell University.

20. George, "Women in the New World." Sociologist Arthur Calhoun, who at the end of the First World War produced a three-volume history of the family, as-

serted that "the divorce movement is largely a part of feminism. Women rather than men have been the serious sufferers from marital evils and their revolt is marked." Calhoun, *A Social History of the American Family from Colonial Times to the Present* (Cleveland, 1919), 3:271.

21. Quoted in "A Call to Arms against Divorce," *Literary Digest* 88 (March 27, 1926): 30; see also "The Steady March from Altar to Court," *Literary Digest* 92 (Jan. 8, 1927): 30.

22. Charlotte Perkins Gilman, "The New Generation of Women," *Current History* 18 (Aug. 1923): 731–37. The phenomenon of women retaining their last names after marriage had not reached Muncie, Ind., in the 1920s: "There is occasional talk . . . of a woman's 'keeping her own name,' but no woman in Middletown follows this practice, and it is sharply frowned upon by the group." Lynd and Lynd, *Middletown*, 112 n.6.

23. Lynd and Lynd, *Middletown*, 127; May, *Great Expectations*, 119; Mabel Potter Daggett, "Make Over Marriage If You Would Cure Divorce: That's What the Judges Say," *Good Housekeeping* 80 (June 1925): 56–57, 174–84; Cole Porter, "Where Would You Get Your Coat?" *Fifty Million Frenchmen* (1929). On the brief burst of popularity enjoyed by French divorces for Americans in the 1920s, see Dorothy D. Bromley, "The Market Value of a Paris Divorce," *Harper's* 154 (May 1927): 669–81; Paul H. Jacobson, *American Marriage and Divorce* (New York, 1959), 105.

24. Charlotte Perkins Gilman had established her reputation with the publication of *Women and Economics* (Boston, 1898), a widely read argument for female economic independence. See also her "Toward Monogamy," *Nation* 118 (June 11, 1924): 671–73 (financial freedom of the new woman is the most significant reason for the social changes). Pathbreaking Denver juvenile court judge Ben B. Lindsey, whose *Companionate Marriage*, written with Wainwright Evans (Garden City, N.Y., 1927), caused a furious outcry, is quoted in "Is Marriage Breaking Down?" *Literary Digest* 76 (Feb. 17, 1923): 36. Similar arguments were presented in Edwin E. Slossom, "Semi-Detached Marriage," *Independent* 102 (May 8, 1920): 209–11 (entry of women into professions will involve changes in marriage); "Marriage, Divorce, and the Federal Constitution," *World's Work* 46 (May 1923): 19–21 (divorce statistics reflect women's greater social and economic independence); George L. Koehn, "Is Divorce a Social Menace?" *Current History* 16 (May 1922): 294–99 (same); W. L. George, "Women in the New World: Her New Job—Earning Her Own Living," *Good Housekeeping* 76 (Jan. 1923): 14–15, 152–54 (same); Doris Stevens, "Uniformity in Divorce," *Forum* 76 (Sept. 1926): 322–32 (same).

25. V. F. Calverton, "Careers for Women—A Survey of Results," *Current History* 29 (Jan. 1929): 633–38; the New York *World* was quoted in *Literary Digest* 92 (Jan. 8, 1927): 30; Robert Grant, "Marriage and Divorce," *Yale Review* 14 (Jan. 1925): 223–38. Americans seemed compelled to recycle their history, or at least their historical reasoning. In a 1996 article discussing divorce trends since the

1960s, Robyn E. Blumner argued that women's success competing with men in the market economy has given them a "sense of self-worth. It raised their expectations for lifetime fulfillment." Blumner then precisely—if perhaps unwittingly—recapitulated Judge Grant's seventy-year-old explanation for an increase in the divorce rate: "No longer were women willing to suffer silently in a relationship that was emotionally empty. And more importantly, women with independent means and personal pride no longer had to put up with philandering husbands." Blumner, "Blame Social Forces, Not the Law, for Divorce," *St. Petersburg Times*, March 3, 1996, 8D.

26. William H. Chafe, *The Paradox of Change: American Women in the Twentieth Century* (New York, 1991), 65.

27. Quoted in ibid., 66.

28. Ibid., 72. In contrast to Chafe, J. Stanley Lemons has argued that while reconversion after World War I reduced the female workforce, its peacetime level remained much higher than that of the prewar decade. Lemons, *Woman Citizen*, 21–25. For a discussion of the continuing vitality of separate gendered spheres of employment in the 1920s, see Dorothy M. Brown, *Setting a Course: American Women in the 1920's* (Boston, 1987): 77–99.

29. Mary Anderson, "The Growing Army of Women Workers," *Current History* 17 (March 1923): 1003–8. Anderson, a veteran trade unionist born in Sweden, was head of the Women's Bureau from its founding in 1920 until 1944. Under her direction, the Department of Labor produced Mary E. Pidgeon's *Women in Industry: A Series of Papers to Aid Study Groups*, Bulletin of the Women's Bureau, no. 91 (Washington, D.C., 1931). Pidgeon discussed the responsibility of married women workers for family support at ibid., 19–20.

30. Crystal Eastman, "Now We Can Begin," *Liberator* 3 (Dec. 1920): 23–24, reprinted in June Sochen, ed., *The New Feminism in Twentieth-Century America* (Lexington, Mass., 1971), 64–69. In addition to her feminist work, Eastman was a noted social investigator and peace activist. See Sylvia A. Law, "Crystal Eastman: Organizer for Women's Rights, Peace, and Civil Liberties in the 1910s," *Valparaiso University Law Review* 28 (1994): 1305. For contemporary evidence that little has changed since Eastman's day, see Arlie Hochschild and Anne Machung, *The Second Shift* (New York, 1989).

31. Pidgeon, *Women in Industry*, 21.

32. F. Scott Fitzgerald, "Imagination and a Few Mothers," *Ladies' Home Journal*, June 1923; Abraham Myerson, *The Nervous Housewife* (Boston, 1920); Myerson, "Remedies for the Housewife's Fatigue," *Ladies' Home Journal*, July 1930; Sinclair Lewis, *Main Street* (New York, 1920), 85. A good discussion of the acrid treatment of domesticity in Sinclair Lewis's novels is found in Glenna Matthews, *"Just a Housewife": The Rise and Fall of Domesticity in America* (New York, 1987): 172–77, 185–86, 200–202. For a housewife's defense of her career as a contented one, see Marian Castle, "I Rebel at Rebellion," *Woman's Journal*, July 1930.

33. W. L. George, "Women in the New World: What Is a Home?" *Good House-keeping* 76 (April 1923): 79, 234–38; George, "Women in the New World: No Housewives, No Homes," ibid. (May 1923): 90, 226–29. Two years later the magazine published another call for wives to receive salaries for housework. This time the editors commented that the "average wife does more work for less personal gain than any other free-born human being." William Johnston, "Should Wives Be Paid Wages?" ibid., 80 (March 1925): 30–31, 202–4. The following year the editors published an article calling for husbands to do housework along with their wives. Beth La Y'La, "Should Husbands Do Housework?" ibid., 82 (Jan. 1926): 18–19, 101. Carrie Chapman Catt argued for an outer limit to a woman's workday at home in "An Eight-Hour Day for the Housewife—Why Not?" *Pictorial Review*, Nov. 1928.

34. Henry R. Carey, "This Two-Headed Monster—The Family," *Harper's* 156 (Jan. 1928): 162–71. The editorial staff of *Harper's* noted a wide range of responses to Carey's pungent avowals. One letter writer thanked Carey for reaffirming that housework was a woman's job. Other correspondents "vigorously contested" Carey's claims, one woman stating that Carey's views were tantamount to a belief that women were not people. The editorial comments and excerpts from the letters are found in ibid. (March 1928): 527–28.

35. Havelock Ellis, Introduction to V. F. Calverton and S. D. Schmalhausen, *Sex in Civilization* (New York, 1929), 21–22.

36. On Freud's impact on the culture of the 1920s, see Frederick Lewis Allen, *Only Yesterday: An Informal History of the Nineteen-Twenties* (New York, 1931), 98–112; Sara M. Evans, *Born for Liberty: A History of Women in America* (New York, 1989), chap. 8, "Flappers, Freudians, and All That Jazz," 175–96.

37. Beatrice M. Hinkle, "The Chaos of Modern Marriage," *Harper's* 152 (Dec. 1925): 9. The 1938 study was cited in Stephanie Coontz, *The Way We Never Were: American Families and the Nostalgia Trap* (New York, 1992), 194.

38. Anonymous, "The Single Woman's Dilemma," *Harper's* 167 (Oct. 1933): 547–55. For accounts of the controversy generated by this article, see the summary of the many letters to the editor received by *Harper's* in its "Personal and Otherwise" column, 168 (Dec. 1933): [unnumbered pages]. For the *Catholic World's* scathing editorial condemning *Harper's* for publishing such a tale, see "The Last Word in Sex Morals," *Catholic World* 138 (Dec. 1933): 263–64.

39. Hartt, "Habit of Getting Divorces—II: Its Growth since the War." For a discussion of the impact of Freudian psychoanalysis on ways of thinking about divorce, see Lynne Carol Halem, *Divorce Reform*, 93–97.

40. Phyllis Blanchard and Carlyn Manasses, *New Girls for Old* (New York, 1930), 179–80; Ferenc Molnar, "Miss Q. Wants to Marry: An Enlightened Daughter and Her Mother Discuss Some Matrimonial Problems," *Vanity Fair* 29 (Oct. 1927): 58; Heywood Broun, "Advice to the Love-Lorn: Why Adventures into Matrimony Should Not Be Taken Too Seriously," ibid., 28 (April 1927): 59; Paula

S. Fass, *The Damned and the Beautiful: American Youth in the 1920's* (Oxford, 1977), 75; Dorothy Dunbar Bromley, "Feminist—New Style," *Harper's* 155 (1927): 558. See also Abbott, "What the Newest New Woman Is," 160.

41. Worth Tuttle, "Autobiography of an Ex-Feminist," *Atlantic* 152 (Dec. 1933): 641–49, 153 (Jan. 1934): 73–81; Pearl S. Buck, "America's Medieval Women," *Harper's* 177 (Aug. 1938): 225–32; Anne Shannon Monroe, "When Shall a Woman Divorce Her Husband?" *Good Housekeeping* 73 (Oct. 1921): 74, 96–98. Some commentators not only viewed women's biological nature as an obstacle to success in wage-earning endeavors, they also registered her dependence on men as an emotional handicap. As Mrs. James M. Kelly noted, "A woman of today may enter any profession—and be successful, as lawyer or doctor, in business or on the stump; but if she has not won the admiration of at least one man, she is a failure as a woman, and knows it." "Supply *and* Demand," ibid., 69 (Dec. 1919): 46.

42. Charlotte Muret, "Marriage as a Career," *Harper's* 173 (Aug. 1936): 249–57. A "career woman" was not considered a suitable wife by Italian opera singer Nino Martini. "I Want to Fall in Love!" *Good Housekeeping* 101 (Oct. 1935): 62–63, 210–13. Fellow opera singer Richard Crooks agreed that a woman's place was in the home. Rose Heylbut, "The Things That Matter," ibid., 102 (March 1936): 62–63, 112–14. Also in accord was Jessica Dragonette, 1935's "Queen of the Radio," who wrote "When Love Comes My Way I'll Renounce My Career," ibid., 103 (Aug. 1936): 34–35, 140–42. But radio and opera star Helen Jepson doubted Dragonette would, for in her words, "Love Came My Way—And My Marriage and My Career Are Helping Each Other," ibid. (Dec. 1936): 36–37, 222–25.

43. Judith Lambert, "I Quit My Job," *Forum* 98 (July 1937): 9–15. For a similar story, see Tuttle, "Autobiography of an Ex-Feminist." Even the extremely rare case of a house husband turned out to be rather less than it appeared. David A. Bates lost his job during the Depression, and while his wife worked outside the home, he and she reversed roles. Bates made it clear, however, that their respective backgrounds were unusual: his father had been a grocer, and so the son was familiar with household items. His wife's childhood, on the other hand, had failed to inculcate in her any sense of domestic savoir-faire. Bates was busy teaching her these skills, and he planned for their unusual arrangement to end within the year, by which time his wife would "have become more cognizant of her responsibilities as housewife." Bates, "A Husband Turns Housewife," *Forum* 101 (Jan. 1939): 8–10.

44. An excellent discussion of domesticity and the culture of consumption is presented in Matthews, "*Just a Housewife*," 172–96.

45. William R. P. Emerson, M.D., "Are You a 100% Mother?" *Women's Home Companion* 49 (Jan. 1922): 25, 56.

46. See Barbara Ehrenreich and Deirdre English, *For Her Own Good: 150 Years of the Experts' Advice to Women* (New York, 1979), chap. 5, "Microbes and the Manufacture of Housework," 141–81; Brown, *Setting a Course*, 111–21; Matthews, "*Just a Housewife*." On the technology of housework, see Ruth Schwartz Cowan,

More Work for Mother: The Ironies of Household Technology from the Open Hearth to the Microwave (New York, 1983); Susan Strasser, *Never Done: A History of American Housework* (New York, 1982). The effect on household work patterns of the large-scale disappearance of servants from upper-class and upper-middle-class homes in the 1920s is discussed in David M. Katzman, *Seven Days a Week: Women and Domestic Service in Industrializing America* (New York, 1978), 95, 130.

47. On the Sheppard-Towner Act, see Rosalind Rosenberg, *Divided Lives: American Women in the Twentieth Century* (New York, 1992), 74–77; Lemons, *Woman Citizen*, 153–80; Brown, *Setting a Course*, 53–54. Funding for the act ran out in 1929, and Congress refused to renew it.

48. Leonard McGee, "Nine Common Causes of Unhappy Marriages," *American Magazine* 97 (March 1924): 28–29, 193–98; Lynd and Lynd, *Middletown*, 117. McGee's list of paired commandments received fairly wide currency, as it was reprinted in Rollin Lynde Hartt, "The Habit of Getting Divorces—I: Causes in American Cities," *World's Work* 48 (Aug. 1924): 403–9, which in turn was reprinted in Julia E. Johnsen, ed., *Selected Articles on Marriage and Divorce* (New York, 1925), 28–39. Research by the Lynds confirmed that "thoughtful" men shared McGee's two-edged views of women: "Middletown husbands . . . are likely to speak of women as creatures purer and morally better than men but as relatively impractical, emotional, unstable, given to prejudice, easily hurt, and largely incapable of facing facts or doing hard thinking." *Middletown*, 117.

49. Floyd H. Allport, "Seeing Women As They Are," *Harper's* 158 (March 1929): 398–408. The editorial comments appeared in ibid. (May 1929): 791–92. Pringle Barrett argued in the *Atlantic* that while women's emancipation was "an accomplished fact," a man continued to think of a woman "in relation to him." She called for men to become liberated from this "delusion." Barrett, "The Emancipation of Men," *Atlantic* 153 (June 1934): 665–72.

50. George Jean Nathan, "Once There Was a Princess," *American Mercury* 19 (Feb. 1930): 242; Ludwig Lewisohn, "Is Love Enough?" *Harper's* 166 (April 1933): 544–53; Marle Beynon Ray, "It's Not Always the Woman Who Pays," *Saturday Evening Post* 205 (Sept. 3, 1932): 15, 46–50.

51. Vera Connolly, "Is Any Man Worth Fighting For?" *Good Housekeeping* 96 (Feb. 1933): 34–35, 190–94. *Good Housekeeping*'s editors remarked on that article's lead page that a husband "requires . . . a wife who fills his leisure hours efficiently." The same magazine later reminded women that a man is more successful in business if he is happily married, the responsibility for which, of course, belonged to the wife. Stanley S. Dickinson, "It Pays to Be Happily Married," ibid., 107 (July 1938): 48–50, 145–47. Divorced women responding to a study told Gretta Palmer that marriage was "a woman's task, more than a man's." Palmer, "Why Marriages Go Wrong," ibid., 109 (Nov. 1939): 34–35, 138–41.

52. Harvey Zorbaugh, "The Burden Marriage Bears," *Reader's Digest* 35 (Dec. 1939): 41–43, condensed from an article appearing in *You* (Winter 1939).

Women's task was not eased by novelist Arthur Stringer's sixteen-page tirade in the *North American Review.* Stringer attacked women as dishonest, emotional, unstable parasites who spent half a billion dollars a year on cosmetics. Anthropology, Stringer asserted, "compels us to accept woman . . . as intermediary between the child and the man." Stringer, "Why Women Make No Sense," *North American Review* 247 (Summer 1939): 296–311. Unsurprisingly, psychologist Grace Adams concluded that women did not like themselves and secretly believed that the male sex was better equipped with courage, wisdom, and trustworthiness. Adams questioned why prominent women were never elected to office, pointing to the fact that the women who had served as U.S. senators and representatives were "rather mediocre housewives who happened in their youth to marry men who later became statesmen and still later died in office." Adams speculated that women were averse to voting for other women, and thus that the Nineteenth Amendment had proved to be as ineffective as the Eighteenth. Grace Adams, "Women Don't Like Themselves," ibid., 288–95.

53. Anonymous, "Getting Along with Women," *Harper's* 171 (Oct. 1935): 614–23. In the same month the magazine printed a letter from Beulah Hannah of Lakeland, Fla., which read as if Hannah had seen a preview of the anonymous essay. She wrote that married women with jobs "should hold on to them like grim death and no girl should marry without some money of her own. Nothing is so conducive of a husband's respect as a wife with some independence, and then, too, she can always be free if marriage offers too many indignities." "Personal and Otherwise," ibid., 10.

54. "A Wife," "I Believe in the Double Standard," *American Mercury* 40 (April 1937): 421–26.

55. The letters responding to "I Believe in the Double Standard" are found in *American Mercury* 41 (June 1937): 251–55, xx–xxii, xxx (16 letters), 41 (July): 377–80 (6 letters), (Aug.): 505–6 (4 letters), 42 (Sept.): 212–14 (5 letters), (Oct.): 248–50 (3 letters), (Nov.): 380–81 (2 letters); (Dec.): 508–9 (1 letter), 43 (Jan.): 121–22 (2 letters), (April): 502 (1 letter), 44 (June): 249 (1 letter).

56. Ibid. Perhaps in response to the outpouring of reader sentiment on the "Double Standard" article, another piece of correspondence published on the final month of the deluge commented that the letters printed in the *American Mercury* were more critical than flattering and "epitomize the mental outlook of the average American in a way that is not equalled in any other publication." 44 (June 1938): 251.

57. Perhaps the fundamental problem between the sexes in this period was best encapsulated by D. H. Lawrence, who wrote that "man is willing to accept women as an equal, as a man in skirts, as an angel, a devil, a baby-face, a machine, an instrument, a bosom, a womb, a pair of legs, a servant, an encyclopedia, an ideal or an obscenity; the one thing he won't accept her as is a human being, a real human being of the feminine sex." Quoted in Dorothy L. Sayers, "Are Women Human?

Address Given to a Women's Society, 1938," in Dorothy L. Sayers, *Unpopular Opinions: Twenty-One Essays* (New York, 1947).

58. Katherine Burton, "On Women," *Commonweal* 19 (Feb. 23, 1934): 463–65. Burton pointed to Eleanor Roosevelt and Secretary of Labor Frances Perkins as examples who "show clearly the everlasting desire of women to clean house." Henrietta Ripperger made the same argument, insisting that "What This Country Needs Is a Woman," *Harper's* 172 (Feb. 1936): 373–76.

59. Inez Haynes Irwin, "Should Women Take over the World?" *Good Housekeeping* 107 (July 1938): 40–41, 142–45; Burton, "On Women." There were, of course, articles suggesting that women eschew interests outside the home. See Rose Wiler Lane, "Woman's Place Is in the Home," *Ladies' Home Journal*, Oct. 1936; Mary Roberts Rinehart, "I Speak for Wives," ibid., Feb. 1937, and "It's a Woman's World," ibid., July 1940.

60. The statistics and the quotation are taken from Steven Mintz and Susan Kellogg, *Domestic Revolutions: A Social History of American Family Life* (New York, 1988), 136.

61. On women workers' gains and losses in the Depression, see Susan Ware, *Holding Their Own: American Women in the 1930's* (Boston, 1982), 21–53; Winifred D. Wandersee, *Women's Work and Family Values, 1920–1940* (Cambridge, Mass., 1981), 84–102. An excellent discussion of Depression family life and its consequences for the following generation is presented in Elaine Tyler May, *Homeward Bound: American Families in the Cold War Era* (New York, 1988), 37–57.

62. "They Must Live, Mr. Biggers," *Independent Woman* 17 (Dec. 1938): 176; Dorothy M. Crook, "Not Guilty!" *Independent Woman* 19 (June 1940): 179–80; "When Married Women Work," *Commonweal* 31 (Feb. 9, 1940): 334.

63. *Independent Woman* 17 (Dec. 1938): 376–78, 396.

64. Elisabeth Cushman, "Office Women and Sex Antagonism," *Harper's* 180 (March 1940): 356–63; Senator Wagner is quoted in Chafe, *Paradox of Change*, 71. A 1930–31 National Education Survey of 1,500 school systems found that 77 percent would not hire married women, and that 63 percent dismissed female teachers upon marriage. Under section 213 (which was repealed in 1937), 75 percent of dismissed employees were women. Discrimination against women in state employment and private industry was also widespread, especially in desirable white-collar jobs. See Ware, *Holding Their Own*, 28; Susan M. Hartmann, *The Home Front and Beyond: American Women in the 1940's* (Boston, 1982), 17–18. On the history of employed women, see Alice Kessler-Harris, *Out to Work: A History of Wage-Earning Women in the United States* (New York, 1982).

65. "America Leading the World in Divorces," *Literary Digest* 69 (May 7, 1921): 28.

66. Henry E. O'Keeffe, "Love, Marriage, and Divorce," *Catholic World* 109 (Sept. 1919): 809–13; Grant, "Call to a New Crusade"; Grant, "The Limits of Feminine Independence," *Scribner's* 65 (June 1919): 729–34. Other articles harshly

criticizing America's divorcing in the 1920s include "The Failure of Divorce," *Literary Digest* 66 (Sept. 18, 1920): 116; Howard Chandler Robbins, "Divorce and Remarriage—Or the Family?" *Current History* 18 (Aug. 1923): 748–52; "A Dramatized Sermon on Divorce," *Literary Digest* 70 (July 2, 1921): 33; "Divorce on the Increase," *Catholic World* 118 (Nov. 1923): 263–64; "What a Divorce Lawyer Knows," *Collier's* 76 (Oct. 1, 1925): 20–21; "Is Divorce Ever Justified," *Outlook* 140 (July 15, 1925): 381–82; "A Call to Arms against Divorce," *Literary Digest* 88 (March 27, 1926): 30.

67. "But What about Your Home?" *Collier's* 68 (July 2, 1921): 14; Myers, "Rapid Increase of Divorce"; "The Ashes on the Hearth," *Literary Digest* 79 (Oct. 13, 1923): 34; Charles Fiske, "The Christian Ideal of Marriage," *Forum* 76 (Nov. 1926): 738–43. In "Laws of Marriage and Divorce," F. A. Bosanquet argued that "anything which tends to impair the permanence of marriage prejudices the position of married women." *Nineteenth Century* 89 (June 1921): 1053–61.

68. Pope Pius XI, "Encyclical Letter: On Christian Marriage," *Catholic Mind* 29 (Jan. 22, 1931): 21–64.

69. Ibid. Companionate and experimental marriages came in for particular censure as "hateful abominations . . . which reduce our truly cultured natures to the barbarous standards of savage peoples." Ibid.

70. "No Surrender on Marriage," *Literary Digest* 108 (Jan. 24, 1931): 30; Theodore Dreiser, "Marriage and Divorce: A Problem of Sex and Society," *Forum* 64 (July 1920): 26–36.

71. Both Hughes and Grant were quoted in "Divorce," *Current Opinion* 73 (Nov. 1922): 580–81; the *New Republic* criticism is found in "The Civilizing of Divorce," *New Republic* 55 (Aug. 1, 1928): 266–67. Grant practiced the modern morals he preached, at least as may be evidenced by his 1921 engagement to a woman who had been twice divorced. See "The Religion of Freedom Expounded by Dr. Grant," *Current Opinion* 74 (March 1923): 341–43. On the emerging religious view of divorce, see Joseph F. Newton, "What God Hath Not Joined," *Atlantic* 131 (June 1923): 721–27; A. Maude Royden, "What Is Marriage?" ibid., 132 (Sept. 1923): 297–307; John H. Holmes, "Marriage and Divorce: The Views of a Liberal Churchman," *Forum* 80 (Oct. 1928): 551–57.

72. This voluminous correspondence was discussed in a two-part article by Walter Davenport, "Grounds for Divorce," *Collier's* 78 (July 17, 1926): 20, 40–41, (July 24): 14, 41.

73. "How Marriage Can Be Saved," *Literary Digest* 70 (July 9, 1921): 30; Edwin Markham, "The Decadent Tendency in Current Fiction," *Current History* 18 (Aug. 1923): 715–23. This criticism of fictionalized marriage is echoed in Koehn, "Is Divorce a Social Menace?"; Elizabeth C. Adams, "The Will to Love: A Postscript to a Discussion of Divorce," *Atlantic* 133 (Feb. 1924): 194–96; Grant, "Marriage and Divorce"; Vera L. Connolly, "Every Man for Himself: There Is Only One Reason for Divorce," *Good Housekeeping* 86 (Feb. 1928): 18–19, 165ff.; "The

Protestant Church's Survey of Marriage Evils," *Literary Digest* 100 (Feb. 23, 1929): 26–27.

74. Newton, "What God Hath Not Joined."

75. Charles G. Norris, *Brass* (New York, 1921); M. E. Ashmun, *Support* (New York, 1922); Robert Herrick, *Homely Lilla* (New York, 1923).

76. For an excellent discussion of the themes of divorce novels in this period, see Barnett, *Divorce and the American Divorce Novel*, 95–140. A discussion of American novels' historical dimensions during this period is provided in Nelson Manfred Blake, *Novelists' America: Fiction as History, 1910–1940* (Syracuse, N.Y., 1969).

77. Gina Kaus, "As Long As We Both Shall Live," *Good Housekeeping* 103 (Sept. 1936): 38–39, 198–203; Lynd and Lynd, *Middletown*, 114; Sanger is quoted in Brown, *Setting a Course*, 103. The ever-upward spiral of romantic rhetoric which set such unrealistic expectations about marriage was best parodied by George Bernard Shaw: "When two people are under the influence of the most violent, most insane, most delusive, and most transient of passions, they are required to swear that they will remain in that excited, abnormal and exhausting condition until death do them part." Quoted in Jon Winokur, ed., *The Portable Curmudgeon* (New York, 1987), 191.

78. Katherine F. Gerould, "Romantic Divorce," *Scribner's* 88 (Nov. 1930): 485–92; Ursula Parrott, *Ex-Wife* (New York, 1929); Katherine Mansfield, "Marriage à la Mode," *Sphere* 87 (Dec. 31, 1921), reprinted in Anthony Alpers, ed., *The Stories of Katherine Mansfield* (Auckland, 1984), 431–40; Maude Parker, "Till the Courts Do Us Part," *Good Housekeeping* 85 (Aug. 1927): 38–39, 106–12. *Philip and His Wife*, Margaret Deland's 1894 novel, anticipated by a generation this trend toward romantic divorce. In Deland's tale the husband believes that since he and his wife are no longer in love, it would be immoral for them to stay married. The wife does not object. *Philip and His Wife* is discussed in Barnett, *Divorce and the American Divorce Novel*, 95–105.

79. A. P. Herbert, *Holy Deadlock* (London, 1934); "Divorce Long a Thorn to British," *Literary Digest* 122 (Dec. 19, 1936): 19–20; "English Divorce: A. P. Herbert Fights to Put Liberalizing Measure through Commons," *Literary Digest* 123 (Jan. 30, 1937): 13–14. Herbert was a maverick member of Parliament as well as a novelist, and he attacked English divorce law in both guises. Herbert's entertaining account of the passage of his divorce bill is found in his *The Ayes Have It: The Story of the Marriage Bill* (New York, 1938). In "Blackmail within the Law," an anonymous English barrister outlined the nonfictional scenario of Herbert's *Holy Deadlock* procedure. A husband merely had to provide his wife's solicitor with the address of the hotel in which he spent one night with a "woman unknown." A divorce trial upon such evidence would take between five and ten minutes. *Living Age* 325 (May 16, 1925): 360–67.

80. "Marriage Is Gone," *Catholic World* 140 (Dec. 1934): 263–63; "The Menace of Divorce," ibid. (January 1935): 387–91; Lewisohn, "Is Love Enough?"; Adela

Rogers St. Johns, "The Married Life of Doug and Mary," *Photoplay* (Feb. 1927): 34, 134–36.

81. Gretta Palmer, "New Rules for Divorce Collectors," *Good Housekeeping* 107 (July 1938): 28–29, 83–86. The shifting mores may also be clearly seen in Hollywood's work product. A Bryn Mawr College study of movies released in 1931–32 found that twenty-two of twenty-four films touching the subject evinced a favorable treatment of divorce. Hornell Hart, "Changing Social Attitudes and Interests," in Report of the President's Research Committee on Social Trends, *Recent Social Trends in the United States* (New York, 1933), 417.

82. Ogden Nash, "I Never Even Suggested It," "I Do, I Will, I Have," and "The Strange Case of Mr. Ormantude's Bride," *Verses from 1929 On* (New York, 1959), 104, 289–90, 391; Nash, "The Strange Case of the Dead Divorcee," *I'm A Stranger Here Myself* (Boston, 1938), 105; Nash, "Advise outside a Church," in "Three Plaints: And Other Poems," *Saturday Evening Post* 208 (Nov. 16, 1935): 29, reprinted in *Verses from 1929 On*, 24–26. Donald N. Koster traced the shift of opinion toward divorce on the American stage, noting the striking liberalization of attitudes after World War I. "The Theme of Divorce in American Drama, 1871–1939" (Ph.D. diss., Univ. of Pennsylvania, 1942).

83. Gerould, "Romantic Divorce."

2. The Popular Arena of Divorce

1. Arthur Garfield Hays, "Modern Marriage and Ancient Laws," *Nation* 119 (Aug. 20, 1924): 187–89. Hays insisted in his memoirs that "no social purpose is served by dragooning two people into an intimate relationship where they have grown indifferent to or hate each other, and that it is morally indefensible to maintain a marriage relation by legal statute where the real emotional bonds between the couple no longer exist." *City Lawyer: The Autobiography of a Law Practice* (New York, 1942), 179. In "The Divorce Laws of America and Europe," *Current History* 20 (May 1924): 249–53, Nancy M. Schoonmaker remarked that Americans are "at last fully convinced" that laws will not force people to remain married when they wish to divorce.

2. Grant, "Domestic Relations and the Child," "Limits of Feminine Independence," "Marriage and Divorce," *Scribner's* 66 (Aug. 1919): 193–98, and "Call to a New Crusade."

3. "Marriage, Divorce, and the Federal Constitution," *World's Work* 46 (May 1923): 19–21.

4. Carey, "This Two-Headed Monster." The editors subsequently published a letter critical of Carey's essay and arguing that mutual incompatibility was "the one sensible [divorce] ground," which unfortunately was legally unrecognized. Ibid. (May 1928): 792.

5. Anonymous, "Ten Years after the Divorce: I Would Not Divorce Him Now," ibid., 165 (Aug. 1932): 313–21.

6. In his influential 1932 compilation of family laws, Professor Chester G. Vernier felt compelled to advise his audience that "despite any impression to the contrary which [the lay reader] may have received from the reading of novels and newspapers, no statute now existing names incompatibility of temper as a cause for absolute divorce." Vernier, *American Family Laws*, vol. 2, *Divorce and Separation* (Stanford, Calif., 1932): 65. The single exception could be found in the territory of the Virgin Islands, which had carried over the divorce provisions of the Danish law that had formerly governed the territory. See Lester B. Orfield, "Divorce for Temperamental Incompatibility," *Michigan Law Review* 52 (1954): 662–63.

7. Hartt, "The Habit of Getting Divorces—I: Causes in American Cities"; Schoonmaker, "Divorce Laws of America and Europe." Judge Grant was more blunt: "Let us either welcome with open arms incompatibility as a ground for divorce or cease to masquerade as moralists by deliberate hoodwinking of our courts by falsehood." Grant, "Marriage and Divorce."

8. On orthodox formalism, see Morton J. Horwitz, *The Transformation of American Law, 1870–1960: The Crisis of Legal Orthodoxy* (New York, 1992), 9–32; G. Edward White, *Tort Law in America: An Intellectual History* (New York, 1985), 20–37.

9. Edward A. Purcell, Jr., *The Crisis of Democratic Theory: Scientific Naturalism and the Problem of Value* (Lexington, Ky., 1973), 11.

10. Oliver Wendell Holmes, Jr., "The Path of the Law," *Harvard Law Review* 10 (1897): 461. On Holmes and instrumentalism, see Morton White, *Social Thought in America: The Revolt against Formalism* (London, 1976), 59–75; P. S. Atiyah and Robert S. Summers, *Form and Substance in Anglo-American Law: A Comparative Study of Legal Reasoning, Legal Theory, and Legal Institutions* (Oxford, 1987), 240–50.

11. John Chipman Gray, *The Nature and Sources of the Law* (New York, 1909), chap. 5; Roscoe Pound, "Law in Books and Law in Action," *American Law Review* 44 (1910): 1236; Pound, *An Introduction to the Philosophy of Law* (New Haven, 1922), 47; Karl N. Llewellyn, *The Bramble Bush* (1930; rept. New York, 1960). For a summary of the Realist movement, see Wilfrid E. Rumble, Jr., *American Legal Realism: Skepticism, Reform, and Judicial Process* (Ithaca, N.Y., 1968).

12. Horwitz, *Transformation of American Law*, 181–82.

13. Roscoe Pound, "Justice according to Law," *Columbia Law Review* 14 (1914): 103.

14. The adaptation of large portions of the juvenile court philosophy by proponents of therapeutic divorce is discussed in chapter 4.

15. Koehn, "Is Divorce a Social Menace?" As late as 1953 sociologist Ray E. Baber noted that newspaper accounts continued to convey the misleading impression that incompatibility was a widespread legal divorce ground. Baber, *Marriage and the Family*, 2d ed. (New York, 1953), 454.

16. Thurman Arnold, *The Folklore of Capitalism* (New Haven, 1937), 365. J. G. Beamer argued that the American way of divorce illustrated Arnold's "immoral and undercover organization" which is "accepted and tolerated as a necessary evil." Ibid., quoted in Beamer, "The Doctrine of Recrimination in Divorce Proceedings," *University of Kansas City Law Review* 10 (1942): 214. As Albert C. Jacobs noted in 1936, "Free consent divorce exists in the United States today as fact, not merely as a phenomenon of the divorce mill, but as the standard practice throughout the country." Jacobs, "Attacks on Decrees of Divorce," *Michigan Law Review* 34 (1936): 749, 751.

17. Fred S. Hall, "Marriage and the Law," *Annals of the American Academy of Political and Social Science* 160 (March 1933): 110.

18. See Max Rheinstein, *Marriage Stability, Divorce, and the Law*, 3; Riley, *Divorce: An American Tradition*, 14–15; Timothy B. Walker, "Disarming the Litigious Man: A Glance at Fault and California's New Divorce Legislation," *Pacific Law Journal* 1 (1970): 183; Phillips, *Putting Asunder*, 566.

19. Walker, "Disarming the Litigious Man," 189–90 and n.23; Hubert I. Teitelbaum, "The Pennsylvania Divorce Law," title 23, *Pennsylvania Statutes Annotated* (1955), 348–49.

20. O'Neill, "Divorce as a Moral Issue," 139.

21. Herbert Croly, *The Promise of American Life* (1909; rept. Cambridge, Mass., 1965), 346.

22. Llewellyn, essay in *My Philosophy of Law: Credos of Sixteen American Scholars* (Boston, 1941), 185.

23. T. J. Jackson Lears, "From Salvation to Self-Realization: Advertising and the Therapeutic Roots of the Consumer Culture, 1880–1930," in Richard Wightman and T. J. Jackson Lears, eds., *The Culture of Consumption: Critical Essays in American History, 1880–1980* (New York, 1983), 4.

24. Gerould, "Divorce," 463.

25. F. MacKenzie, "Spiritual Values and the Family in Court," *Law and Contemporary Problems* 18 (1953): 21–22.

26. Gerould, "Divorce"; Henry H. Foster, Jr., "Family Law in a Changing Society," in F. James Davis et al., *Society and the Law: New Meanings for an Old Profession* (New York, 1962), 229 n.2.

27. Krauss v. Krauss, 163 La. 218, 226, 111 So. 683, 58 A.L.R. 457 (1927).

28. Tschida v. Tschida, 170 Minn. 235, 237, 212 N.W. 193, 194 (1927). Rare indeed are the features of American culture that have no antecedents. While the proliferation of Freudian ideas belongs to the period after World War I, Robert L. Griswold has presented evidence that a "less restrained" definition of cruelty began to emerge in appellate opinions as early as the mid-nineteenth century. He identified a shift "from social and moral considerations to medical and psychological criteria," as well as an emphasis upon "individual autonomy at the expense of social order." Griswold, "The Evolution of the Doctrine of Mental Cruelty in

Victorian American Divorce, 1790–1900," *Journal of Social History* 20 (1986): 127. See also his *Family and Divorce in California, 1850–1890: Victorian Illusions and Everyday Realities* (Albany, 1982).

29. Joseph Walter Bingham, essay in *My Philosophy of Law*, 13.

30. Otto Kahn-Freund, "Observations on the Possible Cooperation of Teachers of Law and Teachers of Social Science in Family Law," *Journal of Legal Education* 9 (1956): 76 (reprinted in *Kansas Law Review* 5 [1957]: 363–65).

31. H. L. Mencken, "Sententiae," in *The Vintage Mencken* (1955), reprinted in George Carruth and Eugene Ehrlich, eds., *The Harper Book of American Quotations* (New York, 1988), 373; Phillips, *Putting Asunder*, 148; Walter Wadlington, "Divorce without Fault without Perjury," *Virginia Law Review* 52 (1966): 36–37. Adultery constituted the only universal divorce ground in the United States. South Carolina represents a partial exception to this rule. It experimented with divorce for ten years beginning in 1868. But from 1878 until the restoration of fault grounds in 1949, the Palmetto State forbade divorce entirely. J. D. Sumner, Jr., "The South Carolina Divorce Act of 1949," *South Carolina Law Quarterly* 3 (1951): 253–59.

32. On the requirements for desertion actions from the end of World War I until the end of World War II, see James M. Henderson, *Nelson on Divorce and Annulment*, 2d ed., vol. 1 (Chicago, 1945), chap. 4.

33. Albert C. Jacobs and Julius Goebel, Jr., *Cases and Other Materials on Domestic Relations*, 4th ed. (Brooklyn, 1961), 410; Rheinstein, *Marriage Stability, Divorce, and the Law*, 124. The Iowa Code, for example, rendered cruelty sufficient to warrant divorce as "such inhuman treatment as to endanger the life of his wife." A husband could proffer similar grounds. Iowa Code 1939, §§ 0475–76.

34. Friedman and Percival, "Who Sues for Divorce?" 79–80.

35. "American Divorce Rate Still Increasing," *World's Work* 38 (July 1919): 297. On the popularity of the cruelty ground, see Baber, *Marriage and the Family*, 458.

36. Hensley was quoted in "Are Changing Conventions Menacing the Marriage Institution?" *Current Opinion* 74 (March 1923): 338–40; Stevens, "Uniformity in Divorce"; Anonymous, "Who Gets the Children?" *Harper's* 161 (Sept. 1930): 455–63; "Divorce Report," *Time* 30 (July 19, 1937): 60–61; William L. Prosser, "Divorce: The Reno Method and Others," *Forum* 100 (Dec. 1938): 296–91. Also noting the ease of establishing cruelty were John Gilland Brunini, "States' Rights and Divorce," *Commonweal* 20 (Oct. 19, 1934): 577–79; and the discussion by "Mr. Con" in "Pro and Con: Legalize Divorce By Mutual Consent?" *Readers' Digest* 34 (Jan. 1939): 91–96.

37. Walker, "Disarming the Litigious Man," 194–97; Rheinstein, *Marriage Stability, Divorce, and the Law*, 53–54. As Judge Paul W. Alexander observed, "If the plaintiff extends mercy to the defendant, the law punishes him for it." Quoted in Walker, "Disarming the Litigious Man," 195. Condonation itself subsumed a bizarre twist, for its continued effectiveness as a bar was conditioned upon

"conjugal kindness" by the offending spouse. Subsequent marital miscues, not themselves substantial enough to be independent grounds for divorce, might be sufficient to allow the once-estopped condoner to revive the original divorce action. See Wadlington, "Divorce without Fault without Perjury," 39.

38. John Sirjamaki, *The American Family in the Twentieth Century* (Cambridge, Mass., 1953), 181. Sociologist Ray E. Baber's quip that "if a marriage becomes intolerable to either husband or wife, it may be dissolved; but if it becomes intolerable to both, the state rules that in the interests of society it must be maintained!" overstated the formal law, but only slightly. Baber, *Marriage and the Family*, 479.

39. Louis Harris, *Love, Marriage, and Divorce in History and Law* (Boston, 1930), 99, quoted in Andrew G. Truxal and Francis E. Merrill, *The Family in American Culture* (New York, 1947), 679.

40. Vernier, *Divorce and Separation*, secs. 62, 80; Rheinstein, *Marriage Stability, Divorce, and the Law*, 54–59; Alvah L. Stinson, *Woman under the Law* (Boston, 1914), 343; Sirjamaki, *American Family*, 181.

41. Monroe, "When Shall a Woman Divorce Her Husband?" Gerould, "Divorce"; Grant, "Marriage and Divorce," 193–98.

42. "Divorce by Collusion," *Commonweal* 17 (Jan. 25, 1933): 340. The article noted that burgeoning divorce rates had altered the attitudes of couples contemplating marriage, making the wedding vows increasingly more provisional. Brides and grooms were thus "potential partners to a collusive divorce at the very altar." Ibid. *Commonweal* was undoubtedly not thinking of Ogden Nash in this context, but his couplet may come back to the reader's mind: "It is pleasant, George, and necessary / To pretend the arrangement is temporary." Nash, "Advice outside a Church."

43. Beamer, "Doctrine of Recrimination," 213; Wadlington, "Divorce without Fault without Perjury," 38–39. See also Paul Sayre, "Divorce for the Unworthy: Specific Grounds for Divorce," *Law and Contemporary Problems* 18 (1953): 28–29.

44. Beamer, "Doctrine of Recrimination," 213, 243, 253–54; Note, "Recrimination as a Defense in Divorce Actions," *Iowa Law Review* 28 (1943): 349.

45. Beamer, "Doctrine of Recrimination."

46. Hale, "Freedom in Divorce." William Seagle also attacked recrimination in "Right to Consolation."

47. Ludwig Lewisohn, "On Love in Marriage," *Nation* 119 (Oct. 19, 1924): 464–65; Royden, "What Is Marriage?"

48. Gerould, "Divorce," 460, 465–67; "Decency in Divorce," *Nation* 127 (Sept. 5, 1928): 214–15. The *Nation* editorialized that it was wrong to "insist that before a divorce is granted one party must violently attack the character of the other." Ibid. Stephen Ewing expressed the same opinion in "The Mockery of American Divorce," *Harper's* 157 (July 1928): 153–64.

49. Royden, "What Is Marriage?" In 1924 *Atlantic* published a poignant story by a man whose wife had ceased to love him and desired a divorce to marry another.

The author wanted happiness for his wife and so intended to accede to her wish. But to do so, the law demanded that he "accuse her of a crime." Nonetheless, he concluded, this distasteful act would ultimately serve everyone's best interest. The author made no mention of the more common alternative, that she accuse him of a marital outrage. Burnham Hall, "Shall I Divorce My Wife?" *Atlantic* 134 (Aug. 1924): 155–62. Anticipating some skeptical readers, the editors appended a comment that the story was "absolutely true." Ibid.

50. Mabel Potter Daggett, "What the Judges Told Us about Divorce," *Good Housekeeping* 80 (April 1925): 28–29, 156–69, "What the Judges Say about Divorce," ibid. (May 1925): 36–37, 104–21, and "Make Over Marriage If You Would Cure Divorce." Similar judicial commentary is also compiled in Connolly, "Every Man for Himself"; Ewing, "Mockery of American Divorce," 153–64.

51. Judges McCourt, Sherman, and Hill were quoted in Daggett, "What the Judges Say about Divorce." My reading of the evidence shows that trial judges rejected the dictates of their appellate superiors on the requirement of establishing actual marital fault, spurred on by an avalanche of litigants. Historian Robert L. Griswold, on the contrary, has argued for "great congruence between appellate court rulings and lower court conceptions of marital cruelty." Griswold, "Evolution of the Doctrine of Mental Cruelty in Victorian American Divorce," 142 n.3. But beginning in the 1920s, the popular culture raced far beyond the cruelty ground and—with the complicity of the trial bench—established a working jurisprudence of mutual consent divorce, a legal outpost never reached by appellate courts. Even when presented with relatively clear legislative mandates to remove considerations of fault from divorce cases, appellate courts often found ways to retain the jurisprudence with which they were most comfortable: ascertaining culpability.

52. Quoted in Daggett, "What the Judges Told Us about Divorce." Judge Shields's opinion about the support for dissatisfied spouses reflected the strength of litigants not only in the United States but also in Canada. Historian James G. Snell recounted the divorce paradigm north of the United States: "The customary rules of marriage and divorce coexisted with the formal divorce regime and interacted with the needs and position of individual couples and spouses to produce a strikingly complex divorce environment. Always operating with the constraints of that environment, divorcing couples in early twentieth-century Canada were able to turn the system back on itself, using it to meet at least some of the their own ends. Mutual consent was the most prominent characteristic of a process in which couples took advantage of loopholes in the system to operate (to some extent at least) as the participants desired." Snell, *In the Shadow of the Law*, 191–92.

53. The "fire-escape" metaphor is that of Judge A. F. Hollenbeck, Trinidad, Colo., quoted in Daggett, "Make Over Marriage If You Would Cure Divorce"; the "divorce easy and rapid" quote is Markleville, Calif., judge L. T. Price's, ibid.; the

"how far is the factory" quote is Daggett's, "What the Judges Say about Divorce"; Judge Dawson was quoted in "Make Over Marriage If You Would Cure Divorce."

54. Judge Orr was quoted in Ewing, "Mockery of American Divorce"; Judge Hill's comment appeared in Daggett, "What the Judges Say about Divorce." Judge L. T. Price, quoted in Daggett, "Make Over Marriage If You Would Cure Divorce," agreed with Judge Hill that children sometimes suffer more within a ruptured household.

55. Judge Miller was quoted in Daggett, "What the Judges Say about Divorce"; I. M. Rubinow, "Marriage Rate Increasing despite Divorces," *Current History* 29 (Nov. 1928): 289–94. Judge Lindsey was a popular subject of rabid commentary in the periodicals, both pro and con. See "Is Marriage Breaking Down?" *Literary Digest* 76 (Feb. 17, 1923): 36; "Are Changing Conventions Menacing the Marriage Institution?" *Current Opinion* 64 (March 1923): 338–40; Martin, "Race Wars and Marriage"; Joseph Collins, M.D., "The Doctor Looks at Companionate Marriage," *Outlook* 147 (Dec. 21, 1927): 492–94, 503; Charlotte Perkins Gilman, "Divorce and Birth Control," *Outlook* 148 (Jan. 25, 1928): 130–31, 153; M. G. L. Black, "A Business Woman on Companionate Marriage," ibid. (Feb. 22, 1928): 286–87; Fulton Oursler, "A Critic of Companionate Marriage," ibid. (April 25, 1928): 648.

56. On the question of which institution was more problematic, Judge William A. Kittinger of Anderson, Ind., said the "chief trouble . . . is not with divorce but with marriage." A bevy of judges agreed: W. W. McComish, Kansas City, Kans.; R. A. Richards, Sparta, Wash.; F. W. Wilson, Dalles, Oreg.; Samuel W. Johnson, Brighton, Colo. (all quoted in Daggett; "What the Judges Say about Divorce"); George Tazwell, Portland, Oreg.; and Frank E. Hutchinson, Lebanon, Ind. (quoted in Daggett, "Make Over Marriage If You Would Cure Divorce"). Daggett's quote is from "What the Judges Say about Divorce." Judge W. A. Reynolds was quoted in Daggett, "What the Judges Told Us about Divorce."

Midwestern and western judges seemed most comfortable with the changing divorce mores. Paul H. Landis even suggested that many easterners migrated west to take advantage of liberalized divorce law. "More mobile" westerners lacked an "established integrated society" and were less bothered by the loss of the traditional "institutional" family. Landis, "Divorce in Our Time," *Forum* 105 (June 1946): 865–72. Similar observations about the higher divorce rate in the West may be found in Daggett, "What the Judges Say about Divorce"; Ewing, "Mockery of American Divorce"; Joseph Kirk Folsom, *The Family: Its Sociology and Social Psychiatry* (New York, 1934), 371, 373; John H. Mariano, *A Psychoanalytic Lawyer Looks at Marriage and Divorce* (New York, 1952), 110–16. Substantially higher divorce rates obtained in the West than in any other part of the country during the period covered by this study. Jacobson, *American Marriage and Divorce*, table 48, at 100.

57. Robert S. Lynd and Helen Merrell Lynd, *Middletown in Transition* (New York, 1937), 161.

58. Ewing, "Mockery of American Divorce," 153–64.

59. *Middletown*, 114 n.8. In his study of Canadian divorce during this same period, James G. Snell observed that the way in which unhappy couples seized "control of divorce . . . was reflected in their behaviour and their language. Couples frequently spoke as though a divorce was theirs to give rather than the state's." Snell, *In the Shadow of the Law*, 194. Of course, uncontested divorces did not always reflect a mutual decision to sever the matrimonial bonds. The *Jersey Journal* noted in 1933 that some defendants lacked the funds to hire counsel to rebut the divorce charge, while others declined to fight because they felt certain of an unfavorable verdict. Still other nonlitigants objected to exposing intimate details to public scrutiny, while a final group may even have been unaware of the proceedings, since they were served with notice by publication and had not "read the right newspapers." The *Jersey Journal*'s comments were excerpted in "For Easier Divorce," *Literary Digest* 116 (July 29, 1933): 18–19.

60. *Middletown*, 121–122 and tables 11 and 12, 521.

61. Ibid., 122–23.

62. Roscoe Pound, Foreword to "A Symposium in the Law of Divorce," *Iowa Law Review* 28 (1943): 184.

63. Kaus, "As Long As We Both Shall Live." V. F. Calverton contrasted the respectability of divorce in the 1930s with his reminiscences that as recently as the time immediately before World War I, his mother would refer to divorced women as "indecent and immoral creatures," to which his father—a man who read Karl Marx at breakfast—would echo, "Ditto." V. F. Calverton, "Marriage à la Mode," in "Morals in Marriage: A Debate," *Forum* 97 (June 1937): 345–51.

64. Halem, *Divorce Reform*, 138–39.

65. Halem also posited the "proponents of an incompatibility ground [as] the true inventors of no-fault divorce laws." Ibid., 140. There are serious doubts about this claim; see chap. 3 below.

66. These statistics are compiled in Jacobson, *American Marriage and Divorce*, 127.

67. Rubinow, "Marriage Rate Increasing despite Divorces."

68. Such was the experience of New York Supreme Court Justice William Harman Black, related by Connolly, "Every Man for Himself." Justice Black's perspective on alimony may be gauged by his opinion that women's penchant for luxuries was a leading cause for divorce. Ibid.

69. Jacobson, *American Marriage and Divorce*, 120, table 57.

70. A. Wile, M.D., and Mary Day Winn, "Facing Divorce," *Survey Graphic* 14 (Jan. 1929): 418. The authors did concede that alimony should be provided a woman who had given her husband "those youthful years when she might have been laying the foundations of business success for herself." Ibid.

71. Frances Parkinson Keyes, "The Right to Happiness," *Good Housekeeping* 100 (April 1935): 34–35, 102–10. Six years earlier Keyes had similarly doubted that a "young, healthy, childless woman should ever be granted alimony." Keyes, "Happily Ever After," ibid., 88 (June 1929): 38–39, 206–13.

72. "Maniacal Wives," *Time* 26 (July 22, 1935): 35. *News-Week* reported the next year that the Illinois Supreme Court had affirmed a law cutting off alimony to childless women after two years. The court's judgment freed "several hundred men, behind in such payments, from alimony jails." "Upheld," *News-Week* 7 (May 2, 1936): 20. Mencken's quote, from *A Book of Burlesques*, is reprinted in Jill Bauer, *From "I Do" to "I'll Sue": An Irreverent Compendium for Survivors of Divorce* (New York, 1993), 171.

73. Anonymous, "Wives-in-Law," *Harper's* 177 (June 1938): 106–8. Two novels of the period explored the difficulties faced in a second marriage when the husband has to maintain alimony payments to his first wife. Faith Baldwin, *Alimony* (New York, 1928); Dorothy Walworth, *Rainbow at Noon* (New York, 1935).

74. Robert Neuner, "Proposed New Techniques in the Law of Divorce: II. Modern Divorce Law—The Compromise Solution," *Iowa Law Review* 28 (1943): 282.

75. Halem, *Divorce Reform*, 150. To exacerbate the relative dearth of financial transfer, some of the early articles describe alimony in such as way as to include child support.

76. Lewisohn, "Is Love Enough?"

77. C. G. Peele, "Social and Psychological Effects of the Availability and the Granting of Alimony on the Spouses," *Law and Contemporary Problems* 6 (1939): 283.

78. Dreiser, "Marriage and Divorce"; Gilman, "Divorce and Birth Control"; James P. Lichtenberger, *Divorce: A Social Interpretation* (New York, 1931): 139; Gerould, "Divorce." Judge Price is quoted in Daggett, "What the Judges Say about Divorce." The connection between divorce and juvenile delinquency was often made, for example, in "Divorce and Children," *Literary Digest* 116 (Sept. 9, 1933): 30.

79. "The Chief Victims of Divorce," *Literary Digest* 109 (May 2, 1931): 24; O'Keefe, "Love, Marriage, and Divorce"; Robbins, "Divorce and Remarriage—Or the Family?" Dorothea Brande, "At Least We're More Honest," *Scribner's* 98 (Dec. 1935): 368–71; William Johnston, "Divorced Children," *Good Housekeeping* 89 (Dec. 1926): 30–31, 199–202; Ernest Mowrer, "Divorce and Readjustment," in *Annals of the American Academy of Political and Social Science* 160 (March 1932): 195–96.

80. Rebecca West, "Divorce," *Forum* 76 (Aug. 1926): 161–70; "The Alarming Increase in Divorce," *Literary Digest* 95 (Dec. 3, 1927): 34; Ewing, "Mockery of American Divorce"; Anonymous, "Who Gets the Children?" *Harper's* 161 (Sept. 1930): 455–63. The "social ostracism" quote is from the Richmond *Times-Dispatch*, quoted in "The Divorce Mill Slackening," *Literary Digest* 107 (November 15, 1930): 26. On the traumas facing postdivorce children and their parents, see Dora Russell, "Is Divorce Worth the Price," *Nation* 136 (Jan. 25, 1933): 84–85, and two anonymous articles published by *Harper's*: "Ten Years after the Divorce: I Would Not Divorce Him Now," 165 (Aug. 1932): 313–21; "The Aftermath of Divorce," 169 (Aug. 1934): 365–73.

81. "I Have Four Parents," *Saturday Evening Post* 209 (Feb. 6, 1937): 7, 51–52. This essay, in condensed form, also appeared as the lead article in *Readers' Digest* 30 (May 1937): 1–5.

82. Gretchen, "I'll Take My Parents Separately," *Harper's* 176 (March 1938): 441–44.

83. Alexander's comments were reported in John S. Bradway, ed., *Proceedings of the Institute of Family Law* (Durham, N.C., 1959), 179.

3. Early Nonfault Experiments

1. Phillips, *Putting Asunder*, 439–54; Orfield, "Divorce for Temperamental Incompatibility," 659. Orfield noted that legislative divorces, which were unregulated, prevailed in the early national period and were not entirely eliminated until the last quarter of the nineteenth century. "We are told," wrote Roscoe Pound, "that the legislature was appealed to in cases that were too flimsy or too whimsical for the courts." Foreword to "Symposium in the Law of Divorce," 187.

2. 1881 Code of Washington, sec. 2000, pp. 340–341, repealed by Laws 1921, ch. 109, p. 332.

3. Stinson, *Woman under the Law*, 348.

4. Jacobson, *American Marriage and Divorce*, 109. On migratory divorces, see Riley, *Divorce: An American Tradition*, 119, 130, 135–44; Phillips, *Putting Asunder*, 531.

5. Note, *California Law Review* 35 (1947): 109; "Marriage and Divorce in Denmark," *Nation* 110 (April 24, 1920): 563–65; "They Shall Not Pass," ibid. (May 15, 1920): 640; Hays, "Modern Marriage and Ancient Laws"; Schoonmaker, "Divorce Laws of America and Europe"; Hale, "Freedom in Divorce"; Edwin Bjorkman, "Sweden's Solution of Divorce," *Forum* 76 (Oct. 1926): 543–50; Bromley, "Market Value of a Paris Divorce." See also Katherine Anthony, "Marriage Laws in Russia," *New Republic* 26 (May 4, 1921): 301–2; "Decency in Divorce," *Nation* 127 (Sept. 5, 1928): 214–15.

6. Ewing, "Mockery of American Divorce." The *Nation* pointed to an additional advantage in the Scandinavian divorce principles: the elimination of collusion as a bar. "Persons who have both been unfaithful may receive a divorce upon request, the British farce of collusion being thus simply accepted and rendered harmless." "They Shall Not Pass," 640.

7. Viggo Bentzon, *Familieretten* (Copenhagen, 1924), 155, quoted in Orfield, "Divorce for Temperamental Incompatibility," 663. After the transfer of the Virgin Islands to American sovereignty in 1917, incompatibility of temper was one of the grounds recognized in the Code of Laws of the Municipality of St. Croix in 1920 and the similar code enacted for St. Thomas and St. John the following year. Each code contained the incompatibility provision in its title III, ch. 44, sec. 7,

204 / NOTES TO CHAPTER THREE

subdivision 8. The history of the Virgin Islands' nonfault statute is traced in Orfield, "Divorce for Tempermental Incompatibility," 662–63, and by the United States Court of Appeals for the Third Circuit in Burch v. Burch, 195 F.2d 799, 805–6 (3rd Cir. 1952).

8. New Mexico Laws 1933, ch. 54, pp. 71–72; Alaska Laws 1935, ch. 54, p. 120; Oklahoma Laws 1953, ch. 22, p. 59; Nevada Laws 1967, ch. 278, pp. 805–6; Delaware Laws 1968, ch. 296, p. 1064; Kansas Laws 1969, ch. 286, pp. 738–39.

9. Friedman and Percival, *Roots of Justice*, 287; Michael Grossberg, *Governing the Hearth: Law and the Family in Nineteenth-Century America* (Chapel Hill, N.C., 1985), x; Robert L. Griswold, "Evolution of the Doctrine of Mental Cruelty in Victorian American Divorce," 141 n.3. For an assessment of the appellate report as a historical document, see White, "Appellate Opinion as Historical Source Material."

10. Orfield discusses some nineteenth-century antecedents to New Mexico's statute in "Divorce for Temperamental Incompatibility," 659–60. The course of incompatibility in New Mexico is sketched in Wadlington, "Divorce without Fault without Perjury," 47–50. N.M. Laws 1871–72, p. 28; N.M. Laws 1887, ch. 33; N.M. Laws 1901, ch. 62, sec. 22. While the impotency ground is not based on fault, it frustrates the traditional procreative purposes of the union. Nondisclosure of pregnancy and commission of a felony, while not conventional fault grounds either, focus on behaviors that may harm the marriage. Interestingly, section 23 of the 1901 act provided that when couples had permanently separated, either may request that a court divide their property or dispose of their children, or, in the wife's case only, award alimony. The statute apparently allowed the couple to separate without judicial approval.

11. N.M. Laws 1933, ch. 54, p. 71. In Poteet v. Poteet, 45 N.M. 214, 114 P.2d 91 (1941), the New Mexico Supreme Court wondered whether the state legislature had intended that the new divorce ground of incompatibility supplement the 1901 provision pertaining to rights of separated couples to have the court decide child custody and resolve financial arrangements. That the state's highest court had to speculate as to the legislature's intent only a few years after the enactment of the new divorce law suggests the difficulty of ascertaining legislative motives.

12. Chavez v. Chavez, 39 N.M. 480, 50 P.2d 264 (1935).

13. Hoff v. Hoff, 48 Mich. 281, 12 N.W. 160 (1882), quoted in *Chavez*. In *Hoff* the trial court had awarded both husband and wife a divorce on the ground of the extreme cruelty of each toward the other. The appellate court took pains to remind the trial judge that the recrimination doctrine forbade this evenhandedness.

14. *Chavez*, 39 N.M. at 487, 50 P.2d at 268.

15. Id. at 493, 50 P.2d at 272.

16. *Poteet*, 114 P.2d at 91. The supreme court opinion contains excerpts of both the wife's pleadings and the trial court's opinion.

17. Id., 114 P.2d at 91–92.

18. Id., 114 P.2d at 92.

19. Id., 114 P.2d at 93–94.

20. Id., 114 P.2d at 93, 96.

21. Pavletich v. Pavletich, 50 N.M. 224, 174 P.2d 826, 829 (1946).

22. Id., 174 P.2d at 830–32. Beamer's article is found at *University of Kansas City Law Review* 10 (1942): 213–56. The *Pavletich* veto of recrimination was praised in Wanda Lee Spears, "Domestic Relations—The Modern Trend toward Rejection of Recrimination," *Kentucky Law Journal* 36 (1948): 342–46.

23. Id., 174 P.2d at 832–33. *Pavletich* generated a bit of legal notoriety. See the discussion in Orfield, "Divorce for Temperamental Incompatibility," 667. *Pavletich* was also noted in *Virginia Law Review* 33 (1947): 355; *Minnesota Law Review* 31 (1947): 744; *Mississippi Law Journal* 18 (1947): 471; *Kentucky Law Journal* 36 (1948): 342. Similar fears of a degeneration into trial marriage were later expressed in Oklahoma, which adopted incompatibility in 1953. Burl Harris, "Divorce: Incompatibility as Ground for," *Oklahoma Law Review* 7 (1954): 99–102.

24. Clark v. Clark, 54 N.M. 364, 225 P.2d 147 (1950).

25. Id., 225 P.2d at 149. Two justices dissented on the *Pavletich* rationale: a finding of incompatibility should end the trial court's inquiry. In the majority opinion Justice (no longer Chief Justice) Sadler revealed that he had fallen one vote short of completely overruling *Pavletich* and so had to settle for its severe restriction. Id. at 148–49. As one commentator noted about incompatibility after *Clark*, "the concept of fault continues to exist in New Mexico though in an attenuated fashion." Orfield, "Divorce for Temperamental Incompatibility," 667.

26. Perhaps the problem was that in the vast majority of instances neither the parties nor the divorce courts believed in recrimination. Most cases were uncontested, and rare must have been the plaintiff sloppy enough to prove the case against his or her own position. Moreover, other divorce courts shared New Mexico trial judge Albert R. Kool's view that recrimination was "cruel and inhuman." In Wisconsin the state "divorce counsel" represented the official public interests in divorce suits. According to one report, the "divorce counsel" had recommended denial of dissolution in over 100 suits on the basis of the recrimination doctrine. The Wisconsin trial courts had followed his recommendation in only one case. N. P. Feinsinger and Kimball Young, "Recrimination and Related Doctrines in the Wisconsin Law of Divorce as Administered in Dane County," *Wisconsin Law Review* 6 (1931): 195, 213 n.39.

27. Robert Earl Lee, *North Carolina Family Law*, 4th ed., 1 (Charlottesville, Va., 1979): 347.

28. Bassett v. Bassett, 56 N.M. 739, 250 P.2d 487, 495 (1952); see also Hines v. Hines, 64 N.M. 377, 328 P.2d 944 (1958). The statistics bore him out. In 1948, for example, nearly seven-eighths of New Mexico divorce decrees were premised on incompatibility. This rate dwarfs the percentages for desertion (7.6), neglect to provide (1.9), cruelty (.8), and drunkenness (.4). Not one adultery divorce was

recorded in New Mexico in 1948. Jacobson, *American Marriage and Divorce*, table 59, p. 123, and text at 126.

29. Garner v. Garner, 85 N.M. 324, 512 P.2d 84 (1973); State ex rel. DuBois v. Ryan, 85 N.M. 575, 514 P.2d 851 (1973). Although recrimination was not formally annulled until the *Garner* decision, the victorious appellee in that case actually requested that the Supreme Court penalize her ex-spouse for filing a "frivolous appeal" suggesting the viability of recrimination. The court declined the request.

30. Wadlington, "Divorce without Fault without Perjury," 52; Shearer v. Shearer, 356 F.2d 391, 399–400 (3rd Cir. 1965), cert. denied, 86 S.Ct. 1463 (1966). In her otherwise scathing attack on "Our Scandalous Divorce Laws," Dorothy Dunbar Bromley had kind words for New Mexico's legal experiment. Apparently unaware of incompatibility's rocky road on appeal, Bromley lauded the statute unstintingly: "The only state where a self-respecting man or woman can come into court and terminate a marriage without at least offering proof of prolonged separation is New Mexico. This state admits as a ground for divorce plain incompatibility, in reality the most common cause for divorce, marriage counsellors will tell you." Bromley, "Our Scandalous Divorce Laws," *American Mercury* 66 (March 1948): 272–77.

31. Bliss Kelly, "Preventing Divorces: Oklahoma City's Family Clinic," *American Bar Association Journal* 45 (June 1959): 566; Oklahoma Laws 1953, ch. 22, p. 59; Chappell v. Chappell, 298 P.2d 768 (Okla. 1956); Wadlington, "Divorce without Fault without Perjury," 47. In a Symposium on the Law of Domestic Relations in Oklahoma, Richard T. Sonberg criticized the Oklahoma court in terms nearly identical to the Third Circuit's comments about New Mexico. "Grounds for Divorce in Oklahoma," *Oklahoma Law Review* 14 (1961): 403.

32. Dever v. Dever, 50 R.I. 179, 146 A.478, 479 (1929).

33. Baber, *Marriage and the Family*, 518. See Sirjamaki, *American Family in the Twentieth Century*, 184. By positing mutual consent as the operating paradigm of American divorce, I do not mean to suggest that all decisions by divorcing couples were free and voluntary. Undoubtedly, many individuals merely acquiesced in a divorce decision made by their spouses, a capitulation reflecting either a power imbalance within the relationship or a felt helplessness in the face of legal process. My review of the literature, both popular and formal, suggests only that those who mutually gave free consent greatly outnumbered those who grudgingly did so, and that the cultural tone of the former group dominated the public discourse.

34. Baber, *Marriage and the Family*, 518.

35. Seagle, "Right to Consolation," 39–44. The great length of most living apart statutes was also criticized in Bromley, "Our Scandalous Divorce Laws." Generally, however, the popular press ignored living-apart laws, as did the divorcing population. In 1948 only 3 percent of all American divorces were obtained under the living-apart statutes, although such laws were in effect in fourteen states and the District of Columbia. Estimates for individual states vary. In North

Carolina, which did not allow divorce on the ground of cruelty, 91 percent of all divorces were on the separation ground. This legal cause was also relatively popular in Louisiana (63 percent), the District of Columbia (24 percent), Vermont (20 percent), and Nevada (14 percent). In the remaining living-apart states, less than one-tenth of marital dissolutions were so premised. Jacobson, *American Marriage and Divorce*, table 59, p. 123, and text at 125–26.

36. Rhode Island Laws 1893, ch. 1187, sec. 1.

37. See Dever v. Dever. The Rhode Island Supreme Court took the ten-year provision quite literally to require a decade of sane contemplation by both parties upon the fate of their relationship. The court denied a divorce in a case in which the couple had lived apart for ten years but the wife had been insane for the final two-and-one-half years. Camire v. Camire, 43 R.I. 489, 113 A. 748 (1921).

38. In one odd twist on the planning-ahead theme, an Arizona husband successfully divorced his spouse on grounds that they had lived apart for the requisite five years. The wife then filed a sixty-page complaint seeking to overturn the divorce because her husband had bribed the Arizona legislature to enact the living-apart statute in order to effect his divorce. The Arizona Supreme Court rejected the wife's suit and affirmed the propriety of the living-apart law. Schuster v. Schuster, 51 Ariz. 1, 73 P.2d 1345 (1937).

39. Jacobson, *American Marriage and Divorce*, table 59, p. 123, and text at 125.

40. Id.

41. Cook v. Cook (*Cook* I), 159 N.C. 46, 74 S.E. 639 (1912); Cook v. Cook (*Cook* II), 164 N.C. 272, 80 S.E. 178 (1913). Limited divorce, also known as divorce *a mensa et thoro*, granted the parties a judicial separation but left them legally married. As a form of relief, it appealed to wives who wished to obtain a support order but not a final divorce. By contrast, absolute divorce, or divorce *a vinculo matrimonii*, constituted a total severing of the bonds of matrimony. See generally Homer H. Clark, Jr., *The Law of Domestic Relations in the United States* 2d ed. (St. Paul, 1988), 266–69; John DeWitt Gregory, Peter N. Swisher, and Sheryl L. Scheible, *Understanding Family Law* (New York, 1993), 208–9.

42. N.C. Laws 1907, ch. 89. Passage of the first living-apart statute in the twentieth century had been far from assured. In the state senate the vote was 23–22. 1907 *North Carolina Senate Journal* (Jan. 31, 1907), 183.

43. In addition to the ten-year separation provision, the living-apart law further required that both husband and wife have resided in North Carolina for ten successive years, and that no children have been born to the marriage. N.C. Laws 1907, ch. 89. In 1913 the latter two requirements were somewhat softened. Thereafter, only the plaintiff need show a ten-year residence, and divorce could be obtained as long as no children were still living. N.C. Laws 1913, ch. 165. No statutory provision required mutual consent.

44. *Cook* II, supra, 80 S.E. at 179. Justice Hoke's position on recrimination is surprising, for in a concurring opinion in Ellett v. Ellett, 157 N.C. 161, 72 S.E. 861, 862 (1911), Hoke had insisted that a marital wrongdoer should be estopped

from prosecuting a divorce action. Hoke maintained that the "doctrine and principle upon which [recrimination] rests lie deeper, and in my opinion, should now and always prevail." Now and always did not last two years.

45. *Cook* II, supra, 80 S.E. at 180.

46. Id.

47. Id. at 181–83. Justice Walker's notion that a wave of malevolent husbands endowed with a capacity for extremely long-range planning was bent on desecrating North Carolina wifeliness was not the only striking conclusion he reached. He also declared that the legislature lacked the power to order the courts to award divorces to any but the injured spouse. Id. at 181.

48. Sanderson v. Sanderson, 178 N.C. 339, 100 S.E. 590 (1919). The "Consolidated Statutes" were adopted by N.C. Laws 1919, ch. 238, sec. 8, effective Aug. 1, 1919. *Sanderson* was handed down on Oct. 22, 1919. The court did not discuss the fact that the lawsuit must have been filed and tried before the effective date of the revision.

49. *Sanderson*, 100 S.E. at 591. It should not be surprising that, as in *Cook* II and *Sanderson*, the wife insisted upon the right to be the injured party. It was only as the injured spouse that she could obtain alimony. See Carnes v. Carnes, 204 N.C. 636, 169 S.E. 22 (1933). Equally unsurprising, given his turnabout on recrimination between *Ellett* and *Cook* II, was the fact that Justice Hoke failed to dissent in *Sanderson*, although it completely undid his opinion in *Cook* II.

50. Lee v. Lee, 182 N.C. 61, 108 S.E. 352 (1921). North Carolina did not allow insanity as a separate divorce ground. Although the Lees had apparently been separated for ten years, the waiting period was reduced to five years shortly before the *Lee* opinion was handed down. N.C. Laws 1921, ch. 63, p. 312.

51. Sitterson v. Sitterson, 191 N.C. 319, 131 S.E. 641 (1926). *Sitterson* is quite unusual as a reported case which was most likely uncontested. No counsel appeared for the husband at the appellate level, and, given the facts, it is almost certain that W. J. never made an appearance himself. Nevertheless, both the trial judge and the supreme court denied Fay relief. In response to the dilemma posed by cases like Fay Sitterson's, the legislature soon amended the law to permit a living-apart divorce in the case of "an involuntary separation . . . in consequence of a criminal act committed by the defendant prior to such divorce proceeding." N.C. Laws 1929, ch. 6.

52. See *Cook* II, 80 S.E. at 181.

53. N.C. Laws 1931, ch. 72.

54. Reeves v. Reeves, 203 N.C. 792, 167 S.E. 129 (1933).

55. Long v. Long, 206 N.C. 706, 175 S.E. 85 (1934). *Long* was followed in Campbell v. Campbell, 207 N.C. 859, 176 S.E. 250 (1934).

56. Parker v. Parker, 210 N.C. 264, 186 S.E. 346 (1936); Reynolds v. Reynolds, 210 N.C. 554, 187 S.E. 768 (1936); Hyder v. Hyder (*Hyder* I), 210 N.C. 486, 187 S.E. 798 (1936). *Hyder* I illustrated the consequences of the supreme court's latest rotation around the wheel of recrimination. Mary Hyder tried to block Govan

Hyder's divorce by alleging that the separation was due to his desertion. The trial court, adhering to what was the then binding—if evanescent—precedent, refused to allow testimony about her allegation, as it was irrelevant under the "either party" statute. In *Hyder* I the supreme court remanded the case for the judge to allow the jury to hear the whole case. The jury did, and found that Govan had indeed deserted Mary, thus disallowing his right to a divorce. Govan's appeal was unavailing. See Hyder v. Hyder (*Hyder* II), 215 N.C. 239, 1 S.E.2d 540 (1939).

57. Brown v. Brown, 213 N.C. 347, 196 S.E. 333, 334 (1938).

58. Brown, 196 S.E. at 335.

59. Id.

60. Byers v. Byers (*Byers* I), 222 N.C. 298, 22 S.E.2d 902, 905 (1942).

61. *Byers* I; Byers v. Byers (*Byers* II), 223 N.C. 85, 25 S.E.2d 466 (1943).

62. *Byers* I, 22 S.E.2d at 903–4. Sara and the children obtained the benefits of the arrangement, spending a monthly average of nearly $470 between 1940 and 1942. Id., 22 S.E.2d at 904.

63. Id., 22 S.E.2d at 905–6. The two laws in question were N.C. Laws 1931, ch. 72, and N. C. Laws 1937, ch. 100.

64. Id., 22 S.E.2d at 906, quoting *Hyder* II, supra, 1 S.E.2d at 541. For a discussion of *Byers* I which comes to a somewhat different conclusion, see Lawrence T. Hammond, Jr., "Domestic Relations—Divorce—Separation by Mutual Consent," *North Carolina Law Review* 40 (1962): 808–11.

65. *Byers* II, 25 S.E.2d at 467, 469–70.

66. Lee, *North Carolina Family Law*, 347. That the supreme court remained an unyielding bulwark of the viability of recrimination may be seen by its full-court defense of the embattled doctrine over the remaining decades: Johnson v. Johnson, 237 N.C. 383, 75 S.E.2d 109 (1953); Pruett v. Pruett, 247 N.C. 752, 117 S.E.2d 724 (1961); Richardson v. Richardson, 257 N.C. 705, 127 S.E.2d 525 (1962); O'Brien v. O'Brien, 266 N.C. 502, 146 S.E.2d 500 (1966); Eubanks v. Eubanks, 273 N.C. 189, 159 S.E.2d 562 (1968); Harrington v. Harrington, 286 N.C. 260, 210 S.E.2d 190 (1975). The *Harrington* decision overturned a court of appeals opinion which had held that adultery should no longer be available as a defense to separation, Harrington v. Harrington, 22 N.C.App. 419, 206 S.E.2d 742 (1974). This reversal goaded the legislature to intervene in an unmistakable way, with the "clear intention . . . to nullify the future effectiveness" of the supreme court's *Harrington* ruling. Lee, *North Carolina Family Law*, 346.

67. Carl N. Everstine, *Divorce in Maryland*, Research Report no. 25, Research Division, Maryland Legislative Council (Feb. 1946): 17–19.

4. The Case of the All-Too-Consenting Adults

1. Paul W. Alexander, "Our Legal Horror Divorce," *Ladies' Home Journal* 66 (Oct. 1949): 124. The story of the slot-machine bill is also told in David G. Wittels,

"Perjury Unlimited," *Saturday Evening Post* 222 (Feb. 18, 1950): 135–38. Reno's reputation as the divorce and gambling mecca earned it the sobriquet of "Gambling Gomorrah." Anthony M. Turano, "Reno the Naughty," *American Mercury* 37 (Feb. 1936): 183–89. On the connection between betting and divorcing in the "Biggest Little City in the World," see Quentin Reynolds, "Relax in Reno," *Collier's* 96 (Dec. 28, 1935): 20–22, 35.

2. Richard H. Wels, "New York: The Poor Man's Reno," *Cornell Law Quarterly* 35 (1950): 303.

3. See Blake, *Road to Reno*, 64–96, 189–202; Jacob, *Silent Revolution*, 30.

4. Noted in Gilman, "Divorce and Birth Control."

5. For descriptions of New York hotel perjury, see Blake's entertaining account in *Road to Reno*, 4–6, 189–94; Walter Gellhorn, *Children and Families in the Courts of New York City* (New York, 1954), 278–303; Wels, "New York: The Poor Man's Reno," 315–18. Not all disposed to divorce could stomach New York's divorce procedure. "Adultery doesn't shock me," a woman informed her lawyer. "But I hate the idea of two witnesses." Hays, *City Lawyer*, 160.

6. New York *Mirror*, Sunday Magazine, Feb. 18, 25, March 4, 1934. The series, by a career corespondent (who retired from the trade when she married her final client), was summarized in Blake, *Road to Reno*, 193–94.

7. Henry Clay Greenberg, "New York's Perjury Mills," *American Magazine* 144 (Oct. 1947): 46–47, 145–47. Greenberg did note that a finding of adultery effectively disqualified the culpable spouse from public office, and he declared—without support—that prevaricating witnesses felt guilty and insecure long after the event. Ibid.

8. "Full Dress," *Time* 25 (Feb. 11, 1935): 16; Horowitz's letter to the editor is captioned "Laughing Ladies," ibid. (Feb. 25, 1935): 6.

9. Reed v. Littleton, 159 Misc. 853, 798 N.Y.S. 798, 800–801 (1936).

10. Quoted in Gellhorn, *Children and Families in the Courts of New York City*, 286.

11. Rheinstein, "Our Dual Law of Divorce: The Law in Action versus the Law of the Books," in The Law School, The University of Chicago, *Conference on Divorce*, Conference Series no. 9 (Feb. 29, 1952), 39–47.

12. Harriet F. Pilpel and Theodora Zavin, *Your Marriage and the Law* (New York, 1952), 283.

13. Joseph R. Clevenger, *Annulments of Marriage, Being a Treatise Covering New York Law and Practice with Composite Forms* (New York, 1946), 27, cited in Blake, *Road to Reno*, 197. The lush variety of annulment grounds was equally apparent twenty years later. See Max Hendler, *Matrimonial Practice in the New York Supreme Court* (New York, 1966), 52–73, 110–32, 157–59. New York's annulment practice was as notorious as its divorce process for featuring perjury. See Blake, *Road to Reno*, 194–99; Gellhorn, *Children and Families in the Courts of New York City*, 290–91.

14. Jacobson, *American Marriage and Divorce*, table A20, p. 172. Calfornia's

high annulment rate was due to its prohibition of remarriage for one year after divorce. See Peter Rowley, "Divorce, New York Style," *Nation* 199 (Dec. 14, 1964): 461–63.

15. Paul W. Alexander, "Family Life Conference Suggests New Judicial Procedures and Attitudes toward Marriage and Divorce," *Journal of the American Judicature Society* 32 (Aug. 1948): 40; Victor J. Baum, "Law and Social Work: Marriage Counseling, a Case in Point," *Journal of Family Law* 3 (Fall 1963): 283; see also Morris Ploscowe, "The Failure of Divorce Reform," *Ohio State Law Journal* 13 (1952): 3–12. The "let the perjury begin" quotation has achieved a niche in divorce folklore, as evidenced by its resurfacing in an article about divorce reform a generation later. George Cantor, "Make Breaking Up Harder to Do? Intervening before Marriage May Be Better," *Detroit News*, Feb. 25, 1996, Outlook.

16. The incident was recounted in Wittels, "Perjury Unlimited," 135–38, and in Henry Noble Hall, "Easy Does It," *Newsweek* 33 (Feb. 14, 1949): 53.

17. Mary Lewis Coakley, "What Do We Get Out of It?" *Catholic World* 173 (June 1951): 210–14. See Fulton J. Sheen, "How to Stay Married Though Unhappy," *Good Housekeeping* 136 (Feb. 1953): 59, 116–20. In 1958 Robert F. Drinan, a Jesuit priest and the dean of the Boston College Law School, addressed the Family Service Association of Greater Boston. The future congressional representative proposed liberal reforms for family life, such as housing assistance, family allowances, and health insurance. In addressing the question of divorce, however, his rhetoric escalated to apocalyptic cliché as he told his audience that "time is running out. The forces of barbarism are at the gates." Drinan, "The Crisis in Family Law," *Vital Speeches* 24 (Aug. 1, 1958): 638–40.

18. *Here's to the Family!* no. 2, *Why Not Get a Divorce?* (New York, 1949), 11.

19. Landis, "Divorce in Our Time"; Mabel A. Elliott and Francis E. Merrill, *Social Disorganization*, rev. ed. (New York, 1941), 597–98, quoted in Roy H. Abrams, "The Concept of Family Stability," *Annals of the American Academy of Political and Social Science* 272 (Nov. 1950): 1–8. On the changed understandings of the American family at mid-twentieth century, see Ogburn and Nimkoff, *Technology and the Changing Family*, chap. 3, "From Economics to Romance," 32–57, and chap. 6, "Shrinking Functions," 123–43; Robin M. Williams, Jr., *American Society: A Sociological Interpretation* (New York, 1951), chap. 4, "Kinship and Family in the United States," 36–77; Robert S. Redmount, "An Analysis of Marriage Trends and Divorce Policies," *Vanderbilt Law Review* 10 (1957): 516–27; Mintz and Kellogg, *Domestic Revolutions*, chap. 6, "The Rise of the Companionate Family, 1900–1930," 107–32. Warren P. Hill hit the mark in observing that "with the family thus stripped of all social utility beyond the mere material provision for offspring, it is small wonder that when love is dead the union tends to fly apart." Hill, "Some Aspects of Family Law," *Ohio State Law Journal* 13 (1952): 2.

20. James P. Kelly, "History and Principles of Catholic Family Law," in Stanley C. Morris, Jr., ed., *Divorce and Family Relations: A Compilation of the Original*

DICTA published by the Virginia Law Weekly, 1949–1950 (Charlottesville, Va., 1950), 14–20.

21. Philip Wylie, "What's Wrong with American Marriages," *Reader's Digest* 49 (Aug. 1946): 37–39 (condensed from *Cosmopolitan,* June 1946); Robert F. Winch, *The Modern Family* (New York, 1952), 389; John McPartland, "Footnote on Sex," *Harper's* 192 (March 1946): 212–14. Margaret Mead commented that the "American marriage ideal is one of the most conspicuous examples of our insistence in hitching our wagons to a star." *Male and Female: A Study of the Sexes in a Changing World* (New York, 1949), 342. See also Ernest W. Burgess, "The End of Romantic Marriage," *Collier's* 121 (Jan. 31, 1948): 12, 61–62.

22. Molly Haskell, *From Reverence to Rape: The Treatment of Women in the Movies,* 2d ed. (Chicago, 1987), 22; *Hamlet,* act 3, scene 1; David L. Cohn, "Are Americans Polygamous?" *Atlantic* 180 (Aug. 1947): 30–33; Truxal and Merrill, *Family in American Culture,* 121–30.

23. Paul H. Landis, "Marriage Has Improved," *Reader's Digest* 62 (June 1953): 13–15 (condensed from *Redbook,* May 1953). As W. Somerset Maugham quipped, American women expected of their husbands "a perfection English women only hope to find in their butlers." Quoted in ibid.

24. U.S. Department of Commerce, Bureau of the Census, *Historical Statistics of the United States, Colonial Times to 1970* (Washington, D.C., 1975), pt. 1, pp. 4, 9, 54–55, 64. Only the percentage of single Americans shrunk during the 1940s, from 31 to 23 percent. Ibid.

25. Samuel Tenenbaum, "The Fate of Wartime Marriages," *American Mercury* 61 (Nov. 1945): 530–36. See also Willard Waller, *War and the Family* (New York, 1940); Harold M. Wayne, "G.I. Divorce Dangers," *Collier's* 114 (Oct. 21, 1944): 13, 80–81. On the rapid increase in marriages and fertility upon the American entry into World War II, see May, *Homeward Bound,* 59; Hartmann, *Home Front and Beyond,* 7, 164. Two marriage peaks surfaced in 1941; one followed the Japanese invasion on Dec. 7, but an earlier one had come in the wake of President Roosevelt's May 21 declaration of unlimited national emergency. Jacobson, *American Marriage and Divorce,* 25–28, table 3 and fig. 3.

26. Tenenbaum, "Fate of Wartime Marriages," 530–36; D'Ann Campbell, *Women at War with America: Private Lives in a Patriotic Era* (Cambridge, Mass., 1984), 89; Reuben Hill and Howard Baker, eds., *Marriage and the Family* (Boston, 1940), 587–88. On marital relations during the war years, see May, *Homeward Bound,* 65–75. In an article written the previous decade, V. F. Calverton had identified the reasons for women's particular cultural vulnerability on this score: "So long as men were the only deviators from conventional morality, moralists never became alarmed at the matter of sexual deviations and violations . . . The dismay of the moralists has grown out of the realization that men have not adopted woman's morality but that women have adopted man's." Calverton, "Marriage à la Mode."

27. The Chattanooga report is described in Reginald Heber Smith, "Dishonest Divorce," *Atlantic* 180 (Dec. 1947): 42–45; "Divorce: The Postwar Wave," *Newsweek* 28 (Oct. 7, 1946): 33–34; "Liquor and Lipstick," *Time* 46 (Oct. 15, 1945): 14–15; "Divorce: National Scandal," *Newsweek* 29 (March 10, 1947): 27–28; Irene Stokes Culman, "You Married Him—Now Stick with Him," *Good Housekeeping* 120 (May 1945): 17.

28. Charlton Ogburn, "The Role of Legal Services in Family Stability," *Annals of the American Academy of Political and Social Science* 272 (Nov. 1950): 127–33; Maxine B. Virtue, *Family Cases in Court* (Durham, N.C., 1956), 229–30.

29. "Divorce Mill: Los Angeles Frees Many More Mismated Couples than Reno," *Life* 19 (July 23, 1945): 55–59. On California's expansive reading of mental cruelty, see Rheinstein, "Our Dual Law of Divorce," 39–47.

30. "Divorce Mill"; Groucho Marx was quoted in Bauer, *From "I Do" to "I'll Sue"*, 208; Wittels, "Perjury Unlimited," 28, 135–38.

31. John Bartlow Martin, "Divorce: A Day in Court," *Saturday Evening Post* 231 (Nov. 1, 1958): 19–21, 64–67; Paul W. Alexander, "The Follies of Divorce: A Therapeutic Approach to the Problem," *American Bar Association Journal* 36 (Feb. 1950): 107–8. A more extensive account confirming the mechanistic routine of Chicago divorce hearings in the 1950s is found in Virtue, *Family Cases in Court*, 52–112.

32. Jessie Barnard, *The Future of Marriage* (New York, 1972), quoted in Kevin J. Gray, *Reallocation of Property on Divorce* (Oxon, Eng., 1977), 6 n.

33. See John M. Eekelaar, "The Place of Divorce in Family Law's New Role," *Modern Law Review* 38 (1975): 242–43.

34. Judicial divorces had only become an option for English spouses in 1857, although private parliamentary bills from the mid-seventeenth-century on had dispensed divorces to a privileged few. The 1857 legislation allowed divorce to be granted to men because of their wives' adultery and to women who could prove that their husband's adultery had been aggravated by some other offense against morals, such as bigamy, incest, sodomy, desertion, cruelty, rape, or bestiality. Only in 1923 were English women granted the right to divorce on the same terms as men. See Ann Sumner Holmes, "The Double Standard in the English Divorce Laws, 1857–1923," *Law and Social Inquiry* 20 (Spring 1995): 601. On the history of English divorce, see generally Lawrence Stone, *Road to Divorce: England, 1530–1987* (Oxford, 1990); Phillips, *Putting Asunder*; Rheinstein, *Marriage Stability, Divorce, and the Law*.

35. Rheinstein, *Marriage Stability, Divorce, and the Law*, 319–20; Dorothy M. Stetson, *A Woman's Issue: The Politics of Family Law Reform in England* (Westport, Conn., 1982), 108–12. The 1937 law had been introduced as a private member bill, with no government endorsement. For an entertaining account of the maneuvering required to achieve its passage by the member of Parliament chiefly responsible, see Herbert, *The Ayes Have It*.

36. Laura Oren, "The Welfare of Women in Laboring Families: England, 1860–1950," in *Clio's Consciousness Raised: New Perspectives on the History of Women,* ed. Mary S. Hartman and Lois Banner (New York, 1974), 236–37.

37. Herbert, *Holy Deadlock;* "Sixty Years Ago," *Solicitors Journal* 66 (1922): 735–36; Stetson, *Woman's Issue,* 169; Church of England, *Putting Asunder: A Divorce Law for Contemporary Society* (London, 1966), 90 (hereafter *Putting Asunder*).

38. Church of England Commission on Christian Doctrine, *Doctrine in the Church of England* (London, 1938, rept. 1982), 200.

39. Elizabeth Wilson, *Only Halfway to Paradise: Women in Postwar Britain, 1945–1968* (London, 1980), 41. The percentage of women workers continued dramatically to increase, reaching 47 percent in 1972. Ibid.

40. Rheinstein, *Marriage Stability, Divorce, and the Law,* 273.

41. United Kingdom, *Report of the Royal Commission on Marriage and Divorce,* Cmd. 9678 (London, 1956), 11 (hereafter *Morton Commission Report*).

42. Quoted in Wilson, *Only Halfway to Paradise,* 90.

43. Robert S. W. Pollard, "The Need for an Inquiry into Divorce," *Contemporary Review* 117 (Jan. 1951): 39–47.

44. Quoted in Paul A. Welsby, *A History of the Church of England, 1945–1980* (New York, 1984), 226. It is hard to imagine a clearer sign of the changed mores than to contrast the role of Queen Elizabeth II in the 1950s in insisting that Princess Margaret reject a divorced suitor with the same queen's demand in the 1990s that Prince Charles and Princess Diana agree to divorce. See Sarah Lyall, "Changing Her Mind, Diana Agrees to Divorce," *New York Times,* Feb. 29, 1996, A1.

45. Oliver R. McGregor, "Equality, Sexual Values, and Permissive Legislation," *Journal of Social Policy* 1 (1972): 51.

46. Robert Cantuar, archbishop of Canterbury, Foreword to Welsby, *History of the Church of England.*

47. Quoted in Reginald Haw, *The State of Matrimony: An Investigation of the Relationship between Ecclesiastical and Civil Marriage,* (London, 1952) 120.

48. Quoted in Arthur R. Winnett, *Church and Divorce* (London, 1968), 18–19. In 1962 Sherwin Bailey pushed this concept even further within the church. In *Common Sense about Sexual Ethics: A Christian View,* he opposed treating ethical principles as legislative sanctions. He argued that where a marriage has broken down, the church's pastoral responsibility was to emphasize the good, and often "a successful second marriage will be the most creative form of reparation for past failure." Quoted in Winnett, *Church and Divorce,* 26.

49. Interesting accounts of this process are found in Welsby, *History of the Church of England,* 226–27; Carol Smart, *The Ties That Bind: Law, Marriage and the Reproduction of Patriarchal Relations* (London, 1984), 60–67.

50. Quoted in Wilson, *Only Halfway to Paradise,* 91.

51. Ibid. That same year John Grigg (Lord Altrincham) argued that the church "must recognize that sexual relations are too complicated to be treated with unqualified moral rigour." *Two Anglican Essays* (London, 1958), 62.

52. With regard to homosexuality, for example, the Wolfendon Committee in 1957 followed the liberal lead of the church in stressing the difference between sin and crime and urging that the law respect privacy in sexual matters. See the discussion in McGregor, "Equality, Sexual Values, and Permissive Legislation," 55–56.

53. Waters v. Waters [1956] P. 344 (D.C.); the quote is from John M. Biggs, *The Concept of Matrimonial Cruelty* (London, 1962), 92.

54. Baker v. Baker [1955] 1 W.L.R. 1011.

55. Crawford v. Crawford [1956] P. 195 (D.C.).

56. Wright v. Wright [1960] P. 85.

57. Ingram v. Ingram [1956] P. 390.

58. Williams v. Williams (1958) *The Times*, 15 March.

59. Davidson v. Davidson [1953] 1 W.L.R. 387.

60. Spicer v. Spicer [1954] 1 W.L.R. 1051.

61. [1942] 2 All.E.R. 637.

62. Id., 638.

63. [1949] P. 277 (C.A.).

64. [1963] 107 *Solicitors Journal* 596.

65. Ibid.

66. *Putting Asunder*, 17, 35.

67. Clark, *Law of Domestic Relations in the United States*, 509 (citation omitted).

68. Research on the ways in which gender roles have been socially constructed is summarized in Judith Lorber and Susan A. Farrell, eds., *The Social Construction of Gender* (Newbury Park, Calif., 1991), and Deborah Rhode, ed., *Theoretical Perspectives on Sexual Differences* (New Haven, 1990).

69. W. Clark Ellzey, "Marriage or Divorce?" *University of Kansas City Law Review* 22 (Fall 1953): 9–17; Ralph S. Banay, "The Trouble with Women," *Collier's* 118 (Dec. 7, 1946): 21, 74–79; Banay, "The Husband Really Pays," ibid., 119 (May 24, 1947): 18–19, 97–98; Banay, "How to Devour Your Husband," ibid., 122 (Oct. 30, 1948): 16–17.

70. Banay, "Trouble with Women," 74–79.

71. Banay, "Husband Really Pays," 97–98.

72. Ibid.

73. Banay, "How to Devour Your Husband," 16–17. Banay's dictum echoed sociologist Willard Waller's earlier assertion that the "modern woman cannot help trying to dominate her husband and cannot help hating him if she succeeds." Waller, *The Family: A Dynamic Interpretation* (New York, 1938), 415–17.

74. "Slur on Women Answered by Our President," *Independent Woman* 26 (Feb. 1947): 51; letter from Marie Laymen Avairy to *Collier's*, 119 (Jan. 11, 1947): 65; letter from Gertrude M. Adams to *Collier's*, 119 (Jan. 18, 1947): 61. Commenting on the popular postwar sport of debunking women's ambitions, one observer characterized Banay's writing as "tak[ing] out his shotgun and let[ting] go with both barrels." Harrison Smith, "Woman, the Scapegoat," *Saturday Review of Literature*

30 (Jan. 18, 1947): 18. See also Kathryn Brummond, "Are Wives People?" *Independent Woman* 25 (Nov. 1946): 329–30.

75. "Letters to the Editor," *Collier's* 119 (Jan. 18, 1947): 61; letter of Donald A. Johnson, ibid., 120 (July 19, 1947): 80.

76. Jacobson, *American Marriage and Divorce*, 126–28; Edwin A. Robson, "The Law and Practice of Divorce: The Judge's Point of View," in *Conference on Divorce*, 3–8; C. Clinton Clad, "You Can't Afford a Divorce," *Saturday Evening Post* 229 (April 20, 1957): 31, 127–30; Gellhorn, *Children and Families in the Courts of New York City*, 341. See also Clad, "The Economics of Divorce," *Phi Delta Delta* 37 (June 1959): 14–17. Kingsley Davis also remarked on the modest scope of alimony orders in "How Much Do We Know about Divorce," *Look* 19 (July 26, 1955): 65–69. A 1955 study reported that the national monthly median child support award was $17.39 per child. John Bartlow Martin, "Divorce: The Depths of Scandal," *Saturday Evening Post* 231 (Nov. 15, 1958), 44–45, 76, 80.

77. Pilpel and Zavin, *Your Marriage and the Law*, 307; Clad, "You Can't Afford a Divorce"; Dan Hopson, Jr., "The Economics of a Divorce: A Pilot Empirical Study at the Trial Court Level," *Kansas Law Review* 11 (1962): 107.

78. Harriet F. Pilpel and Theodora S. Zavin, "Separation Agreements: Their Function and Future," *Law and Contemporary Problems* 18 (1953): 35.

79. Illustrations of the genre include Norman M. Lobsenz, "Are Divorce and Alimony Unfair to Men?" *Reader's Digest* 75 (Oct. 1959): 193–98 (condensed from *Redbook*, Jan. 1959); Alexander Eliot, "Let's Abolish Alimony," *Saturday Evening Post* 237 (Aug. 22, 1964): 12–16; Morris Ploscowe, "Alimony," *Annals of the American Academy of Political and Social Science* 383 (May 1969): 13–22; James Lincoln Collier, "Time to Give Divorced Men a Break," *Reader's Digest* 96 (Feb. 1970): 64–68. Harangues about alimony were, of course, not new. In 1934 New York City magistrate Jonah Goldstein had complained of alimony's unfairness since the "man pays and pays and pays, although the wife in the meantime is earning funds." *The Family in Court* (New York, 1934), 83. See also Anthony M. Turano, "The Alimony Racket," *American Mercury* 29 (June 1933): 237–44.

80. Reprinted in Art Buchwald, "The Seven Year Itch," *American Mercury* 90 (Feb. 1960): 76–78.

81. Eliot, "Let's Abolish Alimony." Even an otherwise balanced account in a standard 1950s sociology textbook devoted the bulk of its discussion on the subject to "alimony careerists," excessive awards, and women who take savage delight in having ex-spouses imprisoned for failure to pay alimony. Baber, *Marriage and the Family*, 480–84.

82. *Time* 64 (Dec. 6, 1954): 2. That Northwestern Mutual selected an unmarried woman to promote the business acumen of married women reflects another twist in the fascinating strand of gendered reality in postwar America.

83. Eliot, "Let's Abolish Alimony," 12–16; "Letters to the Editor," *Saturday Evening Post* 237 (Sept. 19, 1964): 8.

84. Herma Hill Kay, "Equality and Difference: A Perspective on No-Fault Divorce and Its Aftermath," *University of Cincinnati Law Review* 56 (1987): 30.

85. Ibid., 33. Many of the initiative's backers were "males who have been burned by the financial inequities of the present legal system." William J. Lederer and Don D. Jackson, *The Mirages of Marriage* (New York, 1968), 256.

86. Michael Wheeler, *No-Fault Divorce* (Boston, 1974), 51, 136–38.

87. "Letters to the Editor," *Saturday Evening Post* 237 (Sept. 8, 1964): 8; Judge Adesko quoted in Martin, "Divorce: A Day in Court"; Hopson, "Economics of a Divorce," 125; Henry H. Foster, Jr., "Spadework for a Model Divorce Code," *Journal of Family Law* 1 (Spring 1961): 21; Anonymous, quoted in Herbert V. Prochnow and Herbert V. Prochnow, Jr., eds., *A Treasury of Humorous Quotations for Speakers, Writers, and Home Reference* (New York, 1969). For a summary of letter writers' responses to James Lincoln Collier's "Time to Give Divorced Men a Break," see "Divorce Is a Battle with No Winners," *Reader's Digest* 96 (May 1970): 39–41.

88. Margaret Case Harriman, "Woman Needs Man," *Good Housekeeping* 122 (May 1946): 41, 249–51. Marynia F. Farnham and Ferdinand Lundberg's *Modern Woman: The Lost Sex* (New York, 1947) was described by Harrison Smith as the "most comprehensive and damning contribution" to the debate. According to Smith, Farnham and Lundberg viewed feminism as "an aberration dangerous to society and fatal to women." Smith, "Woman, the Scapegoat," 18. Even loquaciousness was dangerous during this thermidorian reaction. See Richard Attridge, "Do Women Have to Talk So Much?" *Saturday Evening Post* 219 (June 28, 1947): 124.

Revisionist historians have raised a challenge to the dominant view emphasizing woman's domestic servitude during the cold war era. Joanne Meyerowitz, for example, has argued that the popular culture manifested a "bifocal vision of women both as feminine and domestic and as public achievers." Meyerowitz, "Beyond the Feminine Mystique: A Reassessment of Popular Mass Culture, 1946–1958," in Joanne Meyerowitz, ed., *Not June Cleaver: Women and Gender in Postwar America, 1945–1960* (Philadelphia, 1994), 232. Meyerowitz's essay serves up a useful corrective to the excesses of Friedanesque rhetoric, namely, that women lived as slaves in the male plantation known as postwar America. But even if many popular periodicals highlighted instances of women's public work, Meyerowitz concedes that the gender line dividing breadwinning from housekeeping remained unbroken. Ibid., 243–44. "The point," as a writer in the *Woman's Home Companion* told its readership in 1956, "is that primary responsibility for home and family engineering are your jobs and you know it." Sidonie M. Gruenberg, "Test Yourself: Do You Exploit Your Husband?" *Woman's Home Companion*, Feb. 1956, 36–37, 67–69.

89. Cole Porter, *Kiss Me, Kate* (1948). This very successful show charmingly told the story of a dramatic troupe's intermingling of Shakepeare's *Taming of the*

Shrew and a modern-day domestication of a virago. Although the song was deleted from the show, the lyrics to "A Woman's Career" satirically illustrate the prevalent view that a woman who breaks what would today be called the glass ceiling pays the price in alienation. Even if a successful actress wins an Oscar, the lyrics insist, "to live with an Oscar won't liven her nights" if she's unable to maintain a relationship with a man.

90. Smith, "Woman, the Scapegoat," 18.

5. The Deceptive Promise of Therapeutic Divorce

1. Andrew J. Polsky, *The Rise of the Therapeutic State* (Princeton, N.J., 1991), 66.

2. A selection of the literature on the origins of the juvenile court would include ibid.; Hamilton Cravens, "Child Saving in Modern America, 1870s-1970s," in Roberta Wollons, ed., *Children at Risk in America: History, Concepts, and Public Policy* (Albany, 1993), 3–31; Alexander W. Pisciotta, "Treatment on Trial: The Rhetoric and Reality of the New York House of Refuge, 1857–1935," *American Journal of Legal History* 29 (April 1985): 151–81; Anthony M. Platt, *The Child Savers: The Invention of Delinquency*, 2d ed. (Chicago, 1977); David J. Rothman, *Conscience and Convenience: The Asylum and Its Alternatives in Progressive America* (Boston, 1980); Ellen Ryerson, *The Best-Laid Plans: America's Juvenile Court Experiment* (New York, 1978); Steven L. Schlossman, *Love and the American Delinquent: The Theory and Practice of "Progressive" Juvenile Justice, 1825–1920* (Chicago, 1977); Sanford J. Fox, "Juvenile Justice Reform: An Historical Perspective," *Stanford Law Review* 22 (June 1970): 1187–1239; J. Herbie DiFonzo, "Deprived of 'Fatal Liberty': The Rhetoric of Child Saving and the Reality of Juvenile Incarceration," *University of Toledo Law Review* 26 (1995): 855.

3. Paul W. Alexander, "Is There a Divorce Evil?" *Ohio Magazine*, April 1945, reprinted in *Congressional Record* 91, A 1222.

4. On the ascendancy of the experts after World War II, see May, *Homeward Bound*, 26–27; Joseph Veroff, Richard A. Kulka, and Elizabeth Douvan, *Mental Health in America: Patterns of Help-Seeking from 1957 to 1976* (New York, 1981), 7–8, 10. According to Christopher Lasch, "The new psychiatric imperialism [of the 1940s and 1950s] not only expanded the doctor's authority over the patient, it ministered to all of 'society as the patient' in Lawrence Frank's memorable phrase." Lasch, *Haven in a Heartless World: The Family Besieged* (New York, 1977), 98, quoting Lawrence K. Frank, *Society as the Patient: Essays on Culture and Personality* (New Brunswick, N.J., 1948).

5. On the illness metaphor for divorce, see text at notes 20–28 below.

6. Halem, *Divorce Reform*, 221.

7. Folsom, *Family*, 365. On the history of the intrepid Judge Lindsey, see Charles E. Larsen, "Ben Lindsey: Symbol of Radicalism in the 1920's," in Harold

M. Hyman and Leonard W. Levy, eds., *Freedom and Reform: Essays in Honor of Henry Steele Commager* (New York, 1967), 255–275; Frank J. Taylor, "A Court to Prevent Divorce," *New Republic* 103 (Aug. 19, 1940): 239–40 (abridged as "Your Don't-Want-a-Divorce Court," *Reader's Digest* 37 [Sept. 1940]: 85–88); John Bartlow Martin, "Divorce: Effort to Save a Troubled Marriage," *Saturday Evening Post* 231 (Nov. 8, 1958): 36, 139–42. The most extensive treatment of Lindsey's iconoclastic career appears in Charles E. Larsen, *The Good Fight: The Life and Times of Ben B. Lindsey* (Chicago, 1972).

The statute creating the conciliation court declared its intention "to provide means for the reconciliation of spouses and the amicable settlement of domestic and family controversies." California Laws 1939, ch. 737, sec. 1730, pp. 513–14.

8. Ewing Cockrell, *Successful Justice* (Charlottesville, Va., 1939), 715; "Milwaukee: Marriages Patched Up," *Newsweek* 31 (Jan. 26, 1948): 27. Maxine Virtue describe the operation of the Milwaukee family court in *Family Cases in Court*, 174–214.

9. Sol Morton Isaac, "Family Law and the Lawyer," *Journal of Family Law* 2 (1962): 47.

10. See, for example, Paul H. Landis, *Making the Most of Marriage* (New York, 1955), 504–5; Ogburn, "Role of Legal Services in Family Stability"; Quintin Johnstone, "Divorce: The Place of the Legal System in Dealing with Marital-Discord Cases," *Oregon Law Review* 31 (1952): 317; Pilpel and Zavin, *Your Marriage and the Law*, 303, 323. For descriptions of the operation of the Toledo court, see Virtue, *Family Cases in Court*, 174–214, and Gertrude Samuels, "Courts for the Family Go on Trial," *New York Times Magazine*, Dec. 20, 1953, 16, 42–43.

11. Quoted in Virtue, *Family Cases in Court*, dedication page.

12. Alexander's crusade in print, in both professional and popular journals, was quite extensive and markedly influential, as repeated citations to Alexander's writings demonstrated. As one illustration of the widespread admiration for his work, note an article in the 1950 *Cornell Law Quarterly* which severely castigated New York's lax and fraudulent divorce procedures as a national disgrace but concluded that "it is possible to have divorce laws which salvage marriages, and the proof of that comes from the Division of Domestic Relations of the Court of Common Pleas in Toledo, Ohio, which for twelve years has been presided over by Judge Paul Alexander, Chairman of the Special Committee on Divorce and Marriage Law and Family Courts of the American Bar Association." The author went on to describe Alexander's therapeutic approach to divorce in glowing terms. Wels, "New York: The Poor Man's Reno," 325.

13. Alexander, "Divorce without 'Guilt' or 'Sin,'" *New York Times Magazine*, July 1, 1951, 14–16.

14. Ibid.

15. Alexander, "Legal Science and the Social Sciences: The Family Court," *Missouri Law Review* 21 (1956): 105, 107.

16. Alexander, "Let's Get the Embattled Spouses Out of the Trenches," *Law and Contemporary Problems* 18 (1953): 98.

17. The fault system "compel[s] the judge to grind out divorces regardless of the real facts, the underlying causes and the effect upon the parties, their families and the state." Paul W. Alexander, Introduction to Virginia Law Weekly, *Divorce and Family Relations*, vi–vii. He also focused criticism on those who "would make of the law a set of dehumanized, mechanized rules, and of the court a human slot machine: in goes the petition; wheels whir; out pops the decree." Alexander, Introduction to Virtue, *Family Cases in Court*, xxxiv.

18. Earl Lomon Koos, "Family Problems and the Court," *Annals of the American Academy of Political and Social Science* 287 (May 1953): 27, 28.

19. Alexander, "Follies of Divorce," 105–8, 168–72, quoted in Judson T. Landis and Mary G. Landis, *Readings in Marriage and the Family* (New York, 1952), 363. In the words of Edmund Bergler, "Divorce is in general a *neurotic* procedure of neurotic people." Bergler, "Six Types of Neurotic Reaction to a Husband's Request for a Divorce," *Marriage and Family Living* 8 (1946): 81, quoted in Fowler V. Harper, *Problems of the Family* (Indianapolis, 1952), 759. That "legal patients" with marital problems should not self-diagnose is also argued in Stanton L. Ehrlich and Charles E. Sproger, "X-ray of Divorce—Recent Developments," *University of Illinois Law Forum*, 1962:601.

20. Emily H. Mudd, "The Social Worker's Function in Divorce Proceedings," *Law and Contemporary Problems* 18 (Winter 1953): 66–71.

21. Mariano, *Psychoanalytic Lawyer Looks at Marriage and Divorce*, Preface. See also Alexander, "Legal Science and the Social Sciences."

22. Mariano, *Psychoanalytic Lawyer Looks at Marriage and Divorce*, chap. 9, "Mixing Chronological Years and Maturity Years," 173–96.

23. Nester C. Kohut, *A Manual on Marital Reconciliations: A Socio-Legal Analysis of Divorce for the Unbroken Marriage* (Chicago, 1964), 11. See also Abraham Stone, "Marital Counseling as Aid to Legal Profession," in Virginia Law Weekly, *Divorce and Family Relations*, 53–58 (reporting that many couples seeking divorce act on impulse); Paul W. Alexander, "A Therapeutic Divorce," in The Law School, The University of Chicago, *Conference on Divorce*, Conference Series, no. 9 (Chicago, Feb. 29, 1952), 51–52 (suggesting that complainants and their counsel automatically—and often incorrectly—assure the court's social worker that the marriage is dead).

24. Kohut, *Manual on Marital Reconciliations*, 7. Emily Marx discussed the medical invalidity of some complaints of cruelty in "Psychosomatics and Judicial Separations," *Fordham Law Review* 20 (1951): 87. Alice O'Leary Ralls, supervisor of the family court of King County, Washington, believed that at least half of divorce filers "are really hoping that something will stop them before it is too late." Ralls, "The King County Family Court," *Washington Law Review* 28 (1953): 26. Some evidence to support Ralls's thesis may be found in the statistics of divorce

dismissals. In a Kansas field study, a group headed by Quintin Johnstone discovered that between 20 and 45 percent of all divorce suits in the late 1940s and early 1950s were dismissed before trial, primarily due to the reconciliation of the parties. However, the study also found that a large percentage of these reconciliations only temporarily forestalled divorce. Johnstone, "Divorce Dismissals: A Field Study," *Kansas Law Review* 1 (1953): 245–57.

25. John S. Bradway, "Why Divorce?" *Duke Law Journal*, 1959:217, 218.

26. Brockenbrough Lamb, "Ethical Considerations as Related to Divorce," in Virginia Law Weekly, *Divorce and Family Relations*, 42–45. For a rare contrary observation that the emotional intensity associated with divorce did not necessarily result in a more neurotic client, see Marie W. Kargman, "The Lawyer as Divorce Counselor," *American Bar Association Journal* 46 (1960): 399.

27. Alexander, "Family Life Conference Suggests New Judicial Procedures and Attitudes toward Marriage and Divorce"; "What Is a Family Court, Anyway?" *Connecticut Bar Journal* 26 (1952): 269.

28. Executive Committee of the Federal Council of the Churches of Christ in America, "An Appeal for Change in Dealing with Divorce Problems," Sept. 19, 1952, quoted in Harper, *Problems of the Family*, 772. According to this church council, scientific experts should aim to "reorient and reeducate" spouses seeking divorce. Ibid. See John H. Mariano, *The Use of Psychotherapy in Divorce and Separation Cases* (New York, 1958), 70 (observing that divorce resulted from "neglect in the treatment of . . . emotional ills").

29. Kohut, *Manual on Marital Reconciliations*, 52–54. Kohut clinched his point by remarking that a "patient can hardly be his own physician!" Ibid., 52. Paul W. Alexander made the same observation in his Introduction to Virginia Law Weekly, *Divorce and Family Relations*, vi.

30. Nester C. Kohut, "Family Courts and Separation Statutes: Correlatives or Non-Correlatives," *Journal of Family Law* 4 (1964): 71–76.

31. Nester C. Kohut, "Therapeutic Separation Agreements," *American Bar Association Journal* 51 (1965): 756–60; See also his *Manual on Marital Reconciliations*, 60, and "Rehabilitation of Broken Marriages," *Practical Lawyer* 10 (1964): 75–91.

32. Kohut, "Therapeutic Separation Agreements." See also William C. Boyden, "Divorce Settlement Agreements," *Illinois Bar Journal* 39 (1950): 110.

33. Kohut, "Therapeutic Separation Agreements." Kohut envisaged that a temporary agreement on issues of custody and maintenance would be appended to the therapeutic separation agreement. For reader response critical of Kohut's proposal, see "Views of Our Readers," *American Bar Association Journal* 51 (1965): 903–4.

34. David Mace, *Marriage* (Garden City, N.Y., 1952), 58.

35. Lasch, *Haven in a Heartless World*, 100; Alexander, "Legal Science and the Social Sciences."

36. Quoted in Goldstein, *Family in Court*, 31–32.

37. Ibid., 76, 81; Ben B. Lindsey and Wainwright Evans, *The Companionate Marriage*, 2d ed. (Garden City, N.Y., 1929), xv, 175. Ernest R. Groves suggested that courts move away from an "atmosphere of criminal procedure to a fact-finding and social-adjusting institution." Groves, *The Marriage Crisis* (New York, 1928), 222. Support for a comprehensive domestic relations court was also articulated by Sophonisba P. Breckinridge, *Social Work and the Courts* (Chicago, 1934), 139; Ernest R. Mowrer, *Family Disorganization*, 2d ed. (Chicago, 1939), 273, 290; Cockrell, *Successful Justice*, 704–24. On the Progressives' development of the scientific/expertise justification for the expanded scope of administrative power generally, see Horwitz, *Transformation of American Law*, 222–25.

38. Reported in Bernard Flexner, Reuben Oppenheimer, and Katherine Lenroot, *The Child, the Family, and the Court*, Children's Bureau Publication no. 193 (Washington, D.C., 1929), 21–22, quoted in Rothman, *Conscience and Convenience*, 216. Ben Lindsey was, as ever, blunt: the House of Human Welfare "would do away with lawyers and the attendant expenses in the great majority of cases." Lindsey and Evans, *Companionate Marriage*, xv.

39. Johnstone, "Divorce," 318; Rothman, *Conscience and Convenience*, 216. On the "minor" role for lawyers in family courts, see Koos, "Family Problems and the Court." In 1967 the United States Supreme Court criticized the belief that "confession is good for the child as the commencement of the assumed therapy of the juvenile court process, and [the child] should be encouraged to assume an attitude of trust and confidence toward the officials of the juvenile process." In re Gault, 387 U.S. 1, 51 (1967).

40. Groves, *Marriage Crisis*, 223.

41. Goldstein, *Family in Court*, 191, 213; Polsky, *Rise of the Therapeutic State*, 55.

42. May, *Homeward Bound*, 26; Benjamin Spock, *The Common Sense Book of Baby and Child Care* (New York, 1946); Brown v. Board of Education, 347 U.S. 483, 494–95 n. 11 (1954); Joseph Veroff, Richard A. Kulka, and Elizabeth Douvan, *The Inner American: A Self-Portrait from 1957 to 1976* (New York, 1981), 194. On the often tortuous linkage between the judiciary, especially the Supreme Court, and social science evidence, see John Monahan and Laurens Walker, *Social Science in Law*, 3d ed. (New York, 1994); Wallace D. Loh, *Social Research in the Judicial Process* (New York, 1984); Donald N. Bersoff and David J. Glass, "The Not-So-*Weisman*: The Supreme Court's Continuing Misuse of Social Science Research," *University of Chicago Law School Roundtable* 2 (1995): 279–304; J. Alexander Tanford, "The Limits of a Scientific Jurisprudence: The Supreme Court and Psychology," *Indiana Law Journal* 66 (1990): 137; Charles Robert Tremper, "Sanguinity and Disillusionment Where Law Meets Social Science," *Law and Human Behavior* 11 (1987): 267; June Lounin Tapp, "Psychology and the Law: An Overture," *Annual Review of Psychology* 27 (1976): 359.

43. Carl A. Weinman, "The Trial Judge Awards Custody," *Law and Contemporary Problems* 10 (1944): 735; Sidney P. Simpson and Ruth Field, "Law and the

Social Sciences," *Virginia Law Review* 32 (1946): 855–67; Charles H. Leclaire, "Reform—The Law of Divorce," *George Washington Law Review* 17 (1949): 380–90.

A sampling of the articles espousing cooperation between law and the social sciences published in legal periodicals from the 1940s until the 1960s includes: Steuart Henderson Britt, "The Social Psychology of Law," *Illinois Law Review* 34 (1940): 802–11; Raphael Lemkin, "Orphans of Living Parents: A Comparative Legal and Socio-legal View," *Law and Contemporary Problems* 10 (1944): 834–54; Thomas A. Cowan, "The Relation of Law to Experimental Social Science," *University of Pennsylvania Law Review* 96 (1948): 484–502; Julius H. Miner, "Conciliation Rather Than Reconciliation," *Illinois Law Review* 43 (1948): 464–94; Karl N. Llewellyn, "Law and the Social Sciences—Especially Sociology," *Harvard Law Review* 62 (1949): 1286–1305; William M. Wherry, "Preventive Law and the Unstable Family," *New York State Bar Association Bulletin* 21 (Oct. 1949): 401–10; Roswell H. Johnson, "Suppressed, Delayed, Damaging, and Avoided Divorces," *Law and Contemporary Problems* 18 (1953): 72–97; David Riesman, "Law and Sociology: Recruitment, Training, and Colleagueship," *Stanford Law Review* 9 (1957): 643; J. E. Hall Williams, "The Relation of Social Work Philosophy to the Study and Practice of Law," *Kansas Law Review* 5 (1957): 366–70; Andrew S. Watson, M.D., "The Law and Behavioral Science Project at the University of Pennsylvania: A Psychiatrist on the Law Faculty," *Journal of Legal Education* 11 (1958): 73–79; Clarence Morris, "Law, Reason, and Sociology," *University of Pennsylvania Law Review* 107 (1958): 147–165; Richard D. Schwartz, "The Law and Behavioral Science Program at Yale: A Sociologist's Account of Some Experiences," *Journal of Legal Education* 12 (1959): 91–98; Allan Barton and Saul Mendlovitz, "The Experience of Injustice as a Research Problem," *Journal of Legal Education* 13 (1960): 24–39; Samuel M. Fahr and Ralph H. Ojemann, "The Use of Social and Behavioral Science Knowledge in Law," *Iowa Law Review* 48 (1962): 59–75; Philip Selznick, "Legal Institutions and Social Controls," *Vanderbilt Law Review* 17 (1963): 79–90; John C. Scanlon and Kenneth Weingarten, "The Role of Statistical Data in the Functioning of the Courts," *Buffalo Law Review* 12 (1963): 522–27; H. M. Fain, "Role and Relationship of Psychiatry to Divorce Law and the Lawyer," *California State Bar Journal* 41 (1966): 46; Lawrence M. Friedman and Jack Ladinsky, "Social Change and the Law of Industrial Accidents," *Columbia Law Review* 67 (1967): 50–82; Hans Zeisel, "Uses of Sociology in the Professions: The Law," *University of Chicago Law School Record* 15 (1967): 6; "A Symposium on Mental Health Concepts in Family Law," *Family Law Quarterly* 1 (1967): 61–87; Paul Bohannan and Karen Huckleberry, "Institutions of Divorce, Family, and the Law," *Law and Society Review* 1 (1967): 81–102; A. L. Tilton, "Psychology, Psychiatry, and Divorce," *Milwaukee Bar Association Gavel* 28 (1968): 12.

44. Alexander, "Public Service by Lawyers in the Field of Divorce," 18; Llewellyn, "Law and the Social Sciences—Especially Sociology," 1305.

45. Kramer's comments appeared in Bradway, *Proceedings of the Institute of Family Law*, 7; Donald Young, "The Behavioral Sciences, Stability, and Change," *Vanderbilt Law Review* 17 (1963): 62.

46. Samuel M. Fahr, "Why Lawyers Are Dissatisfied with the Social Sciences," *Washburn Law Journal* 1 (1961): 163. Sociologist Gilbert Geis responded to law professor Fahr in an article the following year. Geis admitted, however, that the Supreme Court's opinion in *Brown* had intensified concern among some lawyers about the increasing encroachment of social science upon the legal bailiwick. Geis, "The Social Sciences and the Law," *Washburn Law Journal* 1 (1962): 583–84.

47. Paul W. Alexander, Foreword to a "Symposium on Interprofessional Approach to Family Problems," *University of Kansas City Law Review* 22 (1953): 3.

48. Examples include Epaphroditus Peck, *The Law of Persons or Domestic Relations* (Chicago, 1913); Peck, *The Law of Persons and of Domestic Relations* (Chicago, 1920); William E. McCurdy, *Cases on the Law of Persons and Domestic Relations* (Chicago, 1927); Joseph W. Madden, *Cases on Domestic Relations* (St. Paul, 1928); Frederick L. Kane, *Cases on Domestic Relations* (St. Paul, 1936); William Randall Compton, *Cases on Domestic Relations* (St. Paul, 1951); William E. McCurdy, *Cases on the Law of Persons and Domestic Relations*, 4th ed. (Chicago, 1952).

49. In 1940 Joseph W. Madden and William Randall Compton puzzlingly titled their casebook *Cases and Materials on Domestic Relations* (St. Paul, 1940), despite the absence of any noncase materials, as the authors admitted (at p. vii).

50. Noted Harvard scholar William E. McCurdy characterized his 1927 textbook as a "collection of cases." *Cases on the Law of Persons and Domestic Relations*, vii. Nothing in his 1952 edition challenged that bland depiction.

51. The conceptual philosophy which specified that textbook authors were in the business of transmitting received wisdom to students is exemplified in Frederick L. Kane's assertion that "retaining my faith in the efficacy of the case system," he had "edited the cases as little as possible." Kane, *Cases on Domestic Relations*, iii.

52. Albert C. Jacobs, *Cases and Other Materials in Domestic Relations* (Chicago, 1933). The shift from pure casebooks to "cases and materials" texts is detailed in Brainerd Currie, "The Materials of Law Study, Part 3, Nonlegal Materials in the Law School: Beginnings of the Modern Integration Movement," *Journal of Legal Education* 8 (1955): 1–78. See also Albert Ehrenzweig, "The American Casebook: 'Cases and Materials,'" *Georgetown Law Journal* 32 (1944): 224–47. Jacobs's first effort pleased many, but not all: it was criticized for going too far (Chester Vernier, book review, *Harvard Law Review* 47 [1934]: 732); for not going far enough (Robert Angell, book review, *Columbia Law Review* 33 [1933]: 1086); and for not doing it well enough (Donald Slesinger, book review, *University of Chicago Law Review* 1 [1934]: 659).

53. Albert C. Jacobs, *Cases and Other Materials in Domestic Relations*, 2d ed. (Chicago, 1939); Jacobs and Julius Goebel, Jr., *Cases and Other Materials in Domestic*

Relations, 3d ed. (Brooklyn, 1952); Robert Kingsley, book review, *Journal of Legal Education* 5 (1953): 400; Albert A. Ehrenzweig, "Teaching 'Integration'—A Comment on Law and Society," *Journal of Legal Education* 2 (1950): 359.

54. Ehrenzweig, "Teaching 'Integration,'" 359; Jacobs and Goebel, *Cases and Other Materials in Domestic Relations,* 4th ed., ix. In 1956 English scholar Otto Kahn-Freund ridiculed the case teaching method as totally inappropriate: "To teach Family law in terms of 'case law,' . . . is to act like a professor of medicine who not only teaches pathology to students knowing nothing about the anatomy of physiology of the healthy body, but who teaches pathology in terms of the rarest diseases." Kahn-Freund, "Observations on the Possible Cooperation of Teachers of Law and Teachers of Social Science in Family Law."

55. The "second explosion" catchphrase is from Francis A. Allen, "History, Empirical Research, and Law Reform: A Short Comment on a Large Subject," *Journal of Legal Education* 9 (1956): 335; Harper, *Problems of the Family.* Harper's impressionistic shuffling of materials from radically different sources resulted in a deck seen as too stacked in favor of the social sciences. Future casebook author Robert J. Levy criticized Harper's integrative effort for giving "such short shrift to many of the essentials of an introduction to the lawyer's technical tasks that its utility to a group of law students was questionable." Levy, "The Perilous Necessity: Non-Legal Materials in a Family Law Course," *Journal of Family Law* 3 (1963): 151 (reprinted from the *Journal of Legal Education* 15 [1963]: 413–28).

56. Morris Ploscowe and Doris Jonas Freed, *Family Law: Cases and Materials* (Boston, 1963), ix. Other representatives of the "second explosion" in domestic relations casebooks include one coauthored by a psychiatrist (Joseph Goldstein and Jay Katz, *The Family and The Law: Problems for Decision in the Family Law Process* [New York, 1965]), and Caleb Foote, Robert J. Levy, and Frank E. A. Sander, *Cases and Materials on Family Law* (Boston, 1966). The latter text featured the imaginative "Quadrilogue on Divorce Policy" (pp. 769–95), a hypothetical discussion involving a doctor, a professor, a judge, and a bishop.

57. Harry Kalven, Jr., "Some Comments on the Law and Behavioral Science Project at the University of Pennsylvania," *Journal of Legal Education* 11 (1958): 96. For a skeptical glance at the asserted union of law and social science, see Grant Gilmore, *The Ages of American Law* (New Haven, 1977), 86–91.

58. Smith, "Dishonest Divorce." Smith had long advocated reconciliation as the appropriate goal for domestic relations courts. See his "Justice through Conciliation," *Survey* 50 (April 1, 1923): 37. On the significance of and publicity attached to the 1948 report, see Dorothy Thompson, "Divorces Are Not Crimes: They Are Tragedies," *Reader's Digest* 59 (Nov. 1951): 117–18 (condensed from *Ladies' Home Journal* 68 [Aug. 1951]: 11–12); Alexander, "Family Life Conference Suggests New Judicial Procedures and Attitudes toward Marriage and Divorce," 38; and Leclaire, "Reform—The Law of Divorce," 387, 390.

59. See the recommendations of E. Dana Brooks, "Positive Approach to the Divorce Dilemma," in Virginia Law Weekly, *Divorce and Family Relations*, 98–102.

60. Smith, "Dishonest Divorce"; N. Ruth Wood, "Precepts of Modern Uniform Divorce Law," in Virginia Law Weekly, *Divorce and Family Relations*, 103–7. In 1947 Wood had chaired a committee of the National Association of Women Lawyers which had made reform proposals similar to those of Smith and Alexander. But the association had rejected their report as unlikely to be adopted by state legislatures. See Bromley, "Our Scandalous Divorce Laws," 272–77.

61. Paul W. Alexander, "The Follies of Divorce: A Therapeutic Approach to the Problem." *American Bar Association Journal* 36 (Feb. 1950): 107, 172.

62. John S. Bradway, "Proposed New Techniques in the Law of Divorce: I. Family Dissolution—Limits of the Present Litigious Method," *Iowa Law Review* 28 (1943): 262.

63. Lemkin, "Orphans of Living Parents," 851–54; John S. Bradway, "A Suggestion: The Family Lawyer," *American Bar Association Journal* 45 (1959): 831–33, 866.

64. Alexander, "Family Life Conference Suggests New Judicial Procedures and Attitudes toward Marriage and Divorce," 41; see also Law School, The University of Chicago, *Conference on Divorce*, 73. The pervasiveness of the therapeutic divorce movement may be gleaned by the fact that every one of the published articles from the conference dealing with law revision called for implementation of the therapeutic divorce program. The *Virginia Law Weekly*'s 1949–50 DICTA Compendium, *Divorce and Family Relations*, included the voices of several ardent advocates of compulsory conciliation: Thomas J. Cunningham, "Education, Conciliation as Solutions to Divorce," 46–49; William J. Goode, "Compulsory Counseling, Prerequisite to Divorce," 74–77; Dudley F. Sicher, "Comprehensive Divorce Court Needed," 78–87; and Brooks, "Positive Approach to the Divorce Dilemma," 98–102.

65. Alexander, "A Therapeutic Approach to the Problem of Divorce." His penchant for medical and specifically pathological metaphors was unceasing. He criticized writers who confused marriage failure with divorce, comparing that error to an inability to distinguish appendicitis from an appendectomy (Introduction to Virginia Law Weekly, *Divorce and Family Relations*, v). He complained of appearing as a "faintly glorified public mortician," because all he did was "bury dead marriages—thirty thousand to date" ("A Therapeutic Approach to the Problem of Divorce," 51). And he greatly feared that he had "buried a lot of live corpses" ("Family Life Conference Suggests New Judicial Procedures and Attitudes toward Marriage and Divorce," 38). His 1949 *Ladies' Home Journal* article included the subhead "Buried Alive! Judges are the unwilling moticians for thousands of marriages." Alexander, "Our Legal Horror Divorce," 65.

66. Alexander, "Divorce without 'Guilt' or 'Sin.'" This restrictive view was echoed in Milton L. Grossman, "How Can We Make Divorce Realistic?" *New York State Bar Bulletin* 23 (Oct. 1951): 350–63.

67. Otto Kahn-Freund, "Divorce Law Reform?" *Modern Law Review* 19 (1956): 584; Claud Mullins, "Family Relations and Divorce in England," in Virginia Law Weekly, *Divorce and Family Relations*, 25–27.

68. Eric Sachs, "The Judge and the Family Court," in American Bar Association, Section of Family Law, *1960 Summary of Proceedings (Washington, D.C.)* (Chicago, 1960), 66–74.

69. Stephen Keleny, "The Divorce Law Reform Union and Its Divorce Bill," in Section of Family Law, *1960 Summary*, 40–46.

70. Kahn-Freund, "Divorce Law Reform?" 584.

71. Eugene Litwak, "Divorce Law as Social Control," *Social Forces* 24 (March 1956): 217–23, reprinted in Norman W. Bell and Ezra F. Vogel, *A Modern Introduction to the Family* (New York, 1960), 208–17. Litwak noted that law as therapy "focuses on internalization of societal values," but he acknowledged that nonbelievers in therapy may "view it as a punishment." Ibid.

72. See text at note 8 above. On the Los Angeles Conciliation Court, see Taylor, "Court to Prevent Divorce"; Lloyd Shearer, "This Court Saves Foundering Marriages," ibid., 57 (Aug. 1950): 119–22 (condensed from *Christian Herald*, Aug. 1950); Louis H. Burke, "An Instrument of Peace: The Conciliation Court of Los Angeles," *American Bar Association Journal* 42 (1956): 621–24, 690–91; Burke, *With This Ring* (New York, 1958); Burke, "The Conciliation Court of Los Angeles County," *Chicago Bar Record* 40 (1959): 255–64; Roger Alton Pfaff, "A Court That Preserves Marriages," *Phi Delta Delta* 37 (1959): 3–6; Pfaff, "The Conciliation Court of Los Angeles County," *1960 Summary*, 35–39; Burke, "The Role of Conciliation in Divorce Cases," *Journal of Family Law* 1 (1961): 209; Harry M. Fain, "The Lawyer's Role in California's Reconciliation Court Plan," in American Bar Association, Section of Family Law, *1962 Proceedings (San Francisco and Little Rock, Arkansas)* (Chicago, 1962), 211–18; Paul Friggens, "The Walk-In Court That Rescues Rocky Marriages," *Reader's Digest* 81 (Dec. 1962): 107–111 (condensed from *Contemporary*, Nov. 4, 1962).

73. Quoted in Taylor, "Court to Prevent Divorce," 239–40.

74. Martin, "Divorce: Effort to Save a Troubled Marriage."

75. Pfaff, "Conciliation Court of Los Angeles County."

76. Meyer Elkin, "Conciliation Courts: The Reintegration of Disintegrating Families," *Family Coordinator* 22 (Jan. 1973): 66.

77. Judge Burke included a typical reconciliation agreement as an appendix to his *With This Ring*, 270–80. Quoted clauses in the following discussion are drawn from this source. Excerpts also appeared in "Typical Reconciliation Agreement," *California State Bar Journal* 30 (1955): 207–15; Goldstein and Katz, *Family and the Law*, 146–50.

78. Working wives were not uncommon during the 1950s. In 1953, for example, 27.1 percent of married women were employed, and they constituted 56.5 percent of all employed women. See Paul H. Landis, *Making the Most of Marriage*,

56, 58, fig. 7, 9. But the cultural mavens still proclaimed such women as freaks. A 1954 *Esquire* article dubbed wives employed outside the home a "menace," and a *Life* piece cited the paid labor of married women as a "disease." Quoted in Coontz, *Way We Never Were*, 32. Divorce lawyer and columnist Samuel G. Kling maintained that working wives were a "hazard to marital stability," and that "a wife who rebels at being a housewife may do so because she unconsciously resents being a woman." Kling recommended psychoanalysis for such wives. *The Complete Guide to Divorce* (New York, 1963), 13, 33.

79. Burke, *With This Ring*, 32; letter from Judge Burke to Maxine Virtue, quoted in Virtue, *Family Cases in Court*, 258; Friggens, "Walk-In Court That Rescues Rocky Marriages." The counselor was quoted in Martin, "Divorce: Effort to Save a Troubled Marriage."

80. Quoted in Burke, "Instrument of Peace," 624. With a measure of understatement, Judge Burke concluded that the "utilization of a reconciliation agreement, which is readily compiled and signed at the very moment of reconciliation, lends dignity and weight to the promises made." Ibid., 690.

81. The selectivity of the conciliation court rendered all reconciliation statistics virtually meaningless. The claim that the court effected reconciliations in 43 percent of its cases takes on a different coloration when weighed against the statistic that in 1957, for instance, the court only handled 1,380 of the 31,871 divorce, separate maintenance, and annulment suits filed in Los Angeles. See Martin, "Divorce: Effort to Save a Troubled Marriage." Judge Burke presented evidence of his success confusingly in "The Role of Conciliation in Divorce Cases." For criticism of the conciliation court's rosy statistics, see Foote et al., *Cases and Materials on Family Law*, 790–91.

82. Robert J. Levy, *Uniform Marriage and Divorce Legislation: A Preliminary Analysis*, monograph prepared for the Special Committee on Divorce of the National Conference of Commissioners on Uniform State Laws (Chicago, 1968), 123.

83. Evan Frances, "How to Get Marriage Counseling," *Woman's Home Companion* 76 (Aug. 1949): 36, 64. On the origins of the marriage counseling profession in America, see Robert G. Foster, "A Point of View on Marriage Counseling," *Journal of Counseling Psychology* 3 (1956): 212–15, reprinted in Marvin B. Sussman, *Sourcebook in Marriage and the Family*, 2d ed. (Boston, 1963), 460–64.

84. David R. Mace, "Who Needs Marriage Counseling," *Woman's Home Companion* 76 (Aug. 1949): 34–35, 100.

85. "Where to Get a Marriage Counselor When You Need One," *Good Housekeeping* 149 (July 1959): 113–14; Morris Fishbein, M.D., "Beware the Mind-Meddler," *Woman's Home Companion* 75 (Dec. 1948): 36–38, 102; Michael Drury, "Are Marriage Counselors Any Good?" *Cosmopolitan* 134 (Jan. 1953): 104–7. The professional journals also bemoaned the paucity of trained counselors. See Goode, "Compulsory Counseling, Prerequisite to Divorce," 74–77, and Kenneth R. Redden, "Selected Bibliography," in Virginia Law Weekly, *Divorce and Family Relations*, 128.

86. Bill Davidson, "Quack Marriage Counselors: A Growing National Scandal," *Saturday Evening Post* 236 (Jan. 5, 1963): 17–25. Peggy Strait expressed the same fear in "Marriage Counselors—Helpers and Hurters," *New York Times Magazine* (Nov. 3, 1963): 26, 107–8.

87. Veroff et al., *Inner American*, tables 5.11, 5.13, 5.15, at 131–35.

88. Samuel M. Starr, "'Divorcées Anonymous' a Remarkable Success," Virginia Law Weekly, *Divorce and Family Relations*, 50–52. For a brief time in the 1950s, Divorcées Anonymous garnered considerable media attention. See A. Prowitt, "Divorcées Anonymous," *Good Housekeeping* 130 (Feb. 1950): 35; Joseph Millard, "Divorcées Anonymous," *Reader's Digest* 56 (May 1950): 15–18, condensed from *Redbook* (Feb. 1950); "They Mend Broken Marriages," *American Magazine* 149 (June 1950): 107; "Divorcées Anonymous," *Time* 66 (Sept. 26, 1955): 64; Vance Packard, "New Cure for Sick Marriages," *American Magazine* 161 (May 1956): 30–31, 96–100.

89. Mariano, *Psychoanalytic Lawyer Looks at Marriage and Divorce*, 13–14. See his *Shall I Get a Divorce—And How?* (New York, 1946), 116–22 (divorces stem from psychoneuroses), and *Use of Psychotherapy in Divorce and Separation Cases*, 5–6 (psychotherapy as remedy for weak marriages). See also Paul Sayre, "Lawyers as Physicians for Failing Marriages," Virginia Law Weekly, *Divorce and Family Relations*, 50–52.

90. Mariano, *Psychoanalytic Lawyer Looks at Marriage and Divorce*, 260, 207. A general survey of the field, recognizing Mariano as a pioneer in psychoanalytic jurisprudence, is contained in Kohut, *Manual on Marital Reconciliations*, chap. 8, "Rehabilitation of Broken Marriages by Attorneys," 67–83. See also Mariano, "Legal Therapy in Divorce," *Kansas Law Review* 3 (1954): 36–43.

91. Mariano, *Psychoanalytic Lawyer Looks at Marriage and Divorce*, 197; Harriet F. Pilpel, "The Job the Lawyers Shirk," *Harper's* 220 (Jan. 1960): 67–69. See also "The Lawyer as Family Counselor," *University of Kansas City Law Review* 22 (1953): 28–53; Kargman, "Lawyer as Divorce Counselor," 399; Andrew S. Watson, M.D., "The Lawyer as Counselor," *Journal of Family Law* 5 (1965): 7–20.

92. Henry LaCossitt, "The Man Who Doctors Sick Marriages," *Saturday Evening Post* 224 (May 31, 1952): 25, 93–96; M. Z. Gross, "Family Needs a Friend: Michigan's Friend of the Court Plan," *Better Homes and Gardens* 30 (Oct. 1952): 42. See also Edward Pokorny, "Observations by a 'Friend of the Court,'" *Law and Contemporary Problems* 10 (1944): 778–89; "'Friend of the Court' Aids Detroit Judges in Divorce Cases," *Journal of the American Judicature Society* 29 (1946): 166–70.

93. Brigitte M. Bodenheimer, "The Utah Marriage Counseling Experiment: An Account of Changes in Divorce Law and Procedure," *Utah Law Review* 7 (1961): 443.

94. Report of the Reconciliation Committee of the New Jersey Supreme Court, Feb. 14, 1956, excerpted in Goldstein and Katz, *Family and the Law*, 150–53.

95. Ibid.

96. New Jersey Code, title 33.5, secs. 1010.1–1011 (1957).

97. Report of the Reconciliation Committee of the New Jersey Supreme Court, April 14, 1960, excerpted in Goldstein and Katz, *Family and the Law,* 155–56.

98. See, e.g., Johnstone, "Divorce: The Place of the Legal System," 323–24; Johnstone, "Divorce Dismissals," 255–56; Johnson, "Suppressed, Delayed, Damaging, and Avoided Divorces," 72; Donald M. McIntyre, Jr., "Conciliation of Disrupted Marriages by or through the Judiciary," *Journal of Family Law* 4 (1964): 129–30.

99. Robert N. Bellah et al., *Habits of the Heart: Individualism and Commitment in American Life* (Berkeley, Calif., 1985), 47.

6. The Triumph of Naked Divorce

1. See Cal. Civ. Code, sec. 92 (1954).

2. See DeBurgh v. DeBurgh, 39 Cal.2d 858, 250 P.2d 598 (1952).

3. Quoted in Elayne Carol Berg, "Irreconcilable Differences: California Courts Respond to No-Fault Dissolution," *Loyola of Los Angeles Law Review* 7 (1974): 453, 454.

4. Donald Spoto, *Marilyn Monroe: The Biography* (New York, 1993): 290–94.

5. Quoted in Jacob, *Silent Revolution,* 46–47. Robert L. Griswold's study of California in the Victorian era found that Golden State divorces had always been easily obtained. Griswold, *Family and Divorce in California,* 18.

6. Macklin Fleming, "Cases I Have Lost," *American Bar Association Journal* 51 (1965): 641–44. One reader found Fleming's anecdote "a rather sad commentary on the honor accorded the divorce laws in our country by many members of the Bench and Bar at a time when our jails are filled with the products of broken homes." Joseph A. Sullivan, "Is This Divorce American Style?" in "Views of Our Readers," *American Bar Association Journal* 51 (1965): 898, 900.

7. "Charge to the Commission," Governor Edmund G. Brown, May 11, 1966, quoted in *Report of the Governor's Commission on the Family* (Sacramento, Calif., Dec. 1966), 1.

8. Wheeler, *No-Fault Divorce,* 27–28.

9. *Putting Asunder,* 70.

10. Quintin Johnstone, "Family Courts," *University of Kansas City Law Review* 22 (Fall 1953): 18–22. In an article on divorce for the 1956 edition of the *Encyclopedia Americana,* sociologist Paul H. Landis praised the work of family courts but added that in recent years members of his profession had "inclined to the view that once a couple has decided to take legal steps toward breaking their marriage, it is usually too late to achieve a lasting reconciliation." Landis, "Divorce," in *Encyclopedia Americana* 9:208.

11. Thomas M. French, M.D., "Contributions to a Therapeutic Solution to the Divorce Problem: Psychiatry," in The Law School, The University of Chicago, *Conference on Divorce,* 62.

12. Emily H. Mudd, "Contributions to a Therapeutic Solution to the Divorce Problem: Social Work and Marriage Counseling," ibid., 67.

13. Ibid., 68. Mudd compared couples seeking divorce to ten year olds biting, scratching, and beating each other. Ibid., 69.

14. Schaar's and Alexander's comments were recorded in ibid., 72–73. Judge Kross's critique is contained in her article, "Therapeutic Solution of Family Conflicts," ibid., 80.

15. American Bar Association, Family Law Section, *Report of the Subcommittee on the Conciliation Court* (Chicago, June 1961).

16. Thomas Szasz, *Law, Liberty, and Psychiatry: An Inquiry into the Social Uses of Mental Health Practices* (New York, 1963), 248.

17. Paul W. Alexander, "What Is a Family Court, Anyway?" *Connecticut Bar Journal* 26 (1952): 254–55; J. E. Bindeman, "Comment on the Family Court Bill," *Journal of the Bar Association of the District of Columbia* 21 (1954): 122.

18. The latter argument was made by David E. Seidelson, "Systematic Marriage Investigation and Counseling in Divorce Cases: Some Reflections on Its Constitutional Propriety and General Desirability," *George Washinqton Law Review* 36 (1967): 60, 79–89. See the discussion in Levy, *Uniform Marriage and Divorce Leqislation*, 118–30.

19. Johnstone, "Family Courts," 21; Allan Fisher, "A Family Court for the District of Columbia," *Journal of the Bar Association of the District of Columbia* 20 (1953): 577.

20. Quoted in Wheeler, *No-Fault Divorce*, 115. Both Judge Thomas J. Cunningham and reporter John Bartlow Martin observed that some divorce attorneys disliked the Los Angeles Conciliation Court because it dampened their fee-generating ability. Cunningham, "Education, Conciliation as Solutions to Divorce"; Martin, "Divorce: Effort to Save a Troubled Marriage."

21. See, e.g., Gertrude Samuels, "The Family Court—How It Could Work," *New York Times Magazine* (April 29, 1956): 17, 56–60; Sol Morton Isaac, "The Status of Lawyer–Social Worker Cooperation," *Journal of Family Law* 3 (1963): 53–62; Roger Alton Pfaff, "The Role of the Social Worker in the Judicial Process," *American Bar Association Journal* 50 (1964): 565–68.

22. John Bartlow Martin, "Divorce: A Little Nest of Hate," *Saturday Evening Post* 231 (Nov. 22, 1958): 36, 121–26. John H. Mariano expressed a concern that social workers had been trained to view clients in general categories, while lawyers focused on the individual. Mariano, *Psychoanalytic Lawyer Looks at Marriage and Divorce*, 254–56.

23. Quoted in Goldstein and Katz, *Family and the Law*, 160.

24. See, e.g., William M. Kephart, "The Family Court: Some Socio-Legal Implications," *Washington University Legal Ouarterly* 1955 (Feb. 1955): 64; Johnstone, "Divorce: The Place of the Legal System," 322–23.

25. See, e.g., Alexander, "What Is a Family Court, Anyway?"; Max Rheinstein, "The Law of Divorce and the Problem of Marriage Stability," *Vanderbilt Law*

Review 9 (1956): 637; Henry H. Foster, Jr., "Procrustes and the Couch," *Journal of Family Law* 2 (1962): 93.

26. Rheinstein, "Law of Divorce and the Problem of Marriage Stability," 639.

27. Charles W. Tenney, Jr., "The Utopian World of Juvenile Courts," *Annals of the American Academy of Political and Social Science* 383 (May 1969): 107. See also Paul Tappan, *Juvenile Delinquency* (New York, 1949).

28. 383 U.S. 541, 86 S.Ct. 1045, 16 L.Ed.2d 84 (1966). Morris A. Kent, Jr., was a sixteen-year-old charged in the District of Columbia with housebreaking, robbery, and rape. As a minor, he was subject to juvenile court processes unless, after "full investigation," that tribunal waived its jurisdiction and remitted the case for trial before the United States District Court for the District of Columbia. While any term of confinement imposed by the juvenile court would have expired when Kent attained his majority, the youth faced exposure to many decades of imprisonment if he was convicted in a federal trial court. Although Kent's counsel filed a motion for a hearing on the critical issue of waiver, the juvenile court refused to rule on the motion or even to conduct a hearing. Instead, the juvenile judge authorized the jurisdictional waiver with the simple notation that that it had acted after the requisite "full investigation." Kent was tried and convicted in the federal trial court and sentenced to imprisonment for thirty to ninety years. The court of appeals affirmed.

The Supreme Court reversed, noting with some exasperation that the juvenile court's charter was not a "license for arbitrary procedure." 383 U.S. at 553. The justices insisted that the proper exercise of juvenile court powers "assumes procedural regularity sufficient . . . to satisfy the basic requirements of due process and fairness." Id.

29. 387 U.S. 1, 87 S.Ct. 1428, 18 L.Ed.2d 527 (1967). Fifteen-year-old Gerald Gault was convicted of making a lewd telephone call. Had he been an adult, Gault would have faced a small fine and up to two months' imprisonment. 387 U.S. at 29. But the juvenile court of Gila County, Arizona, committed him to the State Industrial School for the remainder of his minority, six years. In reversing the informal and unrecorded procedures followed in Gault's case, the Supreme Court determined that due process for juveniles included adequate and timely written notice of court hearings, advice that the child had the right to be represented by counsel (including court-appointed counsel should the child's family be indigent), enforcement of the privilege against compelled self-incrimination, and the right to confront witnesses who must be placed under oath. 387 U.S. at 31–57.

30. Report by the President's Commission on Law Enforcement and Administration of Justice, "The Challenge of Crime in a Free Society" (1967), cited in In re Gault, 387 U.S. at 14 n.14. See Tenney, "Utopian World of Juvenile Courts," 116. On the "haphazard" arrangement of juvenile court resources, see Polsky, *Rise of the Therapeutic State*, 94–97.

31. Tenney, "Utopian World of Juvenile Courts," 110. See also Will C. Turnbladh, "Midcentury White House Conference of Children and Youth," *Juvenile Court*

Judges Journal 2 (1951): 11–12, 26 (juvenile courts lack the status of other courts and consequently have difficulty attracting high-caliber judges). In 1967 the President's Commission of Law Enforcement bemoaned the disappearance from juvenile courts of the "mature and sophisticate judge, wise and well-versed in law and the science of human behavior." *Task Force Report on Juvenile Delinquency and Youth Crime* (1967), 7. Herma Hill Kay noted that in many urban jurisdictions, juvenile and domestic relations assignments went to junior judges, and even a six-month tour of duty was more than many judges desired. Kay, "A Family Court: The California Proposal," *California Law Review* 56 (Oct. 1968): 1208–9. One family court judge wittily pointed out why most divorce judges disliked their work: "There isn't much satisfaction in being the referee in a series of fixed fights where a one round knockout has been arranged for in advance." Robert W. Hansen, "Three Dimensions of Divorce," *Marquette Law Review* 50 (Aug. 1966): 3.

32. Orman W. Ketcham and Monrad Paulsen, *Cases and Materials Relating to Juvenile Courts* (Brooklyn, 1967).

33. Paul W. Alexander, "Constitutional Rights in Juvenile Court," *American Bar Association Journal* 46 (1960): 1207; David Matza, *Delinquency and Drift* (New York, 1964), 71.

34. In re Gault, 387 U.S. at 17.

35. Kent v. United States, 383 U.S. at 554.

36. In re Gault, 387 U.S. at 18.

37. Henry H. Foster, Jr., "The Future of Family Law," *Annals of the American Academy of Political and Social Science* 383 (May 1969): 143.

38. Alexander, "Constitutional Rights in Juvenile Court," 1209; Tom A. Croxton, "The Kent Case and Its Consequences," *Journal of Family Law* 7 (1967): 1. Ironically, Croxton's plea for cooperative attorneys had been articulated by the court of appeals in the *Kent* decision, in its statement that counsel's role should be limited to presenting "anything on behalf of the child which might help the court in arriving at a decision; it is not to denigrate the [juvenile court] staff's submissions and recommendations." Quoted in Kent v. United States, 383 U.S. at 563. In reversing the appellate court, the Supreme Court sharply criticized this team-player role for an attorney, stating that "if the staff's submissions include materials which are susceptible to challenge or impeachment, it is precisely the role of counsel to 'denigrate' such matter. There is no irrebuttable presumption of accuracy attached to staff reports." Id.

39. Thomas A. Coyne, "Who Will Speak for the Child?" *Annals of the American Academy of Political and Social Science* 383 (May 1969): 34–47; In re Winship, 397 U.S. 358, 90 S.Ct. 1068, 25 L.Ed.2d 368 (1970). The following year the Court drew the line in its criminalization of the juvenile court at the imposition of a jury trial requirement. In McKeiver v. Pennsylvania, 403 U.S. 528, 91 S.Ct. 1976, 29 L.Ed.2d 647 (1971), the Court declined to extend to juveniles the constitutional right to a trial by jury, thus preserving for the juvenile court at least one of the attributes of its independent procedure.

40. Polsky, *Rise of the Therapeutic State*, 191 (citations omitted); for a contemporary perspective, see Karl Birnbaum, "A Court Psychiatrist's View of Juvenile Delinquents," *Annals of the American Academy of Political and Social Science* 261 (Jan. 1949): 57–58. Robert Kramer observed in 1959 that, in their preoccupation with rehabilitation, some juvenile courts "overlook the fact that sometimes people don't want to be reformed, and that sometimes people don't want to be told what to do, even if the advice is wise." Bradway, *Proceedings of the Institute of Family Law*, 9–10.

41. Kephart, "Family Court," 61; Alexander's comments are found in Bradway, *Proceedings of the Institute of Family Law*, 174. Indeed, one hint that the family court idea had not been fully digested by American professionals was the glib nature of its universal acceptance. Quintin Johnstone reported that family courts were acceptable to both divorce liberals and conservatives, even to those opposed to divorce on religious grounds. Johnstone, "Divorce: The Place of the Legal System," 317.

42. Bodenheimer, "Utah Marriage Counseling Experiment."

43. Tenney, "Utopian World of Juvenile Courts," 117.

44. Baber, *Marriage and the Family*, 668.

45. Max Rheinstein was quoted in Bradway, *Proceedings of the Institute of Family Law*, 199.

46. Report of Inter-Agency Committee on Background Materials, National Conference on Family Life, May 1948, *The American Family: A Factual Background* (Washington, D.C., 1949), ii; Virtue, *Family Cases in Court*. The funding problems were discussed in Rheinstein, *Marriage Stability, Divorce, and the Law*, viii–ix; Nester C. Kohut, *Divorce for the Unbroken Marriage* (Madison, Wis., 1973), x–xiv; and in two essays in the *Annals of the American Academy of Political and Social Science* 272 (Nov. 1950): Ogburn, "Role of Legal Services in Family Stability," and Mabel A. Elliott, "Divorce Legislation and Family Instability," 134–47.

47. Alexander, "Family Life Conference Suggests New Judicial Procedures," 43.

48. Jacob T. Zuckerman, "Family Court—Evolving Concepts," *Annals of the Academy of American Political and Social Science* 383 (May 1969): 127–28. See the discussion of this phenomenon by Halem, *Divorce Reform*, 235, 285–86.

49. *National Probation and Parole Association Journal* 5 (1959): 99. See Zuckerman, "Family Court—Evolving Concepts," 126.

50. Quoted in Virtue, *Family Cases in Court*, dedication.

51. Quoted in Robert Blake, *The Decline of Power, 1915–1964* (New York, 1985), 428.

52. Biggs, *Concept of Matrimonial Cruelty*, 2.

53. McGregor, "Equality, Sexual Values, and Permissive Legislation."

54. The memorandum is detailed in *Putting Asunder*, 91–92.

55. The archbishop was not alone among church leaders. On April 3, 1963, a joint statement opposing the seven years' separation proposal was issued by the

heads of the Church of England, the Roman Catholic Church, the Church of Wales, and the Free Church Federal Council. These clerical views were joined by secular opposition three days later in a speech attacking Abse's bill by Sir Jocelyn Simon, president of the Probate, Divorce and Admiralty Division of the High Court. See Olive M. Stone, "The Matrimonial Causes and Reconciliation Bill, 1963," *Journal of Family Law* 3 (1963): 94–95.

56. *Hansard's Parliamentary Debates* (Lords), 5th ser., vol. 250, xcviii, col. 1547, June 21, 1963.

57. As Reginald Haw, vicar of Humberstone, noted in his matrimonial treatise, "It is nothing short of astounding that there was so little realization . . . that worse things can happen to a marriage than adultery." Haw, *State of Matrimony*, 105.

58. *Putting Asunder*, 17–18.

59. Ibid., 28. In its appendix on psychological considerations, for instance, the report noted: "If we concentrate our attention wholly on the actions that are designated 'matrimonial offenses,' we inevitably fail to do justice to the complex of motives in the two interacting persons which finally drives the one to act and the other to treat the action as ground for a divorce petition." Ibid., 144.

60. Ibid., 77. In order to prevent the "automatic" processing of uncontested divorces, the drafters opposed transferring jurisdiction of such cases to county courts. Ibid.

61. Ibid., 68.

62. Ibid. Unafraid to prolong the inquest, *Putting Asunder* proposed that a judge have the power "to adjourn the case in order to secure the attendance of a party not present." Ibid., 70.

63. Ibid.

64. Ibid., 30, 75.

65. Ibid, at 70. The archbishop's group made no reference to the significant shortage of English social workers in the 1960s, nor any suggestion as to how this personnel deficiency could be remedied.

66. Cmnd. 3123 (London, 1966) (hereafter *Field of Choice*). The Law Commission had been established to review all English law "with a view towards its systematic development and reform, including . . . the elimination of anomalies . . . and, generally, the simplification and modernization of the law." Law Commissions Act 1965, sec. 3.

67. *Field of Choice*, 30–31.

68. Ibid., 47–49. The proposals and explanatory text are reprinted in *New Law Journal* 117 (1967): 827–28.

69. Elizabeth II, 1969, ch. 55 (Oct. 22, 1969). The principal change effected by Parliament was that a petitioner who desired to obtain a divorce on the two-year separation ground was required to obtain the consent of the respondent, not merely the absence of objection. For further analysis of the legislation, see George G. Brown, "Divorce Reform Act, 1969," *New Law Journal* 120 (1974): 74; Mary Ann

Glendon, *State, Law, and Family: Family Law in Transition in the United States and Western Europe* (Amsterdam, 1977), 194–96; William Latey, *The Tide of Divorce* (London, 1970), 152–60.

70. Great Britain Law Commission, *Facing the Future: A Discussion Paper on the Ground for Divorce* (London, 1988) (hereafter *Facing the Future*), app. B; Andrew Adonis, "Britain in Focus: Wives Bring Most Divorces," *Financial Times*, Feb. 28, 1996, 10 (reporting statistics from the Feb. 27, 1996, report of the Office of Population, Censuses and Surveys).

71. Id. at 17.

72. Id., 17 and n.80, 30. In its comprehensive report for the 1990s, *Family Law: The Ground for Divorce* (London, 1990), the Law Commission recommended that irretrievable breakdown remain the fulcrum of the divorce question. Breakdown should be "proved by the passage of a twelve month period of time which would both provide solid and objective evidence of the breakdown and enable the parties to resolve its practical consequences before the divorce itself was granted." Great Britain Law Commission, *Twenty-fifth Annual Report, 1990* (London, 1990), 9. For a summary and sharply contrasting critiques of the current British family law proposals, see Jacqueline Brown and Clair Lydon, "Time to Consider and Reflect: A Summary of the Law Commission Report on the Ground for Divorce," *Family Law* 20 (1990): 462–65; Martin Mears, "Getting It Wrong Again?: Divorce and the Law Commission," *Family Law* 21 (1991): 231–33; Janet Walker, "Divorce—Whose Fault?: Is the Law Commission Getting it Right?" *Family Law* 21 (1991): 234–37.

73. *Facing the Future*, 30.

74. News Release from Office of Assembly Member Pearce Young, 5th Assembly District, March 15, 1963, quoted in Howard A. Krom, "California's Divorce Law Reform: An Historical Analysis," *Pacific Law Journal* 1 (1970): 158, reprinted in Kermit L. Hall, ed., *Law, Society, and Domestic Relations: Major Historical Interpretations* (New York, 1987), 350–75.

75. California Assembly Interim Committee on Judiciary Relating to Domestic Relations, "Final Report," 2 Appendix to Journal of the Assembly vol. 23, no. 6, at 25–44 (Reg. Sess. 1965) (hereafter "Final Report").

76. *Transcript of Proceedings on Domestic Relations before the California Assembly Interim Committee on Judiciary*, Jan. 8–9, 1964, 28. See also Krom, "California's Divorce Law Reform," 160–61.

77. "Final Report," 176.

78. Report of the Governor's Commission on the Family, 1.

79. Ibid., 1–2; Philip L. Hammer, "Divorce Reform in California: The Governor's Commission on the Family and Beyond," *Santa Clara Lawyer* 9 (1968): 41.

80. Hammer, "Divorce Reform in California," 41–42.

81. *Report of the Governor's Commission on the Family*, 80–85; see Alexander, "Divorce without 'Guilt' or 'Sin,'" 14–16.

82. *Report of the Governor's Commission on the Family*, 83.

83. Krom, "California's Divorce Law Reform," 160.

84. Ibid., 90.

85. Ibid., 92–93.

86. Monrad Paulsen, "Divorce—Canterbury Style," *Valparaiso University Law Review* 1 (1966): 96.

87. Hansen, "Three Dimensions of Divorce," 1. In his speech the judge related another anecdote which epitomized the disdain family court advocates felt for the fault regime: "'Do I have grounds for divorce?' the lady asked the lawyer. 'Are you married?' the lawyer asked the lady. 'Yes,' answered the lady. 'Then you have grounds for divorce,' answered the lawyer." Ibid., 3. On the importance of making divorce a "time-consuming process," see Aidan R. Gough, "A Suggested Family Court System for California," *Santa Clara Lawyer* 4 (1964): 212–17.

88. 39 Cal.2d 858, 250 P.2d 598 (1952).

89. *Putting Asunder*, 29, quoted in Richard C. Dinkelspiel and Aidan R. Gough, "A Family Court Act for Contemporary California: A Summary of the Report of the California Governor's Commission on the Family," *Journal of the State Bar of California* 42 (1967): 363, adapted and reprinted in *Family Law Quarterly* 1 (Sept. 1967): 70, 77. See also Krom, "California's Divorce Law Reform," 168.

90. Laws 1969, ch. 1608, p. 3325, sec. 8.

91. Richard C. Dinkelspiel and Aidan R. Gough, "The Case for a Family Court—A Summary of the Report of the California Governor's Commission on the Family," *Family Law Quarterly* 1 (1967): 70, 78.

92. Assembly Committee on Judiciary, "Report of 1969 Divorce Reform Legislation," *Journal of California Assembly* 4 (Reg. Sess. 1969): 8058.

93. Krom, "California's Divorce Law Reform," 179 (footnote omitted).

94. Halem, *Divorce Reform*, 244.

95. Assembly Bill 530, sec. 4506 (proposed by assembly member James A. Hayes), quoted in Walker, "Disarming the Litigious Man," 208.

96. Walker, "Disarming the Litigious Man," 208.

97. Ch. 1608, 1969 Cal. Stat. 3323–24 (effective Jan. 1, 1970).

98. Charles W. Johnson, "The Family Law Act: A Guide to the Practitioner," *Pacific Law Journal* 1 (1970): 147, 151.

99. McKim v. McKim, 6 Cal.3d 673, 679, 493 P.2d 868, 871, 100 Cal. Rptr. 140, 143 (1972).

100. Id. at 679, 493 P.2d at 871, 100 Cal. Rptr. at 143, quoting Assembly Committee on Judiciary, "Report of 1969 Divorce Reform Legislation," 8058 (Reg. Sess. 1969).

101. Id. at 680, 493 P.2d at 872, 100 Cal. Rptr. at 144.

102. Id.

103. 28 Cal. App. 3d 108, 104 Cal. Rptr. 472 (1972).

104. Id. at 115–18, 104 Cal. Rptr. at 478–80.

105. The executive director of the Governor's Commission on the Family later attributed the demise of the therapeutic family court to "cost, concern that a family court structure would disrupt existing systems of court calendaring[,] and

perhaps a fear that 'social work' would dilute 'hard legal process.'" Aidan R. Gough, "Divorce without Squalor," *Nation* 210 (Jan. 12, 1970): 17, 20.

106. Kay, "A Family Court," 1244.

107. Halem, *Divorce Reform*, 285. Both Riane Tennehaus Eisler and Allen M. Parkman detailed the story of California assembly leader James A. Hayes, who shepherded key sections of the Family Reform Act through the legislature while engaged in a rancorous divorce proceeding against his wife. Eisler, *Dissolution: No-Fault Divorce, Marriage, and the Future of Women* (New York, 1977), 24–31; Parkman, *No-Fault Divorce: What Went Wrong?* (Boulder, Colo., 1992), 61–62. Michael Wheeler provided similar illustrations from other states. One lawyer lobbying for no-fault admitted an inability to get the attention of legislative leaders until "several . . . were in the midst of divorces and apparently they didn't like what they were experiencing, so our bill went through like gang-busters." An official of a state bar association told Wheeler that key to no-fault reform there was "that the chairman of the senate judiciary committee and the speaker of the house, who had both opposed us in the past, were in the middle of messy marital situations when we reintroduced our bill, and they switched right around." Wheeler, *No-Fault Divorce*, 153.

108. Assembly Committee on Judiciary, "Report of 1969 Divorce Reform Legislation," *Journal of California Assembly* 4 (Reg. Sess. 1969): 8056 II A (2).

109. See Jacob, *Silent Revolution*, 58.

110. Dinkelspiel and Gough, "Case for a Family Court," 74.

111. Rheinstein, "Law of Divorce and the Problem of Marriage Stability," 637.

112. Krom, "California's Divorce Law Reform," 171.

113. Halem, *Divorce Reform*, 251.

114. On the influence of the formal legal apparatus upon divorce negotiations, see Robert H. Mnookin and Lewis Kornhauser, "Bargaining in the Shadow of the Law: The Case of Divorce," *Yale Law Review* 88 (1979): 950.

115. While the analysis in the text has primarily followed the thread of California divorce law, significant domestic relations reforms also occurred on two other major fronts in the 1960s: New York significantly expanded its divorce grounds, and the National Conference of Commissioners on Uniform State Laws drafted a Uniform Marriage and Divorce Act. For accounts of these developments, see Glendon, *Abortion and Divorce in Western Law*; Jacob, *Silent Revolution*.

116. Thompson, *Poverty of Theory and Other Essays*, 96.

Epilogue: The Naked Are Searching for Clothes

1. Doris J. Freed and Henry H. Foster, Jr., "Divorce in the Fifty States: An Overview," *Family Law Quarterly* 11 (1977): 297–313; Eisler, *Dissolution*, 10; Weitzman, *Divorce Revolution*, 18–19; California Laws 1975, ch. 35, p. 59, sec. 1. The almost total deference to unilateral party behavior is described in Lynn D.

Wardle, "No-Fault Divorce and the Divorce Conundrum," *Brigham Young University Law Review*, 1991:107; Berg, "Irreconcilable Differences, 453, 466.

2. Stephen L. Sass, "The Iowa No-Fault Dissolution of Marriage Law in Action," *South Dakota Law Review* 18 (1973): 629, 635, 650.

3. Alan H. Frank, John J. Berman, and Stanley F. Mazur-Hart, "No Fault Divorce and the Divorce Rate: The Nebraska Experience—An Interrupted Time Series Analysis and Commentary," *Nebraska Law Review* 58 (1978): 1, 66.

4. Herma Hill Kay, "Beyond No-Fault: New Directions in Divorce Reform," in Sugarman and Kay, *Divorce Reform at the Crossroads*, 8. An excellent essay contextualing no-fault within a larger trend transforming family law from public to private ordering is presented by Jana B. Singer in "The Privatization of Family Law," *Wisconsin Law Review* 1992:1443–1567.

5. Quoted in Alan Ryan, "Pragmatism Rides Again" (book reiew), *New York Review of Books* 42 (Feb. 16, 1995) 34.

6. Bellah et al., *Habits of the Heart*, 6. On the "Me" decade, see Hall, *Magic Mirror*, 287. A catalog of the social changes affecting family relationships during the years 1965–75 would include, at a minimum, growth of real earnings, increase in government entitlement programs, expanded availability of contraception, development of more publicly asserted feminist ideology, and widespread criticism of traditional institutions and norms. See Victor R. Fuchs, *How We Live* (Cambridge, Mass., 1983), 149–50; Parkman, *No-Fault Divorce*, 59; Coontz, *Way We Never Were*, 150; and Robert T. Michael, "The Rise in Divorce Rates, 1960–1974: Age-Specific Components," *Demography* 15 (1978): 345–47.

7. Milton C. Regan, Jr., *Family Law and the Pursuit of Intimacy* (New York, 1993), 2. See also Bruce C. Hafen, "Individualism and Autonomy in Family Law: The Waning of Belonging," *Brigham Young University Law Review*, 1991:1; Carl E. Schneider, "Moral Discourse and the Transformation of American Family Law," *Michigan Law Review* 83 (1985): 1803.

8. Annamay T. Sheppard, "Women, Families, and Equality: Was Divorce Reform a Mistake?" *Women's Rights Law Reporter* 12 (Fall 1990): 143, 146.

9. Lynn D. Wardle has even argued that no-fault has fostered an increase in physical violence in connection with divorce litigation. Wardle, "Divorce Violence and the No-Fault Divorce Culture," *Utah Law Review*, 1994:741.

10. Norma Basch, *In the Eyes of the Law: Women, Marriage, and Property in Nineteenth-Century New York* (Ithaca, N.Y., 1982), 229.

11. Jacob, *Silent Revolution*, 3, 23.

12. Martha L. Fineman, "Neither Silent, nor Revolutionary." Fineman expands on this point in *Illusion of Equality.*

13. Deborah L. Rhode, *Justice and Gender: Sex Discrimination and the Law* (Cambridge, Mass., 1989), 149. See Gray, *Reallocation of Property on Divorce*, 286–87; Arlene Skolnick, *Embattled Paradise: The American Family in an Age of Uncertainty* (New York, 1991), 200–201.

14. Deborah L. Rhode and Martha Minow, "Reforming the Questions, Ques-

tioning the Reforms: Feminist Perspectives on Divorce Law," in Sugarman and Kay, *Divorce Reform at the Crossroads*, 193. Marie Ashe has written of the "emptiness" of the legal equality approach, in view of its elevation of formal over substantive equality. Ashe, "Mind's Opportunity: Birthing a Poststructuralist Feminist Jurisprudence," *Syracuse Law Review* 38 (1987): 1129, 1138.

15. Mary Ann Mason, *The Equality Trap: Why Working Women Shouldn't Be Treated like Men* (New York, 1988), 25.

16. See Lisa C. Bower, "Unsettling 'Woman': Competing Subjectivities in No-Fault Divorce and Divorce Mediation," in Leslie Friedman Goldstein, ed., *Feminist Jurisprudence: The Difference Debate* (Lanham, Md., 1992), 209–30.

17. Rhode, *Justice and Gender*, 149.

18. Judith S. Wallerstein and Sandra Blakeslee, *Second Chances: Men, Women, and Children a Decade after Divorce* (New York, 1989). Several social science studies are discussed in Barbara Dafoe Whitehead, "Dan Quayle Was Right," *Atlantic* 271 (April 1993): 47–84; Nancy R. Gibbs, "Bringing Up Father," *Time* 141 (June 28, 1993): 53–61. That divorce may inflict lifelong emotional harm is also the premise of Diane Fassel's *Growing Up Divorced: A Road to Healing for Adult Children of Divorce* (New York, 1991). Constance R. Ahrons presents a different reading of the evidence in *The Good Divorce: Keeping Your Family Together When Your Marriage Comes Apart* (New York, 1994).

19. Barbara Dafoe Whitehead, "The New Family Values," *Utne Reader* 57 (May/June 1993): 66, excerpted from *Family Affairs* (Summer 1992); Bellah et al., *Habits of the Heart*, 111; Steven Waldman, "Deadbeat Dads: Wanted for Failure to Pay Child Support," *Newsweek* 119 (May 4, 1992): 46–52; Mary Frances Berry, *The Politics of Parenthood: Child Care, Women's Rights, and the Myth of the Good Mother* (New York, 1993).

20. Trudi Ferguson and Joan S. Dunphy, *Answers to the Mommy Track: How Wives and Mothers in Business Reach the Top and Balance Their Lives* (Far Hills, N.J., 1991), ix; Darcie Sanders and Martha M. Bullen, *Staying Home: From Full-Time Professional to Full-Time Parent* (Boston, 1992), v, ix. A recent letter to the editor of *American Heritage* illustrates the dilemmas of women's social identity and the difficulties of historical generalization. The writer, who signed the letter as "Mrs. Michael T. Van Ornum," identified herself as a professional practicing social worker who had graduated from college summa cum laude. She chided author David Halberstam for what she termed his bias against female full-time homemakers. Quoting from Halberstam's article, "Discovering Sex," Van Ornum declared her own anticipation of fulfillment in the "making of beds, shopping for groceries, matching slipcover materials, eating peanut-butter sandwiches, chauffeuring Cub Scouts and Brownies and lying beside my husband." *American Heritage* 44 (Oct. 1993): 7. On the history of housewifery, see Matthews, *"Just a Housewife"*; Strasser, *Never Done*.

21. Katie Kelley Dorn, *From Briefcase to Diaper Bag: How I Quit My Job, Stayed*

Home with My Kids, and Lived to Tell about It (New York, 1994); Katherine Wyse Goldman, *My Mother Worked and I Turned Out Okay* (New York, 1993). For men, the conversation has barely started. See John Byrne Barry, "Daddytrack: How about Balancing *Fatherhood* and Career?," *Utne Reader* 57 (May/June 1993): 70–73, excerpted from *Mothering* (Spring 1989); Gibbs, "Bringing Up Father"; Jerry Adler et al., "Drums, Sweat, and Tears," *Newsweek* 118 (June 24, 1991): 46–51; Greg Gutfeld, "You Can Do Better! Lifestyle Improvements for Men," *Men's Health* 11 (March 1996): 98; Dan Fost, "The Lost Art of Fatherhood," *American Demographics* 18 (March 1996): 16; Stan Simpson, "Dads Can Make a Positive Difference," *Hartford Courant*, March 11, 1996, A3; Howard Lovy, "Gender Wars: Fathers Strive to Can the Bumbling Mr. Mom Image and Get Some Respect," *Detroit News*, March 13, 1996, MLife; Mark Simpson, "Lost Boys Will Be Boys. Something's Bothering Modern Man. He's Confused, He's Irresponsible, He's Immature," *Independent*, March 16, 1996, Arts 7; Jerry Large, "Fatherhood: It Means Giving 'Good Guy Stuff,'" *Seattle Times*, March 17, 1996, L1; David Blankenhorn, *Fatherless America: Confronting Our Most Urgent Social Problem* (New York, 1995).

22. See generally Regan, *Family Law and the Pursuit of Intimacy*, 137–48; Whitehead, "Dan Quayle Was Right," 71; Kay, "Beyond No-Fault," 19. The proposals summarized in this paragraph and the next include those seeking to factor fault into the adjudication of the marital breakup, as well as those arguing that fault has a critical role to play in the determination of child custody, spousal support, and property division.

23. Barbara Bennett Woodhouse, "Sex, Lies, and Dissipation: The Discourse of Fault in a No-Fault Era," *Georgetown Law Journal* 82 (1994): 2525, 2530.

24. Sugarman, "Dividing Financial Interests on Divorce," in Sugarman and Kay, *Divorce Reform at the Crossroads*, 136–38. Sugarman did not advocate a return to fault but described potential ways to reintroduce culpability in divorce law.

25. Richard Ingleby, "Matrimonial Breakdown and the Legal Process: The Limitations of No-Fault Divorce," *Law and Society Review* 11 (1989): 1.

26. Parkman, *No-Fault Divorce*, xiii, 7–8, 137–40. Martin Zelder argued for a similar limitation in "Inefficient Dissolutions as a Consequence of Public Goods: The Case of No-Fault Divorce," *Journal of Legal Studies* 22 (June 1993): 503.

27. Elizabeth S. Scott, "Rational Decisionmaking about Marriage and Divorce," *Virginia Law Review* 90 (1990): 43–44, 79–91.

28. 1995 Illinois House Bill 2095, called the Marriage Contract Act, proposed that couples could enter into a "marriage contract providing that the marital relationship will not be dissolved or otherwise modified except on a showing by a preponderance of the evidence by one party of the fault the other party." 1995 Washington Senate Bill 5532 and 1996 Indiana Senate Bill 398 contained similar provisions. Indiana state representative Dennis Kruse discussed his bill providing a "convenant marriage" option in Kruse, "Covenant Vows," *Indianapolis Star*, March 12, 1996, A5.

29. Michigan House Bill 4432 (Feb. 14, 1996). Jessie Dalman's divorce legislation generated a very large amount of public attention. For illustrations, see Barbara Vobejda, "Critics Seeking Change, Fault 'No-Fault' Divorce Laws for High Rates," *Washington Post*, March 7, 1996, A3; Dirk Johnson, "Attacking No-Fault Notion, Conservatives Try to Put Blame Back in Divorce," *New York Times*, Feb. 12, 1996, A10; John T. Wark, "Finding Fault," *Detroit News*, Feb. 13, 1996; Jennifer Loven, "No-Fault Divorce Law Coming under Legislative Siege," *Los Angeles Times*, March 3, 1996, A3.

30. Governor Branstad's speech was reprinted as "Iowa 'Vibrant and Growing,'" *Des Moines Register*, Jan. 10, 1996, 11. Branstad expanded his comments in "What Is Best for the Children?" *Des Moines Register*, Feb. 4, 1996, Opinion 1.

31. Micah A. Clark, "The Negative Effects of Easy Divorce," *Indianapolis Star*, March 12, 1996, A5.

32. 1995 Georgia House Bill 30 proposed the outright repeal of no-fault divorce. 1996 Idaho House Bill 470 would require mutual consent in order to grant a no-fault divorce, while 1996 Idaho House Bill 826 proposed a one-year stay in no-fault cases in which one party requested a stay or the family contained minor children, as well as requiring the couple's attendance at counseling sessions during the stay. 1995 Hawaii House Bill 3751 similarly provided for a one-year waiting period and mandatory counseling after a divorce filing in cases with minor children. 1995 Pennsylvania House Bill 958 would condition a divorce upon proof that all children ages six to sixteen had attended at least three counseling sessions between the time of separation and the granting of the decree, while 1995 Pennsylvania House Bill 2003 would require the court to consider holding hearings in no-fault divorce cases. 1996 Virginia House Bill 1188 would limit the availability of divorce upon the ground of separation (the only no-fault alternative under Virginia law) to couples who have been separated for one year, have no minor children, and file jointly for the divorce. 1995 Illinois Senate Bill 1842 would allow a divorce for irreconcilable differences only after a period of separation and would require mutual consent if the couple had been married for more than ten years, if they had a dependant child, or if the wife was pregnant. 1995 Kansas Senate Bill 608 and 1995 Kansas House Bill 3007 would limit no-fault divorce to cases that included mutual consent and no dependent children, while 1995 Kansas Senate Bill 233 would require mandatory reconciliation efforts for would-be divorcees, including three mediation sessions attended by both the wife and the husband.

33. See, e.g., H. S. Erlanger, E. Chambliss, and M. S. Melli, "Participation and Flexibility in Informal Processes: Cautions from the Divorce Context," *Law and Society Review* 21 (1987): 585; Ingleby, "Matrimonial Breakdown and the Legal Process," 14.

34. Austin Sarat and William L. F. Festiner, "Law and Social Relation: Vocabularies of Motive in Lawyer/Client Relations," *Law and Society Review* 22 (1988): 750.

35. Wallerstein and Blakeslee, *Second Chances*, 6–7.

36. Thomas Moore, *Care of the Soul: A Guide to Cultivating Depth and Sacredness in Everyday Life* (New York, 1993): 77.

37. Coontz, *Way We Never Were*, 120. On the declining moral discourse in family law, see Carl E. Schneider, "Marriage, Morals, and the Law: No-Fault Divorce and Moral Discourse," *Utah Law Review*, 1994:503.

38. As Carl E. Schneider has observed, "The people the law seeks to affect themselves think in moral terms. A law which tries to eliminate those terms from its language will both misunderstand the people it is regulating and be misunderstood by them." Schneider, "Rethinking Alimony: Marital Decisions and Moral Discourse," *Brigham Young University Law Review*, 1991:197, 243.

INDEX